Antisemitism

Part One of *The Origins of Totalitarianism*

Hannah Arendt

Antisemitism

A Harvest/HBJ Book

HARCOURT BRACE JOVANOVICH
New York and London

Library of Congress Catalog Card Number: 66-22273

Printed in the United States of America

FGHIJ

TO HEINRICH BLÜCHER

Preface

ANTISEMITISM, a secular nineteenth-century ideology—which in name, though not in argument, was unknown before the 1870's—and religious Jew-hatred, inspired by the mutually hostile antagonism of two conflicting creeds, are obviously not the same; and even the extent to which the former derives its arguments and emotional appeal from the latter is open to question. The notion of an unbroken continuity of persecutions, expulsions, and massacres from the end of the Roman Empire to the Middle Ages, the modern era, and down to our own time, frequently embellished by the idea that modern antisemitism is no more than a secularized version of popular medieval superstitions,[1] is no less fallacious (though of course less mischievous) than the corresponding antisemitic notion of a Jewish secret society that has ruled, or aspired to rule, the world since antiquity. Historically, the hiatus between the late Middle Ages and the modern age with respect to Jewish affairs is even more marked than the rift between Roman antiquity and the Middle Ages, or the gulf—frequently considered to be the most important turning-point of Jewish history in the Diaspora—that separated the catastrophes of the First Crusades from earlier medieval centuries. For this hiatus lasted through nearly two centuries, from the fifteenth to the end of the sixteenth, during which Jewish-Gentile relations were at an all-time low, Jewish "indifference to conditions and events in the outside world" was at an all-time high, and Judaism

[1] The latest example of this view is Norman Cohn's *Warrant for Genocide. The myth of the Jewish world-conspiracy and the "Protocols of the Elders of Zion,"* New York, 1966. The author starts from the implied negation that there is such a thing as Jewish history at all. Jews are in his view "people who . . . lived scattered across Europe from the English Channel to the Volga, with very little in common to them all save their descent from adherents of the Jewish religion" (p. 15). Antisemites, on the contrary, can claim direct and unbroken lineage through space and time from the Middle Ages when "Jews had been seen as agents of Satan, devil-worshippers, demons in human form" (p. 41), and the only qualification to such sweeping generalizations that the learned author of *Pursuit of the Millennium* sees fit to make is that he deals with the "deadliest kind of antisemitism, the kind that results in massacre and attempted genocide" (p. 16). The book also tries rather strenuously to prove that "the mass of the German population was never truly fanaticized against the Jews" and that their extermination "was organized and in the main carried out by the professionals of the SD and the SS," bodies that "did not by any means represent a typical cross-section of German society" (pp. 212 ff.). How one wishes this statement could be squared with the facts! The result is that the work reads as though it were written about forty years ago by an unduly ingenious member of the *Verein zur Bekämpfung des Antisemitismus* of unhappy memory.

became "more than ever a closed system of thought." It was at this time that Jews, without any outside interference, began to think "that the difference between Jewry and the nations was fundamentally not one of creed and faith, but one of inner nature" and that the ancient dichotomy between Jews and Gentiles was "more likely to be racial in origin rather than a matter of doctrinal dissension."[2] This shift in evaluating the alien character of the Jewish people, which became common among non-Jews only much later in the Age of Enlightenment, is clearly the condition *sine qua non* for the birth of antisemitism, and it is of some importance to note that it occurred in Jewish self-interpretation first and at about the time when European Christendom split up into those ethnic groups which then came politically into their own in the system of modern nation-states.

The history of antisemitism, like the history of Jew-hatred, is part and parcel of the long and intricate story of Jewish-Gentile relations under the conditions of Jewish dispersion. Interest in this history was practically nonexistent prior to the middle of the nineteenth century, when it coincided with the rise of antisemitism and its furious reaction to emancipated and assimilated Jewry—obviously the worst possible constellation for establishing reliable historical records.[3] Since then, it has been the common fallacy of Jewish and non-Jewish historiography — though mostly for opposite reasons — to isolate the hostile elements in Christian and Jewish sources and to stress the series of catastrophes, expulsions, and massacres that have punctuated Jewish history just as armed and unarmed conflicts, war, famine, and pestilence have punctuated the history of Europe. Needless to add, it was Jewish historiography, with its strong polemical and apologetical bias, that undertook to trace the record of Jew-hatred in Christian history, while it was left to the antisemites to trace an intellectually not too dissimilar record from ancient Jewish authorities. When this Jewish tradition of an often violent antagonism to Christians and Gentiles came to light, "the general Jewish public was not only outraged but genuinely astonished,"[4] so well had its spokesmen succeeded in convincing themselves and everybody else of the non-fact that Jewish separateness was due exclusively to Gentile hostility and lack of enlightenment. Judaism, it was now maintained chiefly by Jewish historians, had always been superior to other religions in that it believed in human equality and tolerance. That this

---

[2] The quotations are all drawn from Jacob Katz, *Exclusiveness and Tolerance, Jewish-Gentile Relations in Medieval and Modern Times,* New York, 1962 (Chapter 12), an entirely original study, written on the highest possible level, which indeed should have exploded "many cherished notions of contemporary Jewry," as the jacket claims, but did not because it was almost completely ignored by the general press. Katz belongs among the younger generation of Jewish historians, many of whom teach at the Jerusalem University and publish in Hebrew. Why their work is not more speedily translated and published in this country is something of a mystery. With them, the "lachrymose" presentation of Jewish history, against which Salo W. Baron protested nearly forty years ago, has indeed come to an end.

[3] It is interesting to note that the first modern Jewish historian, J. M. Jost, who wrote in Germany in the middle of the last century, was much less prone to the common prejudices of secular Jewish historiography than his more illustrious successors.

[4] Katz, *op. cit.,* p. 196.

self-deceiving theory, accompanied by the belief that the Jewish people had always been the passive, suffering object of Christian persecutions, actually amounted to a prolongation and modernization of the old myth of chosenness and was bound to end in new and often very complicated practices of separation, destined to uphold the ancient dichotomy, is perhaps one of those ironies which seem to be in store for those who, for whatever reasons, try to embellish and manipulate political facts and historical records. For if Jews had anything in common with their non-Jewish neighbors to support their newly proclaimed equality, it was precisely a religiously predetermined, mutually hostile past that was as rich in cultural achievement on the highest level as it was abundant in fanaticism and crude superstitions on the level of the uneducated masses.

However, even the irritating stereotypes of this sort of Jewish historiography rest on a more solid basis of historical fact than the outdated political and social needs of European Jewry in the nineteenth and early twentieth centuries. While Jewish cultural history was infinitely more diverse than it was then assumed, and while the causes of disaster varied with historical and geographical circumstances, it is true that they varied more in the non-Jewish environment than within the Jewish communities. Two very real factors were decisive for the fateful misconceptions that are still current in popular presentations of Jewish history. Nowhere and at no time after the destruction of the temple did Jews possess their own territory and their own state; they always depended for their physical existence upon the protection of non-Jewish authorities, although some means of self-protection, the right to bear arms, were granted to "the Jews in France and Germany well into the thirteenth century."[5] This does not mean that Jews were always deprived of power, but it is true that in any contest of violence, no matter for what reasons, Jews were not only vulnerable but helpless so that it was only natural, especially in the centuries of complete estrangement that preceded their rise to political equality, that all current outbursts of violence should be experienced by them as mere repetitions. Catastrophes, moreover, were understood in Jewish tradition in terms of martyrology, which in turn had its historical basis in the first centuries of our era, when both Jews and Christians had defied the might of the Roman Empire, as well as in medieval conditions when the alternative of submitting to baptism and thus saving themselves from persecution remained open to Jews even when the cause of violence was not religious but political and economic. This factual constellation gave rise to an optical illusion under which both Jewish and non-Jewish historians have suffered ever since. Historiography "has until now dealt more with the Christian dissociation from the Jews than with the reverse,"[6] thus obliterating the otherwise more important fact that Jewish dissociation from the Gentile world, and more specifically from the Christian environment, has been of greater relevance for Jewish history than the reverse, for the obvious reason that the very survival of the people as an identifiable entity depended upon such voluntary separation and not, as was currently assumed, upon the hostility of Christians and non-Jews. Only in the nineteenth and

[5] *Ibid.*, p. 6.
[6] *Ibid.*, p. 7.

twentieth centuries, after emancipation and with the spread of assimilation, has antisemitism played any role in the conservation of the people, since only then did Jews aspire to being admitted to non-Jewish society.

Whereas anti-Jewish sentiments were widespread among the educated classes of Europe throughout the nineteenth century, antisemitism as an ideology remained, with very few exceptions, the prerogative of crackpots in general and the lunatic fringe in particular. Even the dubious products of Jewish apologetics, which never convinced anybody but the convinced, were towering examples of erudition and scholarship compared with what the enemies of Jews had to offer in matters of historical research.[7] When, after the close of the war, I began to organize the material for this book, which had been collected from documentary sources and sometimes excellent monographs over a period of more than ten years, there did not exist a single over-all presentation of its subject matter that could be said to conform to the most elementary standards of historical scholarship. And the situation has hardly changed since. This is all the more deplorable as the need for an impartial, truthful treatment of Jewish history has recently become greater than it has ever been before. Twentieth-century political developments have driven the Jewish people into the storm center of events; the Jewish question and antisemitism, relatively unimportant phenomena in terms of world politics, became the catalytic agent first for the rise of the Nazi movement and the establishment of the organizational structure of the Third Reich, in which every citizen had to prove that he was *not* a Jew, then for a world war of unparalleled ferocity, and finally for the emergence of the unprecedented crime of genocide in the midst of Occidental civilization. That this called not only for lamentation and denunciation but for comprehension seemed to me obvious. This book is an attempt at understanding what at first and even second glance appeared simply outrageous.

Comprehension, however, does not mean denying the outrageous, deducing the unprecedented from precedents, or explaining phenomena by such analogies and generalities that the impact of reality and the shock of experience are no longer felt. It means, rather, examining and bearing consciously the burden that events have placed upon us—neither denying their existence nor submitting meekly to their weight as though everything that in fact happened could not have happened otherwise. Comprehension, in short, means the unpremeditated, attentive facing up to, and resisting of, reality—whatever it may be or might have been.

For this comprehension a certain familiarity with Jewish history in nineteenth-century Europe and the attendant development of antisemitism is indispensable though, of course, not sufficient. The following chapters deal with only those elements in nineteenth-century history which indeed belong among the "origins of totalitarianism." A comprehensive history of antisemitism remains still to be written and is beyond the scope of this book. So long as this lacuna exists, there is enough justification even in terms of mere scholarship to

[7] The only exception is the antisemitic historian Walter Frank, the head of the Nazi *Reichsinstitut für Geschichte des Neuen Deutschlands* and the editor of nine volumes of *Forschungen zur Judenfrage*, 1937-1944. Especially Frank's own contributions can still be consulted with profit.

publish the following chapters as an independent contribution toward a more comprehensive history, although it was originally conceived as a constituent part of the prehistory, as it were, of totalitarianism. Moreover, what is true for the history of antisemitism, that it fell into the hands of non-Jewish crackpots and Jewish apologetics, and was carefully avoided by reputable historians, is true, *mutatis mutandis,* for nearly all elements that later crystallized in the novel totalitarian phenomenon; they had hardly been noticed by either learned or public opinion because they belonged to a subterranean stream of European history where, hidden from the light of the public and the attention of enlightened men, they had been able to gather an entirely unexpected virulence.

Since only the final crystallizing catastrophe brought these subterranean trends into the open and to public notice, there has been a tendency to simply equate totalitarianism with its elements and origins—as though every outburst of antisemitism or racism or imperialism could be identified as "totalitarianism." This fallacy is as misleading in the search for historical truth as it is pernicious for political judgment. Totalitarian politics — far from being simply antisemitic or racist or imperialist or communist — use and abuse their own ideological and political elements until the basis of factual reality, from which the ideologies originally derived their strength and their propaganda value—the reality of class struggle, for instance, or the interest conflicts between Jews and their neighbors—have all but disappeared. It certainly would be a serious error to underestimate the role sheer racism has played and is still playing in the government of the Southern states, but it would be an even more serious fallacy to arrive at the retrospective conclusion that large areas of the United States have been under totalitarian rule for more than a century. The only direct, unadulterated consequence of nineteenth-century antisemitic movements was not Nazism but, on the contrary, Zionism, which, at least in its Western ideological form, was a kind of counterideology, the "answer" to antisemitism. This, incidentally, is not to say that Jewish self-consciousness was ever a mere creation of antisemitism; even a cursory knowledge of Jewish history, whose central concern since the Babylonian exile has always been the survival of the people against the overwhelming odds of dispersion, should be enough to dispel this latest myth in these matters, a myth that has become somewhat fashionable in intellectual circles after Sartre's "existentialist" interpretation of *the* Jew as someone who is regarded and defined as a Jew by others.

The best illustration of both the distinction and the connection between pre-totalitarian and totalitarian antisemitism is perhaps the ludicrous story of the "Protocols of the Elders of Zion." The Nazi use of the forgery as a textbook for global conquest is certainly not part of the history of antisemitism, but only this history can explain why the improbable tale contained enough plausibility to be useful as anti-Jewish propaganda to begin with. What, on the other hand, it can not explain is why the totalitarian claim to global rule, to be exercised by members and methods of a secret society, should become an attractive political goal at all. This latter, politically (though not propagandistically) much more relevant function has its origin in imperialism in general, in its highly explosive continental version, the so-called pan-movements in particular.

This book then is limited in time and place as well as in subject matter. Its analyses concern Jewish history in Central and Western Europe from the time of the court Jews to the Dreyfus Affair insofar as it was relevant to the birth of antisemitism and influenced by it. It deals with antisemitic movements that were still pretty solidly grounded in factual realities characteristic of Jewish-Gentile relations, that is, in the part Jews played in the development of the nation-state on one side and in their role in non-Jewish society on the other. The emergence of the first antisemitic parties in the 1870's and 1880's marks the moment when the limited, factual basis of interest conflict and demonstrable experience was transcended and that road opened which ended in the "final solution." From then on, in the era of imperialism, followed by the period of totalitarian movements and governments, it is no longer possible to isolate the Jewish question or the antisemitic ideology from issues that are actually almost completely unrelated to the realities of modern Jewish history. And this is not merely and not primarily because these matters played such a prominent role in world affairs, but because antisemitism itself was now being used for ulterior purposes that, though their implementation finally claimed Jews as their chief victims, left all particular issues of both Jewish and anti-Jewish interest far behind.

The reader will find the imperialist and totalitarian versions of twentieth-century antisemitism, respectively, in the second and third volumes of this work.

Hannah Arendt

July 1967

Contents

Antisemitism

This is a remarkable century which opened with the Revolution and ended with the Affaire! Perhaps it will be called the century of rubbish.

ROGER MARTIN DU GARD

CHAPTER ONE

Antisemitism as an Outrage to Common Sense

MANY STILL consider it an accident that Nazi ideology centered around antisemitism and that Nazi policy, consistently and uncompromisingly, aimed at the persecution and finally the extermination of the Jews. Only the horror of the final catastrophe, and even more the homelessness and uprootedness of the survivors, made the "Jewish question" so prominent in our everyday political life. What the Nazis themselves claimed to be their chief discovery—the role of the Jewish people in world politics—and their chief interest—persecution of Jews all over the world—have been regarded by public opinion as a pretext for winning the masses or an interesting device of demagogy.

The failure to take seriously what the Nazis themselves said is comprehensible enough. There is hardly an aspect of contemporary history more irritating and mystifying than the fact that of all the great unsolved political questions of our century, it should have been this seemingly small and unimportant Jewish problem that had the dubious honor of setting the whole infernal machine in motion. Such discrepancies between cause and effect outrage our common sense, to say nothing of the historian's sense of balance and harmony. Compared with the events themselves, all explanations of antisemitism look as if they had been hastily and hazardously contrived, to cover up an issue which so gravely threatens our sense of proportion and our hope for sanity.

One of these hasty explanations has been the identification of antisemitism with rampant nationalism and its xenophobic outbursts. Unfortunately, the fact is that modern antisemitism grew in proportion as traditional nationalism declined, and reached its climax at the exact moment when the European system of nation-states and its precarious balance of power crashed.

It has already been noticed that the Nazis were not simple nationalists. Their nationalist propaganda was directed toward their fellow-travelers and not their convinced members; the latter, on the contrary, were never allowed to lose sight of a consistently supranational approach to politics. Nazi "nationalism" had more than one aspect in common with the recent nationalistic propaganda in the Soviet Union, which is also used only to feed the prejudices of the masses. The Nazis had a genuine and never revoked contempt for the narrowness of nationalism, the provincialism of the nation-state, and they repeated time and again that their "movement," international in scope like the Bolshevik movement, was more important to them than any state, which would necessarily be bound to a specific territory. And not only the Nazis, but fifty years of antisemitic history, stand as evidence against the identification of antisemitism with nationalism. The first antisemitic parties in the last decades of the nineteenth century were also among the first that banded together internationally. From the very beginning, they called international congresses and were concerned with a co-ordination of international, or at least inter-European, activities.

General trends, like the coincident decline of the nation-state and the growth of antisemitism, can hardly ever be explained satisfactorily by one reason or by one cause alone. The historian is in most such cases confronted with a very complex historical situation where he is almost at liberty, and that means at a loss, to isolate one factor as the "spirit of the time." There are, however, a few helpful general rules. Foremost among them for our purpose is Tocqueville's great discovery (in *L'Ancien Régime et la Révolution,* Book II, chap. 1) of the motives for the violent hatred felt by the French masses for the aristocracy at the outbreak of the Revolution —a hatred which stimulated Burke to remark that the revolution was more concerned with "the condition of a gentleman" than with the institution of a king. According to Tocqueville, the French people hated aristocrats about to lose their power more than it had ever hated them before, precisely because their rapid loss of real power was not accompanied by any considerable decline in their fortunes. As long as the aristocracy held vast powers of jurisdiction, they were not only tolerated but respected. When noblemen lost their privileges, among others the privilege to exploit and oppress, the people felt them to be parasites, without any real function in the rule of the country. In other words, neither oppression nor exploitation as such is ever the main cause for resentment; wealth without visible function is much more intolerable because nobody can understand why it should be tolerated.

Antisemitism reached its climax when Jews had similarly lost their public functions and their influence, and were left with nothing but their wealth. When Hitler came to power, the German banks were already almost *judenrein* (and it was here that Jews had held key positions for more than a hundred years) and German Jewry as a whole, after a long steady growth in social status and numbers, was declining so rapidly that statisticians predicted its disappearance in a few decades. Statistics, it is true, do not necessarily point to real historical processes; yet it is noteworthy that to a statistician Nazi persecution and extermination could look like a senseless acceleration of a process which would probably have come about in any case.

The same holds true for nearly all Western European countries. The Dreyfus Affair exploded not under the Second Empire, when French Jewry was at the height of its prosperity and influence, but under the Third Republic when Jews had all but vanished from important positions (though not from the political scene). Austrian antisemitism became violent not under the reign of Metternich and Franz Joseph, but in the postwar Austrian Republic when it was perfectly obvious that hardly any other group had suffered the same loss of influence and prestige through the disappearance of the Hapsburg monarchy.

Persecution of powerless or power-losing groups may not be a very pleasant spectacle, but it does not spring from human meanness alone. What makes men obey or tolerate real power and, on the other hand, hate people who have wealth without power, is the rational instinct that power has a certain function and is of some general use. Even exploitation and oppression still make society work and establish some kind of order. Only wealth without power or aloofness without a policy are felt to be parasitical, useless, revolting, because such conditions cut all the threads which tie men together. Wealth which does not exploit lacks even the relationship which exists between exploiter and exploited; aloofness without policy does not imply even the minimum concern of the oppressor for the oppressed.

The general decline of Western and Central European Jewry, however, constitutes merely the atmosphere in which the subsequent events took place. The decline itself explains them as little as the mere loss of power by the aristocracy would explain the French Revolution. To be aware of such general rules is important only in order to refute those recommendations of common sense which lead us to believe that violent hatred or sudden rebellion spring necessarily from great power and great abuses, and that consequently organized hatred of the Jews cannot but be a reaction to their importance and power.

More serious, because it appeals to much better people, is another common-sense fallacy: the Jews, because they were an entirely powerless group caught up in the general and insoluble conflicts of the time, could be blamed for them and finally be made to appear the hidden authors of all evil. The best illustration—and the best refutation—of this explanation, dear to the hearts of many liberals, is in a joke which was told after the first World War. An antisemite claimed that the Jews had caused the war; the reply was: Yes, the Jews and the bicyclists. Why the bicyclists? asks the one. Why the Jews? asks the other.

The theory that the Jews are always the scapegoat implies that the scapegoat might have been anyone else as well. It upholds the perfect innocence of the victim, an innocence which insinuates not only that no evil was done but that nothing at all was done which might possibly have a connection with the issue at stake. It is true that the scapegoat theory in its purely arbitrary form never appears in print. Whenever, however, its adherents painstakingly try to explain why a specific scapegoat was so well suited to his role, they show that they have left the theory behind them and have got themselves involved in the usual historical research—where nothing is ever discovered except that history is made by many groups and that for certain reasons one group was singled out. The so-called scapegoat necessarily ceases to be the innocent victim whom the world blames for all its sins and through whom it wishes to escape punishment; it becomes one group of people among other groups, all of which are involved in the business of this world. And it does not simply cease to be coresponsible because it became the victim of the world's injustice and cruelty.

Until recently the inner inconsistency of the scapegoat theory was sufficient reason to discard it as one of many theories which are motivated by escapism. But the rise of terror as a major weapon of government has lent it a credibility greater than it ever had before.

A fundamental difference between modern dictatorships and all other tyrannies of the past is that terror is no longer used as a means to exterminate and frighten opponents, but as an instrument to rule masses of people who are perfectly obedient. Terror as we know it today strikes without any preliminary provocation, its victims are innocent even from the point of view of the persecutor. This was the case in Nazi Germany when full terror was directed against Jews, *i.e.,* against people with certain common characteristics which were independent of their specific behavior. In Soviet Russia the situation is more confused, but the facts, unfortunately, are only too obvious. On the one hand, the Bolshevik system, unlike the Nazi, never admitted theoretically that it could practice terror against innocent people, and though in view of certain practices this may look like hypocrisy, it makes quite a difference. Russian practice, on the other hand, is even more "advanced" than the German in one respect: arbitrariness of terror is not even limited by racial differentiation, while the old class categories have long since been discarded, so that anybody in Russia may suddenly become a victim of the police terror. We are not concerned here with the ultimate consequence of rule by terror—namely, that nobody, not even the executors, can ever be free of fear; in our context we are dealing merely with the arbitrariness by which victims are chosen, and for this it is decisive that they are objectively innocent, that they are chosen regardless of what they may or may not have done.

At first glance this may look like a belated confirmation of the old scapegoat theory, and it is true that the victim of modern terror does show all the characteristics of the scapegoat: he is objectively and absolutely innocent because nothing he did or omitted to do matters or has any connection with his fate.

There is, therefore, a temptation to return to an explanation which automatically discharges the victim of responsibility: it seems quite adequate to a reality in which nothing strikes us more forcefully than the utter innocence of the individual caught in the horror machine and his utter inability to change his fate. Terror, however, is only in the last instance of its development a mere form of government. In order to establish a totalitarian regime, terror must be presented as an instrument for carrying out a specific ideology; and that ideology must have won the adherence of many, and even a majority, before terror can be stabilized. The point for the historian is that the Jews, before becoming the main victims of modern terror, were the center of Nazi ideology. And an ideology which has to persuade and mobilize people cannot choose its victim arbitrarily. In other words, if a patent forgery like the "Protocols of the Elders of Zion" is believed by so many people that it can become the text of a whole political movement, the task of the historian is no longer to discover a forgery. Certainly it is not to invent explanations which dismiss the chief political and historical fact of the matter: that the forgery is being believed. This fact is more important than the (historically speaking, secondary) circumstance that it is forgery.

The scapegoat explanation therefore remains one of the principal attempts to escape the seriousness of antisemitism and the significance of the fact that the Jews were driven into the storm center of events. Equally widespread is the opposite doctrine of an "eternal antisemitism" in which Jew-hatred is a normal and natural reaction to which history gives only more or less opportunity. Outbursts need no special explanation because they are natural consequences of an eternal problem. That this doctrine was adopted by professional antisemites is a matter of course; it gives the best possible alibi for all horrors. If it is true that mankind has insisted on murdering Jews for more than two thousand years, then Jew-killing is a normal, and even human, occupation and Jew-hatred is justified beyond the need of argument.

The more surprising aspect of this explanation, the assumption of an eternal antisemitism, is that it has been adopted by a great many unbiased historians and by an even greater number of Jews. It is this odd coincidence which makes the theory so very dangerous and confusing. Its escapist basis is in both instances the same: just as antisemites understandably desire to escape responsibility for their deeds, so Jews, attacked and on the defensive, even more understandably do not wish under any circumstances to discuss their share of responsibility. In the case of Jewish, and frequently of Christian, adherents of this doctrine, however, the escapist tendencies of official apologetics are based upon more important and less rational motives.

The birth and growth of modern antisemitism has been accompanied by and interconnected with Jewish assimilation, the secularization and withering away of the old religious and spiritual values of Judaism. What actually happened was that great parts of the Jewish people were at the same time threatened by physical extinction from without and dissolution from within. In this situation, Jews concerned with the survival of their people would, in a curious desperate misinterpretation, hit on the consoling idea that antisemitism, after all, might be an excellent means for keeping the people together, so that the assumption of eternal antisemitism would even imply an eternal guarantee of Jewish existence. This superstition, a secularized travesty of the idea of eternity inherent in a faith in chosenness and a Messianic hope, has been strengthened through the fact that for many centuries the Jews experienced the Christian brand of hostility which was indeed a powerful agent of preservation, spiritually as well as politically. The Jews mistook modern anti-Christian antisemitism for the old religious Jew-hatred —and this all the more innocently because their assimilation had by-passed

Christianity in its religious and cultural aspect. Confronted with an obvious symptom of the decline of Christianity, they could therefore imagine in all ignorance that this was some revival of the so-called "Dark Ages." Ignorance or misunderstanding of their own past were partly responsible for their fatal underestimation of the actual and unprecedented dangers which lay ahead. But one should also bear in mind that lack of political ability and judgment have been caused by the very nature of Jewish history, the history of a people without a government, without a country, and without a language. Jewish history offers the extraordinary spectacle of a people, unique in this respect, which began its history with a well-defined concept of history and an almost conscious resolution to achieve a well-circumscribed plan on earth and then, without giving up this concept, avoided all political action for two thousand years. The result was that the political history of the Jewish people became even more dependent upon unforeseen, accidental factors than the history of other nations, so that the Jews stumbled from one role to the other and accepted responsibility for none.

In view of the final catastrophe, which brought the Jews so near to complete annihilation, the thesis of eternal antisemitism has become more dangerous than ever. Today it would absolve Jew-haters of crimes greater than anybody had ever believed possible. Antisemitism, far from being a mysterious guarantee of the survival of the Jewish people, has been clearly revealed as a threat of its extermination. Yet this explanation of antisemitism, like the scapegoat theory and for similar reasons, has outlived its refutation by reality. It stresses, after all, with different arguments but equal stubbornness, that complete and inhuman innocence which so strikingly characterizes victims of modern terror, and therefore seems confirmed by the events. It even has the advantage over the scapegoat theory that somehow it answers the uncomfortable question: Why the Jews of all people?—if only with the question begging reply: Eternal hostility.

It is quite remarkable that the only two doctrines which at least attempt to explain the political significance of the antisemitic movement deny all specific Jewish responsibility and refuse to discuss matters in specific historical terms. In this inherent negation of the significance of human behavior, they bear a terrible resemblance to those modern practices and forms of government which, by means of arbitrary terror, liquidate the very possibility of human activity. Somehow in the extermination camps Jews were murdered as if in accordance with the explanation these doctrines had given of why they were hated: regardless of what they had done or omitted to do, regardless of vice or virtue. Moreover, the murderers themselves, only obeying orders and proud of their passionless efficiency, uncannily resembled the "innocent" instruments of an inhuman impersonal course of events which the doctrine of eternal antisemitism had considered them to be.

Such common denominators between theory and practice are by themselves no indication of historical truth, although they are an indication of the "timely" character of such opinions and explain why they sound so plausible to the multitude. The historian is concerned with them only insofar as they are themselves part of his history and because they stand in the way of his search for truth. Being a contemporary, he is as likely to succumb to their persuasive force as anybody else. Caution in handling generally accepted opinions that claim to explain whole trends of history is especially important for the historian of modern times, because the last century has produced an abundance of ideologies that pretend to be keys to history but are actually nothing but desperate efforts to escape responsibility.

Plato, in his famous fight against the ancient Sophists, discovered that their "universal art of enchanting the mind by arguments" (*Phaedrus* 261) had nothing to do with truth but aimed at opinions which by their very nature are changing, and which are valid only "at the time of the agreement and as long as the agreement lasts" (*Theaetetus* 172). He also discovered the very insecure position of truth in the world, for from "opinions comes persuasion and not from truth" (*Phaedrus* 260). The most striking difference between ancient and modern sophists is that the ancients were satisfied with a passing victory of the argument at the expense of truth, whereas the moderns want a more lasting victory at the expense of reality. In other words, one destroyed the dignity of human thought whereas the others destroy the dignity of human action. The old manipulators of logic were the concern of the philosopher, whereas the modern manipulators of facts stand in the way of the historian. For history itself is destroyed, and its comprehensibility—based upon the fact that it is enacted by men and therefore can be understood by men—is in danger, whenever facts are no longer held to be part and parcel of the past and present world, and are misused to prove this or that opinion.

There are, to be sure, few guides left through the labyrinth of inarticulate facts if opinions are discarded and tradition is no longer accepted as unquestionable. Such perplexities of historiography, however, are very minor consequences, considering the profound upheavals of our time and their effect upon the historical structures of Western mankind. Their immediate result has been to expose all those components of our history which up to now had been hidden from our view. This does not mean that what came crashing down in this crisis (perhaps the most profound crisis in Western history since the downfall of the Roman Empire) was mere façade, although many things have been revealed as façade that only a few decades ago we thought were indestructible essences.

The simultaneous decline of the European nation-state and growth of antisemitic movements, the coincident downfall of nationally organized Europe and the extermination of Jews, which was prepared for by the victory of antisemitism over all competing isms in the preceding struggle for persuasion of public opinion, have to be taken as a serious indication of the source of antisemitism. Modern antisemitism must be seen in the more general framework of the development of the nation-state, and at the same time its source must be found in certain aspects of Jewish history and specifically Jewish functions during the last centuries. If, in the final stage of disintegration, antisemitic slogans proved the most effective means of inspiring and organizing great masses of people for imperialist expansion and destruction of the old forms of government, then the previous history of the relationship between Jews and the state must contain elementary clues to the growing hostility between certain groups of society and the Jews. We shall show this development in the next chapter.

If, furthermore, the steady growth of the modern mob—that is, of the *déclassés* of all classes—produced leaders who, undisturbed by the question of whether the Jews were sufficiently important to be made the focus of a political ideology, repeatedly saw in them the "key to history" and the central cause of all evils, then the previous history of the relationship between Jews and society must contain the elementary indications of the hostile relationship between the mob and the Jews. We shall deal with the relationship between Jews and society in the third chapter.

The fourth chapter deals with the Dreyfus Affair, a kind of dress rehearsal for the performance of our own time. Because of the peculiar opportunity it offers of seeing, in a brief historical moment, the otherwise hidden potentialities of antisemitism as a major political weapon within the framework of nineteenth-century politics and its relatively well-balanced sanity, this case has been treated in full detail.

The following three chapters, to be sure, analyze only the preparatory elements, which were not fully realized until the decay of the nation-state and the development of imperialism reached the foreground of the political scene.

CHAPTER TWO: The Jews, the Nation-State,
and the Birth of Antisemitism

I: *The Equivocalities of Emancipation
and the Jewish State Banker*

AT THE height of its development in the nineteenth century, the nation-state granted its Jewish inhabitants equality of rights. Deeper, older, and more fateful contradictions are hidden behind the abstract and palpable inconsistency that Jews received their citizenship from governments which in the process of centuries had made nationality a prerequisite for citizenship and homogeneity of population the outstanding characteristic of the body politic.

The series of emancipation edicts which slowly and hesitantly followed the French edict of 1792 had been preceded and were accompanied by an equivocal attitude toward its Jewish inhabitants on the part of the nation-state. The breakdown of the feudal order had given rise to the new revolutionary concept of equality, according to which a "nation within the nation" could no longer be tolerated. Jewish restrictions and privileges had to be abolished together with all other special rights and liberties. This growth of equality, however, depended largely upon the growth of an independent state machine which, either as an enlightened despotism or as a constitutional government above all classes and parties, could, in splendid isolation, function, rule, and represent the interests of the nation as a whole. Therefore, beginning with the late seventeenth century, an unprecedented need arose for state credit and a new expansion of the state's sphere of economic and business interest, while no group among the European populations was prepared to grant credit to the state or take an active part in the development of state business. It was only natural that the Jews, with their age-old experience as moneylenders and their connections with European nobility—to whom they frequently owed local protection and for whom they used to handle financial matters—would be called upon for help; it was clearly in the interest of the new state business to grant the Jews certain privileges and to treat them as a separate group. Under no circumstances could the state afford to see them wholly assimilated into the rest of the population, which refused credit to the state, was reluctant to enter and to develop businesses owned by the state, and followed the routine pattern of private capitalistic enterprise.

Emancipation of the Jews, therefore, as granted by the national state system in Europe during the nineteenth century, had a double origin and an ever-present equivocal meaning. On the one hand it was due to the political and legal structure of a new body politic which could function only under the conditions of political and legal equality. Governments, for their own sake, had to iron out the inequalities of the old order as completely and as quickly as possible. On the other hand, it was the clear result of a gradual extension of specific Jewish privileges, granted originally only to individuals, then through them to a small group of well-to-do Jews; only when this limited group could no longer handle by themselves the ever-growing demands of state business, were these privileges finally extended to the whole of Western and Central European Jewry.[1]

Thus, at the same time and in the same countries, emancipation meant equality *and* privileges, the destruction of the old Jewish community autonomy *and* the conscious preservation of the Jews as a separate group in society, the abolition of special restrictions and special rights *and* the extension of such rights to a growing group of individuals. Equality of condition for all nationals had become the premise of the new body politic, and while this equality had actually been carried out at least to the extent of depriving the old ruling classes of their privilege to govern and the old oppressed classes of their right to be protected, the process coincided with the birth of the class society which again separated the nationals, economically and socially, as efficiently as the old regime. Equality of condition, as the Jacobins had understood it in the French Revolution, became a reality only in America, whereas on the European continent it was at once replaced by a mere formal equality before the law.

The fundamental contradiction between a political body based on equality before the law and a society based on the inequality of the class system prevented the development of functioning republics as well as the birth of a new political hierarchy. An insurmountable inequality of social condition,

---

[1] To the modern historian rights and liberties granted the court Jews during the seventeenth and eighteenth centuries may appear to be only the forerunners of equality: court Jews could live wherever they liked, they were permitted to travel freely within the realm of their sovereign, they were allowed to bear arms and had rights to special protection from local authorities. Actually these court Jews, characteristically called *Generalprivilegierte Juden* in Prussia, not only enjoyed better living conditions than their fellow Jews who still lived under almost medieval restrictions, but they were better off than their non-Jewish neighbors. Their standard of living was much higher than that of the contemporary middle class, their privileges in most cases were greater than those granted to the merchants. Nor did this situation escape the attention of their contemporaries. Christian Wilhelm Dohm, the outstanding advocate of Jewish emancipation in eighteenth-century Prussia, complained of the practice, in force since the time of Frederick William I, which granted rich Jews "all sorts of favors and support" often "at the expense of, and with neglect of diligent legal [that is, non-Jewish] citizens." In *Denkwürdigkeiten meiner Zeit*, Lemgo, 1814-1819, IV, 487.

the fact that class membership on the continent was bestowed upon the individual and, up to the first World War, almost guaranteed to him by birth, could nevertheless exist side by side with political equality. Only politically backward countries, like Germany, had retained a few feudal remnants. There members of the aristocracy, which on the whole was well on its way to transforming itself into a class, had a privileged political status, and thus could preserve as a group a certain special relationship to the state. But these were remnants. The fully developed class system meant invariably that the status of the individual was defined by his membership in his own class and its relationship to another, and not by his position in the state or within its machinery.

The only exceptions to this general rule were the Jews. They did not form a class of their own and they did not belong to any of the classes in their countries. As a group, they were neither workers, middle-class people, landholders, nor peasants. Their wealth seemed to make them part of the middle class, but they did not share in its capitalist development; they were scarcely represented in industrial enterprise and if, in the last stages of their history in Europe, they became employers on a large scale, they employed white-collar personnel and not workers. In other words, although their status was defined through their being Jews, it was not defined through their relationship to another class. Their special protection from the state (whether in the old form of open privileges, or a special emancipation edict which no other group needed and which frequently had to be reinforced against the hostility of society) and their special services to the governments prevented their submersion in the class system as well as their own establishment as a class.[2] Whenever, therefore, they were admitted to and entered society, they became a well-defined, self-preserving group within one of the classes, the aristocracy or the bourgeoisie.

There is no doubt that the nation-state's interest in preserving the Jews as a special group and preventing their assimilation into class society coincided with the Jewish interest in self-preservation and group survival. It is also more than probable that without this coincidence the governments' attempts would have been in vain; the powerful trends toward equalization of all citizens from the side of the state and incorporation of each individual into a class from the side of society, both clearly implying complete Jewish assimilation, could be frustrated only through a combination of government intervention and voluntary co-operation. Official policies for the Jews were, after all, not always so consistent and unwavering as we may believe if we consider only the final results.[3] It is indeed surprising to see how consistently

[2] Jacob Lestschinsky, in an early discussion of the Jewish problem, pointed out that Jews did not belong to any social class, and spoke of a *"Klasseneinschiebsel"* (in *Weltwirtschafts-Archiv,* 1929, Band 30, 123 ff.), but saw only the disadvantages of this situation in Eastern Europe, not its great advantages in Western and Central European countries.

[3] For example, under Frederick II after the Seven Years' War, a decided effort was made in Prussia to incorporate the Jews into a kind of mercantile system. The

Jews neglected their chances for normal capitalist enterprise and business.[4] But without the interests and practices of the governments, the Jews could hardly have preserved their group identity.

In contrast to all other groups, the Jews were defined and their position determined by the body politic. Since, however, this body politic had no other social reality, they were, socially speaking, in the void. Their social inequality was quite different from the inequality of the class system; it was again mainly the result of their relationship to the state, so that, in society, the very fact of being born a Jew would either mean that one was over-privileged—under special protection of the government—or underprivileged, lacking certain rights and opportunities which were withheld from the Jews in order to prevent their assimilation.

The schematic outline of the simultaneous rise and decline of the European nation-state system and European Jewry unfolds roughly in the following stages:

1. The seventeenth and eighteenth centuries witnessed the slow development of nation-states under the tutelage of absolute monarchs. Individual Jews everywhere rose out of deep obscurity into the sometimes glamorous, and always influential, position of court Jews who financed state affairs and handled the financial transactions of their princes. This development affected the masses who continued to live in a more or less feudal order as little as it affected the Jewish people as a whole.

2. After the French Revolution, which abruptly changed political conditions on the whole European continent, nation-states in the modern sense emerged whose business transactions required a considerably larger amount of capital and credit than the court Jews had ever been asked to place at a

---

older general *Juden-reglement* of 1750 was supplanted by a system of regular permits issued only to those inhabitants who invested a considerable part of their fortune in new manufacturing enterprises. But here, as everywhere else, such government attempts failed completely.

[4] Felix Priebatsch ("Die Judenpolitik des fürstlichen Absolutismus im 17. und 18. Jahrhundert," in *Forschungen und Versuche zur Geschichte des Mittelalters und der Neuzeit*, 1915) cites a typical example from the early eighteenth century: "When the mirror factory in Neuhaus, Lower Austria, which was subsidized by the administration, did not produce, the Jew Wertheimer gave the Emperor money to buy it. When asked to take over the factory he refused, stating that his time was taken up with his financial transactions."

See also Max Köhler, "Beiträge zur neueren jüdischen Wirtschaftsgeschichte. Die Juden in Halberstadt und Umgebung," in *Studien zur Geschichte der Wirtschaft und Geisteskultur*, 1927, Band 3.

In this tradition, which kept rich Jews from real positions of power in capitalism, is the fact that in 1911 the Paris Rothschilds sold their share in the oil wells of Baku to the Royal Shell group, after having been, with the exception of Rockefeller, the world's biggest petroleum tycoons. This incident is reported in Richard Lewinsohn, *Wie sie gross und reich wurden*, Berlin, 1927.

André Sayou's statement ("Les Juifs" in *Revue Economique Internationale*, 1932) in his polemic against Werner Sombart's identification of Jews with capitalist development, may be taken as a general rule: "The Rothschilds and other Israelites who were almost exclusively engaged in launching state loans and in the international movement of capital, did not try at all . . . to create great industries."

prince's disposal. Only the combined wealth of the wealthier strata of Western and Central European Jewry, which they entrusted to some prominent Jewish bankers for such purposes, could suffice to meet the new enlarged governmental needs. This period brought with it the granting of privileges, which up to then had been necessary only for court Jews, to the larger wealthy class, which had managed to settle in the more important urban and financial centers in the eighteenth century. Finally emancipation was granted in all full-fledged nation-states and withheld only in those countries where Jews, because of their numbers and the general backwardness of these regions, had not been able to organize themselves into a special separate group whose economic function was financial support of their government.

3. Since this intimate relationship between national government and Jews had rested on the indifference of the bourgeoisie to politics in general and state finance in particular, this period came to an end with the rise of imperialism at the end of the nineteenth century when capitalist business in the form of expansion could no longer be carried out without active political help and intervention by the state. Imperialism, on the other hand, undermined the very foundations of the nation-state and introduced into the European comity of nations the competitive spirit of business concerns. In the early decades of this development, Jews lost their exclusive position in state business to imperialistically minded businessmen; they declined in importance as a group, although individual Jews kept their influence as financial advisers and as inter-European middlemen. These Jews, however—in contrast to the nineteenth-century state bankers—had even less need of the Jewish community at large, notwithstanding its wealth, than the court Jews of the seventeenth and eighteenth centuries, and therefore they frequently cut themselves off completely from the Jewish community. The Jewish communities were no longer financially organized, and although individual Jews in high positions remained representative of Jewry as a whole in the eyes of the Gentile world, there was little if any material reality behind this.

4. As a group, Western Jewry disintegrated together with the nation-state during the decades preceding the outbreak of the first World War. The rapid decline of Europe after the war found them already deprived of their former power, atomized into a herd of wealthy individuals. In an imperialist age, Jewish wealth had become insignificant; to a Europe with no sense of balance of power between its nations and of inter-European solidarity, the non-national, inter-European Jewish element became an object of universal hatred because of its useless wealth, and of contempt because of its lack of power.

The first governments to need regular income and secure finances were the absolute monarchies under which the nation-state came into being. Feudal princes and kings also had needed money, and even credit, but for specific purposes and temporary operations only; even in the sixteenth century, when the Fuggers put their own credit at the disposal of the state, they were not yet thinking of establishing a special state credit. The absolute monarchs at first provided for their financial needs partly through the old method of war and looting, and partly through the new device of tax monopoly. This undermined the power and ruined the fortunes of the nobility without assuaging the growing hostility of the population.

For a long time the absolute monarchies looked about society for a class upon which to rely as securely as the feudal monarchy had upon the nobility. In France an incessant struggle between the guilds and the monarchy, which wanted to incorporate them into the state system, had been going on since the fifteenth century. The most interesting of these experiments were doubtless the rise of mercantilism and the attempts of the absolute state to get an absolute monopoly over national business and industry. The resulting disaster, and the bankruptcy brought about by the concerted resistance of the rising bourgeoisie, are sufficiently well known.[5]

Before the emancipation edicts, every princely household and every monarch in Europe already had a court Jew to handle financial business. During the seventeenth and eighteenth centuries, these court Jews were always single individuals who had inter-European connections and inter-European credit at their disposal, but did not form an international financial entity.[6] Char-

---

[5] The influence, however, of mercantile experiments on future developments can hardly be overrated. France was the only country where the mercantile system was tried consistently and resulted in an early flourishing of manufactures which owed their existence to state interference; she never quite recovered from the experience. In the era of free enterprise, her bourgeoisie shunned unprotected investment in native industries while her bureaucracy, also a product of the mercantile system, survived its collapse. Despite the fact that the bureaucracy also lost all its productive functions, it is even today more characteristic of the country and a greater impediment to her recovery than the bourgeoisie.

[6] This had been the case in England since Queen Elizabeth's Marrano banker and the Jewish financiers of Cromwell's armies, until one of the twelve Jewish brokers admitted to the London Stock Exchange was said to have handled one-quarter of all government loans of his day (see Salo W. Baron, *A Social and Religious History of the Jews*, 1937, Vol. II: *Jews and Capitalism*); in Austria, where in only forty years (1695-1739), the Jews credited the government with more than 35 million florins and where the death of Samuel Oppenheimer in 1703 resulted in a grave financial crisis for both state and Emperor; in Bavaria, where in 1808 80 per cent of all government loans were endorsed and negotiated by Jews (see M. Grunwald, *Samuel Oppenheimer und sein Kreis,* 1913); in France, where mercantile conditions were especially favorable for the Jews, Colbert already praised their great usefulness to the state (Baron, *op. cit., loc. cit.*), and where in the middle of the eighteenth century the German Jew, Liefman Calmer, was made a baron by a grateful king who appreciated services and loyalty to "Our state and Our person" (Robert Anchel, "Un Baron Juif Français au 18e siècle, Liefman Calmer," in *Souvenir et Science,* I, pp. 52-55); and also in Prussia where Frederick II's *Münzjuden* were titled and where, at the end of the eighteenth century, 400 Jewish families formed one of the wealthiest groups in Berlin. (One of the best descriptions of Berlin and the role of the Jews in its society at the turn of the eighteenth century is to be found in Wilhelm Dilthey, *Das Leben Schleiermachers,* 1870, pp. 182 ff.).

acteristic of these times, when Jewish individuals and the first small wealthy Jewish communities were more powerful than at any time in the nineteenth century,[7] was the frankness with which their privileged status and their right to it was discussed, and the careful testimony of the authorities to the importance of their services to the state. There was not the slightest doubt or ambiguity about the connection between services rendered and privileges granted. Privileged Jews received noble titles almost as a matter of course in France, Bavaria, Austria and Prussia, so that even outwardly they were more than just wealthy men. The fact that the Rothschilds had such a hard time getting their application for a title approved by the Austrian government (they succeeded in 1817), was the signal that a whole period had come to an end.

By the end of the eighteenth century it had become clear that none of the estates or classes in the various countries was willing or able to become the new ruling class, that is to identify itself with the government as the nobility had done for centuries.[8] The failure of the absolute monarchy to find a substitute within society led to the full development of the nation-state and its claim to be above all classes, completely independent of society and its particular interests, the true and only representative of the nation as a whole. It resulted, on the other side, in a deepening of the split between state and society upon which the body politic of the nation rested. Without it, there would have been no need—or even any possibility—of introducing the Jews into European history on equal terms.

When all attempts to ally itself with one of the major classes in society had failed, the state chose to establish itself as a tremendous business concern. This was meant to be for administrative purposes only, to be sure, but the range of interests, financial and otherwise, and the costs were so great that one cannot but recognize the existence of a special sphere of state business from the eighteenth century on. The independent growth of state business was caused by a conflict with the financially powerful forces of the time, with the bourgeoisie which went the way of private investment, shunned all state intervention, and refused active financial participation in what appeared to be an "unproductive" enterprise. Thus the Jews were the only part of the population willing to finance the state's beginnings and to tie their destinies to its further development. With their credit and international connections, they were in an excellent position to help the nation-state to

[7] Early in the eighteenth century, Austrian Jews succeeded in banishing Eisemenger's *Entdecktes Judentum*, 1703, and at the end of it, *The Merchant of Venice* could be played in Berlin only with a little prologue apologizing to the (not emancipated) Jewish audience.

[8] The only, and irrelevant, exception might be those tax collectors, called *fermiers-généraux,* in France, who rented from the state the right to collect taxes by guaranteeing a fixed amount to the government. They earned their great wealth from and depended directly upon the absolute monarchy, but were too small a group and too isolated a phenomenon to be economically influential by themselves.

establish itself among the biggest enterprises and employers of the time.⁹

Great privileges, decisive changes in the Jewish condition, were necessarily the price of the fulfillment of such services, and, at the same time, the reward for great risks. The greatest privilege was equality. When the *Münzjuden* of Frederick of Prussia or the court Jews of the Austrian Emperor received through "general privileges" and "patents" the same status which half a century later all Prussian Jews received under the name of emancipation and equal rights; when, at the end of the eighteenth century and at the height of their wealth, the Berlin Jews managed to prevent an influx from the Eastern provinces because they did not care to share their "equality" with poorer brethren whom they did not recognize as equals; when, at the time of the French National Assembly, the Bordeaux and Avignon Jews protested violently against the French government's granting equality to Jews of the Eastern provinces—it became clear that at least the Jews were not thinking in terms of equal rights but of privileges and special liberties. And it is really not surprising that privileged Jews, intimately linked to the businesses of their governments and quite aware of the nature and conditions of their status, were reluctant to accept for all Jews this gift of a freedom which they themselves possessed as the price for services, which they knew had been calculated as such and therefore could hardly become a right for all.¹⁰

Only at the end of the nineteenth century, with the rise of imperialism, did the owning classes begin to change their original estimate of the unproductivity of state business. Imperialist expansion, together with the growing perfection of the instruments of violence and the state's absolute monopoly of them, made the state an interesting business proposition. This meant, of course, that the Jews gradually but automatically lost their exclusive and unique position.

But the good fortune of the Jews, their rise from obscurity to political significance; would have come to an even earlier end if they had been confined to a mere business function in the growing nation-states. By the middle of the last century some states had won enough confidence to get

⁹ The urgencies compelling the ties between government business and the Jews may be gauged by those cases in which decidedly anti-Jewish officials had to carry out the policies. So Bismarck, in his youth, made a few antisemitic speeches only to become, as chancellor of the Reich, a close friend of Bleichroeder and a reliable protector of the Jews against Court Chaplain Stoecker's antisemitic movement in Berlin. William II, although as Crown Prince and a member of the anti-Jewish Prussian nobility very sympathetic to all antisemitic movements in the eighties, changed his antisemitic convictions and deserted his antisemitic protégés overnight when he inherited the throne.

¹⁰ As early as the eighteenth century, wherever whole Jewish groups got wealthy enough to be useful to the state, they enjoyed collective privileges and were separated as a group from their less wealthy and useful brethren, even in the same country. Like the *Schutzjuden* in Prussia, the Bordeaux and Bayonne Jews in France enjoyed equality long before the French Revolution and were even invited to present their complaints and propositions along with the other General Estates in the *Convocation des Etats Généraux* of 1787.

along without Jewish backing and financing of government loans.[11] The nationals' growing consciousness, moreover, that their private destinies were becoming more and more dependent upon those of their countries made them ready to grant the governments more of the necessary credit. Equality itself was symbolized in the availability to all of government bonds which were finally even considered the most secure form of capital investment simply because the state, which could wage national wars, was the only agency which actually could protect its citizens' properties. From the middle of the nineteenth century on, the Jews could keep their prominent position only because they had still another more important and fateful role to play, a role also intimately linked to their participation in the destinies of the state. Without territory and without a government of their own, the Jews had always been an inter-European element; this international status the nation-state necessarily preserved because the Jews' financial services rested on it. But even when their economic usefulness had exhausted itself, the inter-European status of the Jews remained of great national importance in times of national conflicts and wars.

While the need of the nation-states for Jewish services developed slowly and logically, growing out of the general context of European history, the rise of the Jews to political and economic significance was sudden and unexpected to themselves as well as their neighbors. By the later Middle Ages the Jewish moneylender had lost all his former importance, and in the early sixteenth century Jews had already been expelled from cities and trade centers into villages and countryside, thereby exchanging a more uniform protection from remote higher authorities for an insecure status granted by petty local nobles.[12] The turning point had been in the seventeenth century when, during the Thirty Years' War and precisely because of their dispersion, these small, insignificant moneylenders could guarantee the necessary provisions to the mercenary armies of the war-lords in far-away lands and with the aid of small peddlers buy victuals in entire provinces. Since these wars remained half-feudal, more or less private affairs of the princes, involving no interest of other classes and enlisting no help from the people, the Jews' gain in status was very limited and hardly visible. But the number of court Jews increased because now every feudal household needed the equivalent of the court Jew.

As long as these court Jews served small feudal lords who, as members

[11] Jean Capefigue (*Histoire des grandes opérations financières,* Tome III: *Banque, Bourses, Emprunts,* 1855) pretends that during the July Monarchy only the Jews, and especially the house of Rothschild, prevented a sound state credit based upon the Banque de France. He also claims that the events of 1848 made the activities of the Rothschilds superfluous. Raphael Strauss ("The Jews in the Economic Evolution of Central Europe" in *Jewish Social Studies,* III, 1, 1941) also remarks that after 1830 "public credit already became less of a risk so that Christian banks began to handle this business in increasing measure." Against these interpretations stands the fact that excellent relations prevailed between the Rothschilds and Napoleon III, although there can be no doubt as to the general trend of the time.

[12] See Priebatsch, *op. cit.*

of the nobility, did not aspire to represent any centralized authority, they were the servants of only one group in society. The property they handled, the money they lent, the provisions they bought up, all were considered the private property of their master, so that such activities could not involve them in political matters. Hated or favored, Jews could not become a political issue of any importance.

When, however, the function of the feudal lord changed, when he developed into a prince or king, the function of his court Jew changed too. The Jews, being an alien element, without much interest in such changes in their environment, were usually the last to become aware of their heightened status. As far as they were concerned, they went on handling private business, and their loyalty remained a personal affair unrelated to political considerations. Loyalty meant honesty; it did not mean taking sides in a conflict or remaining true for political reasons. To buy up provisions, to clothe and feed an army, to lend currency for the hiring of mercenaries, meant simply an interest in the well-being of a business partner.

This kind of relationship between Jews and aristocracy was the only one that ever tied a Jewish group to another stratum in society. After it disappeared in the early nineteenth century, it was never replaced. Its only remnant for the Jews was a penchant for aristocratic titles (especially in Austria and France), and for the non-Jews a brand of liberal antisemitism which lumped Jews and nobility together and pretended that they were in some kind of financial alliance against the rising bourgeoisie. Such argumentation, current in Prussia and France, had a certain amount of plausibility as long as there was no general emancipation of the Jews. The privileges of the court Jews had indeed an obvious similarity to the rights and liberties of the nobility, and it was true that the Jews were as much afraid of losing their privileges and used the same arguments against equality as members of the aristocracy. The plausibility became even greater in the eighteenth century when most privileged Jews were given minor titles, and at the opening of the nineteenth century when wealthy Jews who had lost their ties with the Jewish communities looked for new social status and began to model themselves on the aristocracy. But all this was of little consequence, first because it was quite obvious that the nobility was on the decline and that the Jews, on the contrary, were continually gaining in status, and also because the aristocracy itself, especially in Prussia, happened to become the first class that produced an antisemitic ideology.

The Jews had been the purveyors in wars and the servants of kings, but they did not and were not expected to engage in the conflicts themselves. When these conflicts enlarged into national wars, they still remained an international element whose importance and usefulness lay precisely in their not being bound to any national cause. No longer state bankers and purveyors in wars (the last war financed by a Jew was the Prussian-Austrian war of 1866, when Bleichroeder helped Bismarck after the latter had been refused the necessary credits by the Prussian Parliament), the Jews had become the financial advisers and assistants in peace treaties and, in a less organized and more indefinite way, the providers of news. The last peace treaties drawn up without Jewish assistance were those of the Congress of Vienna, between the continental powers and France. Bleichroeder's role in the peace negotiations between Germany and France in 1871 was already more significant than his help in war,[13] and he rendered even more important services in the late seventies when, through his connections with the Rothschilds, he provided Bismarck with an indirect news channel to Benjamin Disraeli. The peace treaties of Versailles were the last in which Jews played a prominent role as advisers. The last Jew who owed his prominence on the national scene to his international Jewish connections was Walter Rathenau, the ill-fated foreign minister of the Weimar Republic. He paid with his life for having (as one of his colleagues put it after his death) donated his prestige in the international world of finance and the support of Jews everywhere in the world [14] to the ministers of the new Republic, who were completely unknown on the international scene.

That antisemitic governments would not use Jews for the business of war and peace is obvious. But the elimination of Jews from the international scene had a more general and deeper significance than antisemitism. Just because the Jews had been used as a non-national element, they could be of value in war and peace only as long as during the war everybody tried consciously to keep the possibilities of peace intact, only as long as everybody's aim was a peace of compromise and the re-establishment of a *modus vivendi.* As soon as "victory or death" became a determining policy, and war actually aimed at the complete annihilation of the enemy, the Jews could no longer be of any use. This policy spelled destruction of their collective existence in any case, although the disappearance from the political scene and even extinction of a specific group-life would by no means necessarily have led to their physical extermination. The frequently repeated argument, however, that the Jews would have become Nazis as easily as their German fellow-citizens if only they had been permitted to join the movement, just as they had enlisted in Italy's Fascist party before Italian Fascism introduced race legislation, is only half true. It is true only with respect to the psychology of individual Jews, which of course did not greatly differ from the psychology of their environment. It is patently false in a historical sense. Nazism, even without antisemitism, would have been the deathblow to the existence of the Jewish people in Europe; to consent to it would have

[13] According to an anecdote, faithfully reported by all his biographers, Bismarck said immediately after the French defeat in 1871: "First of all, Bleichroeder has got to go to Paris, to get together with his fellow Jews and to talk it (the five billion francs for reparations) over with the bankers." (See Otto Joehlinger, *Bismarck und die Juden,* Berlin, 1921.)

[14] See Walter Frank, "Walter Rathenau und die blonde Rasse," in *Forschungen zur Judenfrage,* Band IV, 1940. Frank, in spite of his official position under the Nazis, remained somewhat careful about his sources and methods. In this article he quotes from the obituaries on Rathenau in the *Israelitisches Familienblatt* (Hamburg, July 6, 1922), *Die Zeit,* (June, 1922) and *Berliner Tageblatt* (May 31, 1922).

meant suicide, not necessarily for individuals of Jewish origin, but for the Jews as a people.

To the first contradiction, which determined the destiny of European Jewry during the last centuries, that is, the contradiction between equality and privilege (rather of equality granted in the form and for the purpose of privilege) must be added a second contradiction: the Jews, the only non-national European people, were threatened more than any other by the sudden collapse of the system of nation-states. This situation is less paradoxical than it may appear at first glance. Representatives of the nation, whether Jacobins from Robespierre to Clemenceau, or representatives of Central European reactionary governments from Metternich to Bismarck, had one thing in common: they were all sincerely concerned with the "balance of power" in Europe. They tried, of course, to shift this balance to the advantage of their respective countries, but they never dreamed of seizing a monopoly over the continent or of annihilating their neighbors completely. The Jews could not only be used in the interest of this precarious balance, they even became a kind of symbol of the common interest of the European nations.

It is therefore more than accidental that the catastrophic defeats of the peoples of Europe began with the catastrophe of the Jewish people. It was particularly easy to begin the dissolution of the precarious European balance of power with the elimination of the Jews, and particularly difficult to understand that more was involved in this elimination than an unusually cruel nationalism or an ill-timed revival of "old prejudices." When the catastrophe came, the fate of the Jewish people was considered a "special case" whose history follows exceptional laws, and whose destiny was therefore of no general relevance. This breakdown of European solidarity was at once reflected in the breakdown of Jewish solidarity all over Europe. When the persecution of German Jews began, Jews of other European countries discovered that German Jews constituted an exception whose fate could bear no resemblance to their own. Similarly, the collapse of German Jewry was preceded by its split into innumerable factions, each of which believed and hoped that its basic human rights would be protected by special privileges— the privilege of having been a veteran of World War I, the child of a veteran, the proud son of a father killed in action. It looked as though the annihilation of all individuals of Jewish origin was being preceded by the bloodless destruction and self-dissolution of the Jewish people, as though the Jewish people had owed its existence exclusively to other peoples and their hatred.

It is still one of the most moving aspects of Jewish history that the Jews' active entry into European history was caused by their being an inter-European, non-national element in a world of growing or existing nations. That this role proved more lasting and more essential than their function as state bankers is one of the material reasons for the new modern type of Jewish productivity in the arts and sciences. It is not without historical justice that their downfall coincided with the ruin of a system and a political body which, whatever its other defects, had needed and could tolerate a purely European element. The grandeur of this consistently European existence should not be forgotten because of the many undoubtedly less attractive aspects of Jewish history during the last centuries. The few European authors who have been aware of this aspect of the "Jewish question" had no special sympathies for the Jews, but an unbiased estimate of the whole European situation. Among them was Diderot, the only eighteenth-century French philosopher who was not hostile to the Jews and who recognized in them a useful link between Europeans of different nationalities; Wilhelm von Humboldt who, witnessing their emancipation through the French Revolution, remarked that the Jews would lose their universality when they were changed into Frenchmen; [15] and finally Friedrich Nietzsche, who out of disgust with Bismarck's German Reich coined the word "good European," which made possible his correct estimate of the significant role of the Jews in European history, and saved him from falling into the pitfalls of cheap philosemitism or patronizing "progressive" attitudes.

This evaluation, though quite correct in the description of a surface phenomenon, overlooks the most serious paradox embodied in the curious political history of the Jews. Of all European peoples, the Jews had been the only one without a state of their own and had been, precisely for this reason, so eager and so suitable for alliances with governments and states as such, no matter what these governments or states might represent. On the other hand, the Jews had no political tradition or experience, and were as little aware of the tension between society and state as they were of the obvious risks and power-possibilities of their new role. What little knowledge or traditional practice they brought to politics had its source first in the Roman Empire, where they had been protected, so to speak, by the Roman soldier, and later, in the Middle Ages, when they sought and received protection against the population and the local rulers from remote monarchical and Church authorities. From these experiences, they had somehow drawn the conclusion that authority, and especially high authority, was favorable to them and that lower officials, and especially the common people, were dangerous. This prejudice, which expressed a definite historical truth but no longer corresponded to new circumstances, was as deeply rooted in and as unconsciously shared by the vast majority of Jews as corresponding prejudices about Jews were commonly accepted by Gentiles.

The history of the relationship between Jews and governments is rich in examples of how quickly Jewish bankers switched their allegiance from one

[15] Wilhelm von Humboldt, *Tagebücher,* ed. by Leitzmann, Berlin, 1916-1918, I, 475.—The article "Juif" of the *Encyclopédie,* 1751-1765, Vol. IX, which was probably written by Diderot: "Thus dispersed in our time . . . [the Jews] have become instruments of communication between the most distant countries. They are like the cogs and nails needed in a great building in order to join and hold together all other parts."

government to the next even after revolutionary changes. It took the French Rothschilds in 1848 hardly twenty-four hours to transfer their services from the government of Louis Philippe to the new short-lived French Republic and again to Napoleon III. The same process repeated itself, at a slightly slower pace, after the downfall of the Second Empire and the establishment of the Third Republic. In Germany this sudden and easy change was symbolized, after the revolution of 1918, in the financial policies of the Warburgs on one hand and the shifting political ambitions of Walter Rathenau on the other.[16]

More is involved in this type of behavior than the simple bourgeois pattern which always assumes that nothing succeeds like success.[17] Had the Jews been bourgeois in the ordinary sense of the word, they might have gauged correctly the tremendous power-possibilities of their new functions, and at least have tried to play that fictitious role of a secret world power which makes and unmakes governments, which antisemites assigned to them anyway. Nothing, however, could be farther from the truth. The Jews, without knowledge of or interest in power, never thought of exercising more than mild pressure for minor purposes of self-defense. This lack of ambition was later sharply resented by the more assimilated sons of Jewish bankers and businessmen. While some of them dreamed, like Disraeli, of a secret Jewish society to which they might belong and which never existed, others, like Rathenau, who happened to be better informed, indulged in half-antisemitic tirades against the wealthy traders who had neither power nor social status.

This innocence has never been quite understood by non-Jewish statesmen or historians. On the other hand, their detachment from power was so much taken for granted by Jewish representatives or writers that they hardly ever mentioned it except to express their surprise at the absurd suspicions leveled against them. In the memoirs of statesmen of the last century many remarks occur to the effect that there won't be a war because Rothschild in London or Paris or Vienna does not want it. Even so sober and reliable a historian as J. A. Hobson could state as late as 1905: "Does any one seriously suppose that a great war could be undertaken by any European state, or a great state loan subscribed, if the House of Rothschild and its connexions set their face against it?" [18] This misjudgment is as amusing in its naïve assumption

[16] Walter Rathenau, foreign minister of the Weimar Republic in 1921 and one of the outstanding representatives of Germany's new will to democracy, had proclaimed as late as 1917 his "deep monarchical convictions," according to which only an "anointed" and no "upstart of a lucky career" should lead a country. See *Von kommenden Dingen*, 1917, p. 247.

[17] This bourgeois pattern, however, should not be forgotten. If it were only a matter of individual motives and behavior patterns, the methods of the house of Rothschild certainly did not differ much from those of their Gentile colleagues. For instance, Napoleon's banker, Ouvrard, after having provided the financial means for Napoleon's hundred days' war, immediately offered his services to the returning Bourbons.

[18] J. H. Hobson, *Imperialism*, 1905, p. 57 of unrevised 1938 edition.

THE NATION-STATE; THE BIRTH OF ANTISEMITISM

that everyone is like oneself, as Metternich's sincere belief that "the house of Rothschild played a greater role in France than any foreign government," or his confident prediction to the Viennese Rothschilds shortly before the Austrian revolution in 1848: "If I should go to the dogs, you would go with me." The truth of that matter was that the Rothschilds had as little political idea as other Jewish bankers of what they wanted to carry out in France, to say nothing of a well-defined purpose which would even remotely suggest a war. On the contrary, like their fellow Jews they never allied themselves with any specific government, but rather with governments, with authority as such. If at this time and later they showed a marked preference for monarchical governments as against republics, it was only because they rightly suspected that republics were based to a greater extent on the will of the people, which they instinctively mistrusted.

How deep the Jews' faith in the state was, and how fantastic their ignorance of actual conditions in Europe, came to light in the last years of the Weimar Republic when, already reasonably frightened about the future, the Jews for once tried their hand in politics. With the help of a few non-Jews, they then founded that middle-class party which they called "State-party" (*Staatspartei*), the very name a contradiction in terms. They were so naïvely convinced that their "party," supposedly representing them in political and social struggle, ought to be the state itself, that the whole relationship of the party to the state never dawned upon them. If anybody had bothered to take seriously this party of respectable and bewildered gentlemen, he could only have concluded that loyalty at any price was a façade behind which sinister forces plotted to take over the state.

Just as the Jews ignored completely the growing tension between state and society, they were also the last to be aware that circumstances had forced them into the center of the conflict. They therefore never knew how to evaluate antisemitism, or rather never recognized the moment when social discrimination changed into a political argument. For more than a hundred years, antisemitism had slowly and gradually made its way into almost all social strata in almost all European countries until it emerged suddenly as the one issue upon which an almost unified opinion could be achieved. The law according to which this process developed was simple: each class of society which came into a conflict with the state as such became anti-semitic because the only social group which seemed to represent the state were the Jews. And the only class which proved almost immune from anti-semitic propaganda were the workers who, absorbed in the class struggle and equipped with a Marxist explanation of history, never came into direct conflict with the state but only with another class of society, the bourgeoisie, which the Jews certainly did not represent, and of which they were never a significant part.

The political emancipation of the Jews at the turn of the eighteenth century in some countries, and its discussion in the rest of Central and Western Europe, resulted first of all in a decisive change in their attitude toward the state, which was somehow symbolized in the rise of the house of Rothschild. The new policy of these court Jews, who were the first to become full-fledged state bankers, came to light when they were no longer content to serve one particular prince or government through their international relationships with court Jews of other countries, but decided to establish themselves internationally and serve simultaneously and concurrently the governments in Germany, France, Great Britain, Italy and Austria. To a large extent, this unprecedented course was a reaction of the Rothschilds to the dangers of real emancipation, which, together with equality, threatened to nationalize the Jewries of the respective countries, and to destroy the very inter-European advantages on which the position of Jewish bankers had rested. Old Meyer Amschel Rothschild, the founder of the house, must have recognized that the inter-European status of Jews was no longer secure and that he had better try to realize this unique international position in his own family. The establishment of his five sons in the five financial capitals of Europe—Frankfurt, Paris, London, Naples and Vienna—was his ingenious way out of the embarrassing emancipation of the Jews.[19]

The Rothschilds had entered upon their spectacular career as the financial servants of the Kurfürst of Hessen, one of the outstanding moneylenders of his time, who taught them business practice and provided them with many of their customers. Their great advantage was that they lived in Frankfurt, the only great urban center from which Jews had never been expelled and where they formed nearly 10 per cent of the city's population at the beginning of the nineteenth century. The Rothschilds started as court Jews without being under the jurisdiction of either a prince or the Free City, but directly under the authority of the distant Emperor in Vienna. They thus combined all the advantages of the Jewish status in the Middle Ages with those of their own times, and were much less dependent upon nobility or other local authorities than any of their fellow court Jews. The later financial activities of the house, the tremendous fortune they amassed, and their even greater symbolic fame since the early nineteenth century, are sufficiently well known.[20] They entered the scene of big business during the last years of the Napoleonic wars when—from 1811 to 1816—almost half the English subventions to the Continental powers went through their hands. When after the defeat of Napoleon the Continent needed great government loans everywhere for the reorganization of its state machines and the erection of financial structures on the model of the Bank of England, the Rothschilds enjoyed almost a monopoly in the handling of state loans. This lasted for three generations

[19] How well the Rothschilds knew the sources of their strength is shown in their early house law according to which daughters and their husbands were eliminated from the business of the house. The girls were allowed, and after 1871, even encouraged, to marry into the non-Jewish aristocracy; the male descendants had to marry Jewish girls exclusively, and if possible (in the first generation this was generally the case) members of the family.

[20] See especially Egon Cesar Conte Corti, *The Rise of the House of Rothschild*, New York, 1927.

during which they succeeded in defeating all Jewish and non-Jewish competitors in the field. "The House of Rothschild became," as Capefigue put it,[21] "the chief treasurer of the Holy Alliance."

The international establishment of the house of Rothschild and its sudden rise above all other Jewish bankers changed the whole structure of Jewish state business. Gone was the accidental development, unplanned and unorganized, when individual Jews shrewd enough to take advantage of a unique opportunity frequently rose to the heights of great wealth and fell to the depths of poverty in one man's lifetime; when such a fate hardly touched the destinies of the Jewish people as a whole except insofar as such Jews sometimes had acted as protectors and petitioners for distant communities; when, no matter how numerous the wealthy moneylenders or how influential the individual court Jews, there was no sign of the development of a well-defined Jewish group which collectively enjoyed specific privileges and rendered specific services. It was precisely the Rothschilds' monopoly on the issuance of government loans which made it possible and necessary to draw on Jewish capital at large, to direct a great percentage of Jewish wealth into the channels of state business, and which thereby provided the natural basis for a new inter-European cohesiveness of Central and Western European Jewry. What in the seventeenth and eighteenth centuries had been an unorganized connection among individual Jews of different countries, now became the more systematic disposition of these scattered opportunities by a single firm, physically present in all important European capitals, in constant contact with all sections of the Jewish people, and in complete possession of all pertinent information and all opportunities for organization.[22]

The exclusive position of the house of Rothschild in the Jewish world replaced to a certain extent the old bonds of religious and spiritual tradition whose gradual loosening under the impact of Western culture for the first time threatened the very existence of the Jewish people. To the outer world, this one family also became a symbol of the working reality of Jewish internationalism in a world of nation-states and nationally organized peoples. Where, indeed, was there better proof of the fantastic concept of a Jewish world government than in this one family, nationals of five different countries, prominent everywhere, in close co-operation with at least three different governments (the French, the Austrian, and the British), whose frequent conflicts never for a moment shook the solidarity of interest of their state bankers? No propaganda could have created a symbol more effective for political purposes than the reality itself.

The popular notion that the Jews—in contrast to other peoples—were tied together by the supposedly closer bonds of blood and family ties, was to a large extent stimulated by the reality of this one family, which virtually

[21] Capefigue, *op. cit.*

[22] It has never been possible to ascertain the extent to which the Rothschilds used Jewish capital for their own business transactions and how far their control of Jewish bankers went. The family has never permitted a scholar to work in its archives.

represented the whole economic and political significance of the Jewish people. The fateful consequence was that when, for reasons which had nothing to do with the Jewish question, race problems came to the foreground of the political scene, the Jews at once fitted all ideologies and doctrines which defined a people by blood ties and family characteristics.

Yet another, less accidental, fact accounts for this image of the Jewish people. In the preservation of the Jewish people the family had played a far greater role than in any Western political or social body except the nobility. Family ties were among the most potent and stubborn elements with which the Jewish people resisted assimilation and dissolution. Just as declining European nobility strengthened its marriage and house laws, so Western Jewry became all the more family-conscious in the centuries of their spiritual and religious dissolution. Without the old hope for Messianic redemption and the firm ground of traditional folkways, Western Jewry became overconscious of the fact that their survival had been achieved in an alien and often hostile environment. They began to look upon the inner family circle as a kind of last fortress and to behave toward members of their own group as though they were members of a big family. In other words, the antisemitic picture of the Jewish people as a family closely knit by blood ties had something in common with the Jews' own picture of themselves.

This situation was an important factor in the early rise and continuous growth of antisemitism in the nineteenth century. Which group of people would turn antisemitic in a given country at a given historical moment depended exclusively upon general circumstances which made them ready for a violent antagonism to their government. But the remarkable similarity of arguments and images which time and again were spontaneously reproduced have an intimate relationship with the truth they distort. We find the Jews always represented as an international trade organization, a world-wide family concern with identical interests everywhere, a secret force behind the throne which degrades all visible governments into mere façade, or into marionettes whose strings are manipulated from behind the scenes. Because of their close relationship to state sources of power, the Jews were invariably identified with power, and because of their aloofness from society and concentration upon the closed circle of the family, they were invariably suspected of working for the destruction of all social structures.

II: *Early Antisemitism*

IT IS an obvious, if frequently forgotten, rule that anti-Jewish feeling acquires political relevance only when it can combine with a major political issue, or when Jewish group interests come into open conflict with those of a major class in society. Modern antisemitism, as we know it from Central and Western European countries, had political rather than economic causes, while complicated class conditions produced the violent popular hatred of Jews in Poland and Rumania. There, due to the inability of the governments to solve the land question and give the nation-state a minimum of equality through liberation of the peasants, the feudal aristocracy succeeded not only in maintaining its political dominance but also in preventing the rise of a normal middle class. The Jews of these countries, strong in number and weak in every other respect, seemingly fulfilled some of the functions of the middle class, because they were mostly shopkeepers and traders and because as a group they stood between the big landowners and the propertyless classes. Small property holders, however, can exist as well in a feudal as in a capitalist economy. The Jews, here as elsewhere, were unable or unwilling to develop along industrial capitalist lines, so that the net result of their activities was a scattered, inefficient organization of consumption without an adequate system of production. The Jewish positions were an obstacle for a normal capitalistic development because they looked as though they were the only ones from which economic advancement might be expected without being capable of fulfilling this expectation. Because of their appearance, Jewish interests were felt to be in conflict with those sections of the population from which a middle class could normally have developed. The governments, on the other hand, tried halfheartedly to encourage a middle class without liquidating the nobility and big landowners. Their only serious attempt was economic liquidation of the Jews—partly as a concession to public opinion, and partly because the Jews were actually still a part of the old feudal order. For centuries they had been middlemen between the nobility and peasantry; now they formed a middle class without fulfilling its productive functions and were indeed one of the elements that stood in the way of industrialization and capitalization.[23] These Eastern European conditions, however, although they constituted the essence of the Jewish mass question, are of little importance in our context. Their political significance was limited to backward countries where the ubiquitous hatred of Jews made it almost useless as a weapon for specific purposes.

Antisemitism first flared up in Prussia immediately after the defeat by Napoleon in 1807, when the "Reformers" changed the political structure so that the nobility lost its privileges and the middle classes won their freedom to develop. This reform, a "revolution from above," changed the half-feudal structure of Prussia's enlightened despotism into a more or less modern nation-state whose final stage was the German Reich of 1871.

Although a majority of the Berlin bankers of the time were Jews, the Prussian reforms did not require any considerable financial help from them. The outspoken sympathies of the Prussian reformers, their advocacy of Jewish emancipation, was the consequence of the new equality of all citizens, the abolition of privilege, and the introduction of free trade. They were not interested in the preservation of Jews as Jews for special purposes. Their

[23] James Parkes, *The Emergence of the Jewish Problem, 1878-1939*, 1946, discusses these conditions briefly and without bias in chapters iv and vi.

reply to the argument that under conditions of equality "the Jews might cease to exist" would always have been: "Let them. How does this matter to a government which asks only that they become good citizens?" [24] Emancipation, moreover, was relatively inoffensive, for Prussia had just lost the eastern provinces which had a large and poor Jewish population. The emancipation decree of 1812 concerned only those wealthy and useful Jewish groups who were already privileged with most civic rights and who, through the general abolition of privileges, would have suffered a severe loss in civil status. For these groups, emancipation meant not much more than a general legal affirmation of the status quo.

But the sympathies of the Prussian reformers for the Jews were more than the logical consequence of their general political aspirations. When, almost a decade later and in the midst of rising antisemitism, Wilhelm von Humboldt declared: "I love the Jews really only *en masse; en détail* I rather avoid them," [25] he stood of course in open opposition to the prevailing fashion, which favored individual Jews and despised the Jewish people. A true democrat, he wanted to liberate an oppressed people and not bestow privileges upon individuals. But this view was also in the tradition of the old Prussian government officials, whose consistent insistence throughout the eighteenth century upon better conditions and improved education for Jews have frequently been recognized. Their support was not motivated by economic or state reasons alone, but by a natural sympathy for the only social group that also stood outside the social body and within the sphere of the state, albeit for entirely different reasons. The education of a civil service whose loyalty belonged to the state and was independent of change in government, and which had severed its class ties, was one of the outstanding achievements of the old Prussian state. These officials were a decisive group in eighteenth-century Prussia, and the actual predecessors of the Reformers; they remained the backbone of the state machine all through the nineteenth century, although they lost much of their influence to the aristocracy after the Congress of Vienna.[26]

Through the attitude of the Reformers and especially through the emancipation edict of 1812, the special interests of the state in the Jews became manifest in a curious way. The old frank recognition of their usefulness as Jews (Frederick II of Prussia exclaimed, when he heard of possible mass-conversion: "I hope they won't do such a devilish thing!") [27] was gone. Emancipation was granted in the name of a principle, and any allusion to

---

[24] Christian Wilhelm Dohm, *Über die bürgerliche Verbesserung der Juden,* Berlin and Stettin, 1781, I, 174.

[25] *Wilhelm und Caroline von Humboldt in ihren Briefen,* Berlin, 1900, V, 236.

[26] For an excellent description of these civil servants who were not essentially different in different countries, see Henri Pirenne, *A History of Europe from the Invasions to the XVI Century,* London, 1939, pp. 361-362: "Without class prejudices and hostile to the privileges of the great nobles who despised them, . . . it was not the King who spoke through them, but the anonymous monarchy, superior to all, subduing all to its power."

[27] See *Kleines Jahrbuch des Nützlichen und Angenehmen für Israeliten,* 1847.

special Jewish services would have been sacrilege, according to the mentality of the time. The special conditions which had led to emancipation, though well known to everybody concerned, were now hidden as if they were a great and terrible secret. The edict itself, on the other hand, was conceived as the last and, in a sense, the most shining achievement of change from a feudal state into a nation-state and a society where henceforth there would be no special privileges whatsoever.

Among the naturally bitter reactions of the aristocracy, the class that was hardest hit, was a sudden and unexpected outburst of antisemitism. Its most articulate spokesman, Ludwig von der Marwitz (prominent among the founders of a conservative ideology), submitted a lengthy petition to the government in which he said that the Jews would now be the only group enjoying special advantages, and spoke of the "transformation of the old awe-inspiring Prussian monarchy into a new-fangled Jew-state." The political attack was accompanied by a social boycott which changed the face of Berlin society almost overnight. For aristocrats had been among the first to establish friendly social relationship with Jews and had made famous those salons of Jewish hostesses at the turn of the century, where a truly mixed society gathered for a brief time. To a certain extent, it is true, this lack of prejudice was the result of the services rendered by the Jewish moneylender who for centuries had been excluded from all greater business transactions and found his only opportunity in the economically un-productive and insignificant but socially important loans to people who had a tendency to live beyond their means. Nevertheless, it is remarkable that social relationships survived when the absolute monarchies with their greater financial possibilities had made the private loan business and the individual small court Jew a thing of the past. A nobleman's natural resentment against losing a valuable source of help in emergencies made him want to marry a Jewish girl with a rich father rather than hate the Jewish people.

Nor was the outburst of aristocratic antisemitism the result of a closer contact between Jews and nobility. On the contrary, they had in common an instinctive opposition to the new values of the middle classes, and one that sprang from very similar sources. In Jewish as well as in noble families, the individual was regarded first of all as a member of a family; his duties were first of all determined by the family which transcended the life and importance of the individual. Both were a-national and inter-European, and each understood the other's way of life in which national allegiance was secondary to loyalty to a family which more often than not was scattered all over Europe. They shared a conception that the present is nothing more than an insignificant link in the chain of past and future generations. Anti-Jewish liberal writers did not fail to point out this curious similarity of prin-ciples, and they concluded that perhaps one could get rid of nobility only by first getting rid of the Jews, and this not because of their financial connections but because both were considered to be a hindrance to the true development of that "innate personality," that ideology of self-respect, which the liberal middle classes employed in their fight against the concepts of birth, family, and heritage.

These pro-Jewish factors make it all the more significant that the aristocrats started the long line of antisemitic political argumentation. Neither economic ties nor social intimacy carried any weight in a situation where aristocracy openly opposed the egalitarian nation-state. Socially, the attack on the state identified the Jews with the government; despite the fact that the middle classes, economically and socially, reaped the real gains in the reforms, politically they were hardly blamed and suffered the old contemptuous aloofness.

After the Congress of Vienna, when during the long decades of peaceful reaction under the Holy Alliance, Prussian nobility had won back much of its influence on the state and temporarily become even more prominent than it had ever been in the eighteenth century, aristocratic antisemitism changed at once into mild discrimination without further political significance.[28] At the same time, with the help of the romantic intellectuals, conservatism reached its full development as one of the political ideologies which in Germany adopted a very characteristic and ingeniously equivocal attitude toward the Jews. From then on the nation-state, equipped with conservative arguments, drew a distinct line between Jews who were needed and wanted and those who were not. Under the pretext of the essential Christian character of the state—what could have been more alien to the enlightened despots!—the growing Jewish intelligentsia could be openly discriminated against without harming the affairs of bankers and businessmen. This kind of discrimination which tried to close the universities to Jews by excluding them from the civil services had the double advantage of indicating that the nation-state valued special services higher than equality, and of preventing, or at least postponing, the birth of a new group of Jews who were of no apparent use to the state and even likely to be assimilated into society.[29] When, in the eighties, Bismarck went to considerable trouble to protect the Jews against Stoecker's antisemitic propaganda, he said *expressis verbis* that he wanted to protest only against the attacks upon "moneyed Jewry . . . whose interests are tied to the conservation of our state institutions" and that his friend Bleichroeder, the Prussian banker, did not complain about attacks on Jews in general (which he might have overlooked) but on rich Jews.[30]

[28] When the Prussian Government submitted a new emancipation law to the *Vereinigte Landtage* in 1847, nearly all members of the high aristocracy favored complete Jewish emancipation, See I. Elbogen, *Geschichte der Juden in Deutschland,* Berlin, 1935, p. 244.

[29] This was the reason why Prussian kings were so very much concerned with the strictest conservation of Jewish customs and religious rituals. In 1823 Frederick William III prohibited "the slightest renovations," and his successor, Frederick William IV, openly declared that "the state must not do anything which could further an amalgamation between the Jews and the other inhabitants" of his kingdom. Elbogen, *op. cit.,* pp. 223, 234.

[30] In a letter to *Kultusminister* v. Puttkammer in October, 1880. See also Herbert von Bismarck's letter of November, 1880, to Tiedemann. Both letters in Walter

The seeming equivocation with which government officials on the one hand protested against equality (especially professional equality) for the Jews, or complained somewhat later about Jewish influence in the press and yet, on the other, sincerely "wished them well in every respect," [31] was much more suited to the interests of the state than the earlier zeal of the reformer. After all, the Congress of Vienna had returned to Prussia the provinces in which the poor Jewish masses had lived for centuries, and nobody but a few intellectuals who dreamed of the French Revolution and the Rights of Man had ever thought of giving them the same status as their wealthy brethren—who certainly were the last to clamor for an equality by which they could only lose.[32] They knew as well as anybody else that "every legal or political measure for the emancipation of the Jews must necessarily lead to a deterioration of their civic and social situation." [33] And they knew better than anybody else how much their power depended upon their position and prestige within the Jewish communities. So they could hardly adopt any other policy but to "endeavor to get more influence for themselves, and keep their fellow Jews in their national isolation, pretending that this separation is part of their religion. Why? . . . Because the others should depend upon them even more, so that they, as *unsere Leute,* could be used exclusively by those in power." [34] And it did turn out that in the twentieth century, when emancipation was for the first time an accomplished fact for the Jewish masses, the power of the privileged Jews had disappeared.

Thus a perfect harmony of interests was established between the powerful Jews and the state. Rich Jews wanted and obtained control over their fellow Jews and segregation from non-Jewish society; the state could combine a policy of benevolence toward rich Jews with legal discrimination against the Jewish intelligentsia and furtherance of social segregation, as expressed in the conservative theory of the Christian essence of the state.

While antisemitism among the nobility remained without political consequence and subsided quickly in the decades of the Holy Alliance, liberals

---

Frank, *Hofprediger Adolf Stoecker und die christlich-soziale Bewegung,* 1928, pp. 304, 305.

[31] August Varnhagen comments on a remark made by Frederick William IV. "The king was asked what he intended to do with the Jews. He replied: 'I wish them well in every respect, but I want them to feel that they are Jews.' These words provide a key to many things." *Tagebücher,* Leipzig, 1861, II, 113.

[32] That Jewish emancipation would have to be carried out against the desires of Jewish representatives was common knowledge in the eighteenth century. Mirabeau argued before the *Assemblée Nationale* in 1789: "Gentlemen, is it because the Jews don't want to be citizens that you don't proclaim them citizens? In a government like the one you now establish, all men must be men; you must expel all those who are not or who refuse to become men." The attitude of German Jews in the early nineteenth century is reported by J. M. Jost, *Neuere Geschichte der Israeliten. 1815-1845,* Berlin, 1846, Band 10.

[33] Adam Mueller (see *Ausgewählte Abhandlungen,* ed. by J. Baxa, Jena, 1921, p. 215) in a letter to Metternich in 1815.

[34] H. E. G. Paulus, *Die jüdische Nationalabsonderung nach Ursprung, Folgen und Besserungsmitteln,* 1831.

and radical intellectuals inspired and led a new movement immediately after the Congress of Vienna. Liberal opposition to Metternich's police regime on the continent and bitter attacks on the reactionary Prussian government led quickly to antisemitic outbursts and a veritable flood of anti-Jewish pamphlets. Precisely because they were much less candid and outspoken in their opposition to the government than the nobleman Marwitz had been a decade before, they attacked the Jews more than the government. Concerned mainly with equal opportunity and resenting most of all the revival of aristocratic privileges which limited their admission to the public services, they introduced into the discussion the distinction between individual Jews, "our brethren," and Jewry as a group, a distinction which from then on was to become the trademark of leftist antisemitism. Although they did not fully understand why and how the government, in its enforced independence from society, preserved and protected the Jews as a separate group, they knew well enough that some political connection existed and that the Jewish question was more than a problem of individual Jews and human tolerance. They coined the new nationalist phrases "state within the state," and "nation within the nation." Certainly wrong in the first instance, because the Jews had no political ambitions of their own and were merely the only social group that was unconditionally loyal to the state, they were half right in the second, because the Jews, taken as a social and not as a political body, actually did form a separate group within the nation.[35]

In Prussia, though not in Austria or in France, this radical antisemitism was almost as short-lived and inconsequential as the earlier antisemitism of nobility. The radicals were more and more absorbed by the liberalism of the economically rising middle classes, which all over Germany some twenty years later clamored in their diets for Jewish emancipation and for realization of political equality. It established, however, a certain theoretical and even literary tradition whose influence can be recognized in the famous anti-Jewish writings of the young Marx, who so frequently and unjustly has been accused of antisemitism. That the Jew, Karl Marx, could write the same way these anti-Jewish radicals did is only proof of how little this kind of anti-Jewish argument had in common with full-fledged antisemitism. Marx as an individual Jew was as little embarrassed by these arguments against "Jewry" as, for instance, Nietzsche was by his arguments against Germany. Marx, it is true, in his later years never wrote or uttered an opinion on the Jewish question; but this is hardly due to any fundamental change of mind. His exclusive preoccupation with class struggle as a phenomenon inside society, with the problems of capitalist production in which Jews were not involved as either buyers or sellers of labor, and his utter neglect of political questions, automatically prevented his further inspection of the state structure, and thereby of the role of the Jews. The strong influence of Marxism on the labor movement in Germany is among the chief reasons why German

[35] For a clear and reliable account of German antisemitism in the nineteenth century see Waldemar Gurian, "Antisemitism in Modern Germany," in *Essays on Anti-Semitism*, ed. by K. S. Pinson, 1946.

revolutionary movements showed so few signs of anti-Jewish sentiment.[36] The Jews were indeed of little or no importance for the social struggles of the time.

The beginnings of the modern antisemitic movement date back everywhere to the last third of the nineteenth century. In Germany, it began rather unexpectedly once more among the nobility, whose opposition to the state was again aroused by the transformation of the Prussian monarchy into a fell-fledged nation-state after 1871. Bismarck, the actual founder of the German Reich, had maintained close relations with Jews ever since he became Prime Minister; now he was denounced for being dependent upon and accepting bribes from the Jews. His attempt and partial success in abolishing most feudal remnants in the government inevitably resulted in conflict with the aristocracy; in their attack on Bismarck they represented him as either an innocent victim or a paid agent of Bleichroeder. Actually the relationship was the very opposite; Bleichroeder was undoubtedly a highly esteemed and well-paid agent of Bismarck.[37]

Feudal aristocracy, however, though still powerful enough to influence public opinion, was in itself neither strong nor important enough to start a real antisemitic movement like the one that began in the eighties. Their spokesman, Court Chaplain Stoecker, himself a son of lower middle-class parents, was a much less gifted representative of conservative interests than his predecessors, the romantic intellectuals who had formulated the main tenets of a conservative ideology some fifty years earlier. Moreover, he discovered the usefulness of antisemitic propaganda not through practical or theoretical considerations but by accident, when he, with the help of a great demagogic talent, found out it was highly useful for filling otherwise empty halls. But not only did he fail to understand his own sudden successes; as court chaplain and employee of both the royal family and the government, he was hardly in a position to use them properly. His enthusiastic audiences were composed exclusively of lower middle-class people, small shopkeepers and tradesmen, artisans and old-fashioned craftsmen. And the anti-Jewish sentiments of these people were not yet, and certainly not exclusively, motivated by a conflict with the state.

III: *The First Antisemitic Parties*

THE SIMULTANEOUS RISE of antisemitism as a serious political factor in Germany, Austria, and France in the last twenty years of the nineteenth cen-

[36] The only leftist German antisemite of any importance was E. Duehring who, in a confused way, invented a naturalistic explanation of a "Jewish race" in his *Die Judenfrage als Frage der Rassenschädlichkeit für Existenz, Sitte und Cultur der Völker mit einer weltgeschichtlichen Antwort*, 1880.

[37] For antisemitic attacks on Bismarck see Kurt Wawrzinek, *Die Entstehung der deutschen Antisemitenparteien. 1873-1890*. Historische Studien, Heft 168, 1927.

tury was preceded by a series of financial scandals and fraudulent affairs whose main source was an overproduction of ready capital. In France a majority of Parliament members and an incredible number of government officials were soon so deeply involved in swindle and bribery that the Third Republic was never to recover the prestige it lost during the first decades of its existence; in Austria and Germany the aristocracy was among the most compromised. In all three countries, Jews acted only as middlemen, and not a single Jewish house emerged with permanent wealth from the frauds of the Panama Affair and the *Gründungsschwindel*.

However, another group of people besides noblemen, government officials, and Jews were seriously involved in these fantastic investments whose promised profits were matched by incredible losses. This group consisted mainly of the lower middle classes, which now suddenly turned antisemitic. They had been more seriously hurt than any of the other groups: they had risked small savings and had been permanently ruined. There were important reasons for their gullibility. Capitalist expansion on the domestic scene tended more and more to liquidate small property-holders, to whom it had become a question of life or death to increase quickly the little they had, since they were only too likely to lose all. They were becoming aware that if they did not succeed in climbing upward into the bourgeoisie, they might sink down into the proletariat. Decades of general prosperity slowed down this development so considerably (though it did not change its trend) that their panic appears rather premature. For the time being, however, the anxiety of the lower middle classes corresponded exactly to Marx's prediction of their rapid dissolution.

The lower middle classes, or petty bourgeoisie, were the descendants of the guilds of artisans and tradesmen who for centuries had been protected against the hazards of life by a closed system which outlawed competition and was in the last instance under the protection of the state. They consequently blamed their misfortune upon the Manchester system, which had exposed them to the hardships of a competitive society and deprived them of all special protection and privileges granted by public authorities. They were, therefore, the first to clamor for the "welfare state," which they expected not only to shield them against emergencies but to keep them in the professions and callings they had inherited from their families. Since an outstanding characteristic of the century of free trade was the access of the Jews to all professions, it was almost a matter of course to think of the Jews as the representatives of the "applied system of Manchester carried out to the extreme," [38] even though nothing was farther from the truth.

This rather derivative resentment, which we find first in certain conservative writers who occasionally combined an attack on the bourgeoisie with an attack on Jews, received a great stimulus when those who had hoped for help from the government or gambled on miracles had to accept the

[38] Otto Glagau, *Der Bankrott des Nationalliberalismus und die Reaktion*, Berlin, 1878. The same author's *Der Boersen- und Gruendungsschwindel*, 1876, is one of the most important antisemitic pamphlets of the time.

rather dubious help of bankers. To the small shopkeeper the banker appeared to be the same kind of exploiter as the owner of a big industrial enterprise was to the worker. But while the European workers, from their own experience and a Marxist education in economics, knew that the capitalist filled the double function of exploiting them and giving them the opportunity to produce, the small shopkeeper had found nobody to enlighten him about his social and economic destiny. His predicament was even worse than the worker's and on the basis of his experience he considered the banker a parasite and usurer whom he had to make his silent partner, even though this banker, in contrast to the manufacturer, had nothing whatsoever to do with his business. It is not difficult to comprehend that a man who put his money solely and directly to the use of begetting more money can be hated more bitterly than the one who gets his profit through a lengthy and involved process of production. Since at that time nobody asked for credit if he could possibly help it—certainly not small tradesmen—bankers looked like the exploiters not of working power and productive capacity, but of misfortune and misery.

Many of these bankers were Jews and, even more important, the general figure of the banker bore definite Jewish traits for historical reasons. Thus the leftist movement of the lower middle class and the entire propaganda against banking capital turned more or less antisemitic, a development of little importance in industrial Germany but of great significance in France and, to a lesser extent, in Austria. For a while it looked as though the Jews had indeed for the first time come into direct conflict with another class without interference from the state. Within the framework of the nation-state, in which the function of the government was more or less defined by its ruling position above competing classes, such a clash might even have been a possible, if dangerous, way to normalize the Jewish position.

To this social-economic element, however, another was quickly added which in the long run proved to be more ominous. The position of the Jews as bankers depended not upon loans to small people in distress, but primarily on the issuance of state loans. Petty loans were left to the small fellows, who in this way prepared themselves for the more promising careers of their wealthier and more honorable brethren. The social resentment of the lower middle classes against the Jews turned into a highly explosive political element, because these bitterly hated Jews were thought to be well on their way to political power. Were they not only too well known for their relationship with the government in other respects? Social and economic hatred, on the other hand, reinforced the political argument with that driving violence which up to then it had lacked completely.

Friedrich Engels once remarked that the protagonists of the antisemitic movement of his time were noblemen, and its chorus the howling mob of the petty bourgeoisie. This is true not only for Germany, but also for Austria's Christian Socialism and France's Anti-Dreyfusards. In all these cases, the aristocracy, in a desperate last struggle, tried to ally itself with the conservative forces of the churches—the Catholic Church in Austria and France, the Protestant Church in Germany—under the pretext of fighting liberalism with the weapons of Christianity. The mob was only a means to strengthen their position, to give their voices a greater resonance. Obviously they neither could nor wanted to organize the mob, and would dismiss it once their aim was achieved. But they discovered that antisemitic slogans were highly effective in mobilizing large strata of the population.

The followers of Court Chaplain Stoecker did not organize the first antisemitic parties in Germany. Once the appeal of antisemitic slogans had been demonstrated, radical antisemites at once separated themselves from Stoecker's Berlin movement, went into a full-scale fight against the government, and founded parties whose representatives in the Reichstag voted in all major domestic issues with the greatest opposition party, the Social Democrats.[39] They quickly got rid of the compromising initial alliance with the old powers; Boeckel, the first antisemitic member of Parliament, owed his seat to votes of the Hessian peasants whom he defended against "Junkers and Jews," that is against the nobility which owned too much land and against the Jews upon whose credit the peasants depended.

Small as these first antisemitic parties were, they at once distinguished themselves from all other parties. They made the original claim that they were not a party among parties but a party "above all parties." In the class- and party-ridden nation-state, only the state and the government had ever claimed to be above all parties and classes, to represent the nation as a whole. Parties were admittedly groups whose deputies represented the interests of their voters. Even though they fought for power, it was implicitly understood that it was up to the government to establish a balance between the conflicting interests and their representatives. The antisemitic parties' claim to be "above all parties" announced clearly their aspiration to become the representative of the whole nation, to get exclusive power, to take possession of the state machinery, to substitute themselves for the state. Since, on the other hand, they continued to be organized as a party, it was also clear that they wanted state power as a party, so that their voters would actually dominate the nation.

The body politic of the nation-state came into existence when no single group was any longer in a position to wield exclusive political power, so that the government assumed actual political rule which no longer depended upon social and economic factors. The revolutionary movements of the left, which fought for a radical change of social conditions, had never directly touched this supreme political authority. They had challenged only the power of the bourgeoisie and its influence upon the state, and were therefore always ready to submit to government guidance in foreign affairs, where the interests of an assumedly unified nation were at stake. The numerous programs of the antisemitic groups, on the other hand, were, from the beginning, chiefly concerned with foreign affairs; their revolutionary impulse was

[39] See Wawrzinek, *op. cit.* An instructive account of all these events, especially with respect to Court Chaplain Stoecker, in Frank, *op. cit.*

directed against the government rather than a social class, and they actually aimed to destroy the political pattern of the nation-state by means of a party organization.

The claim of a party to be beyond all parties had other, more significant, implications than antisemitism. If it had been only a question of getting rid of the Jews, Fritsch's proposal, at one of the early antisemitic congresses,[40] not to create a new party but rather to disseminate antisemitism until finally all existing parties were hostile to Jews, would have brought much quicker results. As it was, Fritsch's proposal went unheeded because antisemitism was then already an instrument for the liquidation not only of the Jews but of the body politic of the nation-state as well.

Nor was it an accident that the claim of the antisemitic parties coincided with the early stages of imperialism and found exact counterparts in certain trends in Great Britain which were free of antisemitism and in the highly antisemitic pan-movements on the Continent.[41] Only in Germany did these new trends spring directly from antisemitism as such, and antisemitic parties preceded and survived the formation of purely imperialist groups such as the Alldeutscher Verband and others, all of which also claimed to be more than and above party groups.

The fact that similar formations without active antisemitism—which avoided the charlatan aspect of the antisemitic parties and therefore seemed at first to have far better chances for final victory—were finally submerged or liquidated by the antisemitic movement is a good index to the importance of the issue. The antisemites' belief that their claim to exclusive rule was no more than what the Jews had in fact achieved, gave them the advantage of a domestic program, and conditions were such that one had to enter the arena of social struggle in order to win political power. They could pretend to fight the Jews exactly as the workers were fighting the bourgeoisie. Their advantage was that by attacking the Jews, who were believed to be the secret power behind governments, they could openly attack the state itself, whereas the imperialist groups, with their mild and secondary antipathy against Jews, never found the connection with the important social struggles of the times.

The second highly significant characteristic of the new antisemitic parties was that they started at once a supranational organization of all antisemitic groups in Europe, in open contrast to, and in defiance of, current nationalistic slogans. By introducing this supranational element, they clearly indicated that they aimed not only at political rule over the nation but had already planned a step further for an inter-European government "above all nations." [42] This second revolutionary element meant the fundamental break

[40] This proposition was made in 1886 in Cassel, where the *Deutsche Antisemitische Vereinigung* was founded.

[41] For an extensive discussion of the "parties above parties" and the pan-movements see chapter viii.

[42] The first international anti-Jewish congress took place in 1882 in Dresden, with about 3,000 delegates from Germany, Austria-Hungary, and Russia; during the discussions, Stoecker was defeated by the radical elements who met one year later in

with the status quo; it has been frequently overlooked because the anti-semites themselves, partly because of traditional habits and partly because they consciously lied, used the language of the reactionary parties in their propaganda.

The intimate relationship between the peculiar conditions of Jewish existence and the ideology of such groups is even more evident in the organization of a group beyond nations than in the creation of a party beyond parties. The Jews very clearly were the only inter-European element in a nationalized Europe. It seemed only logical that their enemies had to organize on the same principle, if they were to fight those who were supposed to be the secret manipulators of the political destiny of all nations.

While this argument was sure to be convincing as propaganda, the success of supranational antisemitism depended upon more general considerations. Even at the end of the last century, and especially since the Franco-Prussian War, more and more people felt that the national organization of Europe was antiquated because it could no longer adequately respond to new economic challenges. This feeling had been a powerful supporting argument for the international organization of socialism and had, in turn, been strengthened by it. The conviction that identical interests existed all over Europe was spreading through the masses.[43] Whereas the international socialist organizations remained passive and uninterested in all foreign policy issues (that is in precisely those questions where their internationalism might have been tested), the antisemites started with problems of foreign policy and even promised solution of domestic problems on a supranational basis. To take ideologies less at their face value and to look more closely at the actual programs of the respective parties is to discover that the socialists, who were more concerned with domestic issues, fitted much better into the nation-state than the antisemites.

Of course this does not mean that the socialists' internationalist convictions were not sincere. These were, on the contrary, stronger and, incidentally, much older than the discovery of class interests which cut across the boundaries of national states. But the very awareness of the all-importance of class struggle induced them to neglect that heritage which the French Revolution had bequeathed to the workers' parties and which alone might have led them to an articulate political theory. The socialists kept implicitly intact the original concept of a "nation among nations," all of which belong to the family of mankind, but they never found a device by which to trans-

---

Chemnitz and founded the Alliance Antijuive Universelle. A good account of these meetings and congresses, their programs and discussions, is to be found in Wawrzinek, *op. cit.*

[43] The international solidarity of the workers' movements was, as far as it went, an inter-European matter. Their indifference to foreign policy was also a kind of self-protection against both active participation in or struggle against the contemporary imperialist policies of their respective countries. As far as economic interests were concerned, it was all too obvious that everybody in the French or British or Dutch nation would feel the full impact of the fall of their empires, and not just capitalists and bankers.

form this idea into a working concept in the world of sovereign states. Their internationalism, consequently, remained a personal conviction shared by everybody, and their healthy disinterest in national sovereignty turned into a quite unhealthy and unrealistic indifference to foreign politics. Since the parties of the left did not object to nation-states on principle, but only to the aspect of national sovereignty; since, moreover, their own inarticulate hopes for federalist structures with eventual integration of all nations on equal terms somehow presupposed national liberty and independence of all oppressed peoples, they could operate within the framework of the nation-state and even emerge, in the time of decay of its social and political structure, as the only group in the population that did not indulge in expansionist fantasies and in thoughts of destroying other peoples.

The supranationalism of the antisemites approached the question of international organization from exactly the opposite point of view. Their aim was a dominating superstructure which would destroy all home-grown national structures alike. They could indulge in hypernationalistic talk even as they prepared to destroy the body politic of their own nation, because tribal nationalism, with its immoderate lust for conquest, was one of the principal powers by which to force open the narrow and modest limits of the nation-state and its sovereignty.[44] The more effective the chauvinistic propaganda, the easier it was to persuade public opinion of the necessity for a supranational structure which would rule from above and without national distinctions by a universal monopoly of power and the instruments of violence.

There is little doubt that the special inter-European condition of the Jewish people could have served the purposes of socialist federalism at least as well as it was to serve the sinister plots of supranationalists. But socialists were so concerned with class struggle and so neglectful of the political consequences of their own inherited concepts that they became aware of the existence of the Jews as a political factor only when they were already confronted with full-blown antisemitism as a serious competitor on the domestic scene. Then they were not only unprepared to integrate the Jewish issue into their theories, but actually afraid to touch the question at all. Here as in other international issues, they left the field to the supranationalists who could then seem to be the only ones who knew the answers to world problems.

By the turn of the century, the effects of the swindles in the seventies had run their course and an era of prosperity and general well-being, especially in Germany, put an end to the premature agitations of the eighties. Nobody could have predicted that this end was only a temporary respite, that all unsolved political questions, together with all unappeased political hatreds, were to redouble in force and violence after the first World War. The antisemitic parties in Germany, after initial successes, fell back into insignificance; their leaders, after a brief stirring of public opinion, disap-

[44] Compare chapter viii.

peared through the back door of history into the darkness of crackpot confusion and cure-all charlatanry.

IV: *Leftist Antisemitism*

WERE IT NOT for the frightful consequences of antisemitism in our own time, we might have given less attention to its development in Germany. As a political movement, nineteenth-century antisemitism can be studied best in France, where for almost a decade it dominated the political scene. As an ideological force, competing with other more respectable ideologies for the acceptance of public opinion, it reached its most articulate form in Austria.

Nowhere had the Jews rendered such great services to the state as in Austria, whose many nationalities were kept together only by the Dual Monarchy of the House of Hapsburg, and where the Jewish state banker, in contrast to all other European countries, survived the downfall of the monarchy. Just as at the beginning of this development in the early eighteenth century, Samuel Oppenheimer's credit had been identical with the credit of the House of Hapsburg, so "in the end Austrian credit was that of the *Creditanstalt"*—a Rothschild banking house.[45] Although the Danube monarchy had no homogeneous population, the most important prerequisite for evolution into a nation-state, it could not avoid the transformation of an enlightened despotism into a constitutional monarchy and the creation of modern civil services. This meant that it had to adopt certain institutions of the nation-state. For one thing, the modern class system grew along nationality lines, so that certain nationalities began to be identified with certain classes or at least professions. The German became the dominating nationality in much the same sense as the bourgeoisie became the dominating class in the nation-states. The Hungarian landed aristocracy played a role that was even more pronounced than, but essentially similar to, that played by the nobility in other countries. The state machinery itself tried its best to keep the same absolute distance from society, to rule above all nationalities, as the nation-state with respect to its classes. The result for the Jews was simply that the Jewish nationality could not merge with the others and could not become a nationality itself, just as it had not merged with other classes in the nation-state, or become a class itself. As the Jews in nation-states had differed from all classes of society through their special relationship to the state, so they differed from all other nationalities in Austria through their special relationship to the Hapsburg monarchy. And just as everywhere else each class that came into open conflict with the state turned antisemitic, so in Austria each nationality that not only engaged in the all-pervading struggle of the nationalities but came into open conflict with the monarchy

[45] See Paul H. Emden, "The Story of the Vienna *Creditanstalt*," in *Menorah Journal*, XXVIII, 1, 1940.

itself, started its fight with an attack upon the Jews. But there was a marked difference between these conflicts in Austria, and those in Germany and France. In Austria they were not only sharper, but at the outbreak of the first World War every single nationality, and that meant every stratum of society, was in opposition to the state, so that more than anywhere else in Western or Central Europe the population was imbued with active antisemitism.

Outstanding among these conflicts was the continuously rising state hostility of the German nationality, which accelerated after the foundation of the Reich and discovered the usefulness of antisemitic slogans after the financial crash of 1873. The social situation at that moment was practically the same as in Germany, but the social propaganda to catch the middleclass vote immediately indulged in a much more violent attack on the state, and a much more outspoken confession of nonloyalty to the country. Moreover, the German Liberal Party, under the leadership of Schoenerer, was from the beginning a lower middle-class party without connections or restraints from the side of the nobility, and with a decidedly left-wing outlook. It never achieved a real mass basis, but it was remarkably successful in the universities during the eighties where it organized the first closely knit students' organization on the basis of open antisemitism. Schoenerer's antisemitism, at first almost exclusively directed against the Rothschilds, won him the sympathies of the labor movement, which regarded him as a true radical gone astray.[46] His main advantage was that he could base his antisemitic propaganda on demonstrable facts: as a member of the Austrian Reichsrat he had fought for nationalization of the Austrian railroads, the major part of which had been in the hands of the Rothschilds since 1836 due to a state license which expired in 1886. Schoenerer succeeded in gathering 40,000 signatures against its renewal, and in placing the Jewish question in the limelight of public interest. The close connection between the Rothschilds and the financial interests of the monarchy became very obvious when the government tried to extend the license under conditions which were patently to the disadvantage of the state as well as the public. Schoenerer's agitation in this matter became the actual beginning of an articulate antisemitic movement in Austria.[47] The point is that this movement, in contrast to the German Stoecker agitation, was initiated and led by a man who was sincere beyond doubt, and therefore did not stop at the use of antisemitism as a propaganda weapon, but developed quickly that Pan-German ideology which was to influence Nazism more deeply than any other German brand of antisemitism.

[46] See F. A. Neuschaefer, *Georg Ritter von Schoenerer*, Hamburg, 1935, and Eduard Pichl, *Georg Schoenerer*, 1938, 6 vols. Even in 1912, when the Schoenerer agitation had long lost all significance, the Viennese *Arbeiterzeitung* cherished very affectionate feelings for the man of whom it could think only in the words Bismarck had once uttered about Lassalle: "And if we exchanged shots, justice would still demand that we admit even during the shooting: He is a man; and the others are old women." (Neuschaefer, p. 33.)

[47] See Neuschaefer, *op. cit.,* pp. 22 ff., and Pichl, *op. cit.,* I, 236 ff.

Though victorious in the long run, the Schoenerer movement was temporarily defeated by a second antisemitic party, the Christian-Socials under the leadership of Lueger. While Schoenerer had attacked the Catholic Church and its considerable influence on Austrian politics almost as much as he had the Jews, the Christian-Socials were a Catholic party who tried from the outset to ally themselves with those reactionary conservative forces which had proved so helpful in Germany and France. Since they made more social concessions, they were more successful than in Germany or in France. They, together with the Social Democrats, survived the downfall of the monarchy and became the most influential group in postwar Austria. But long before the establishment of an Austrian Republic, when, in the nineties, Lueger had won the Mayoralty of Vienna by an antisemitic campaign, the Christian-Socials already adopted that typically equivocal attitude toward the Jews in the nation-state—hostility to the intelligentsia and friendliness toward the Jewish business class. It was by no means an accident that, after a bitter and bloody contest for power with the socialist workers' movement, they took over the state machinery when Austria, reduced to its German nationality, was established as a nation-state. They turned out to be the only party which was prepared for exactly this role and, even under the old monarchy, had won popularity because of their nationalism. Since the Hapsburgs were a German house and had granted their German subjects a certain predominance, the Christian-Socials never attacked the monarchy. Their function was rather to win large parts of the German nationality for the support of an essentially unpopular government. Their antisemitism remained without consequence; the decades when Lueger ruled Vienna were actually a kind of golden age for the Jews. No matter how far their propaganda occasionally went in order to get votes, they never could have proclaimed with Schoenerer and the Pan-Germanists that "they regarded antisemitism as the mainstay of our national ideology, as the most essential expression of genuine popular conviction and thus as the major national achievement of the century." [48] And although they were as much under the influence of clerical circles as was the antisemitic movement in France, they were of necessity much more restrained in their attacks on the Jews because they did not attack the monarchy as the antisemites in France attacked the Third Republic.

The successes and failures of the two Austrian antisemitic parties show the scant relevance of social conflicts to the long-range issues of the time. Compared with the mobilization of all opponents to the government as such, the capturing of lower middle-class votes was a temporary phenomenon. Indeed, the backbone of Schoenerer's movement was in those German-speaking provinces without any Jewish population at all, where competition with Jews or hatred of Jewish bankers never existed. The survival of the Pan-Germanist movement and its violent antisemitism in these provinces, while it subsided in the urban centers, was merely due to the fact that these

---

[48] Quoted from Pichl, *op. cit.*, I, p. 26.

provinces were never reached to the same extent by the universal prosperity of the pre-war period which reconciled the urban population with the government.

The complete lack of loyalty to their own country and its government, for which the Pan-Germanists substituted an open loyalty to Bismarck's Reich, and the resulting concept of nationhood as something independent of state and territory, led the Schoenerer group to a veritable imperialist ideology in which lies the clue to its temporary weakness and its final strength. It is also the reason why the Pan-German party in Germany (the Alldeutschen), which never overstepped the limits of ordinary chauvinism, remained so extremely suspicious and reluctant to take the outstretched hands of their Austrian Germanist brothers. This Austrian movement aimed at more than rise to power as a party, more than the possession of the state machinery. It wanted a revolutionary reorganization of Central Europe in which the Germans of Austria, together with and strengthened by the Germans of Germany, would become the ruling people, in which all other peoples of the area would be kept in the same kind of semiservitude as the Slavonic nationalities in Austria. Because of this close affinity to imperialism and the fundamental change it brought to the concept of nationhood, we shall have to postpone the discussion of the Austrian Pan-Germanist movement. It is no longer, at least in its consequences, a mere nineteenth-century preparatory movement; it belongs, more than any other brand of antisemitism, to the course of events of our own century.

The exact opposite is true of French antisemitism. The Dreyfus Affair brings into the open all other elements of nineteenth-century antisemitism in its mere ideological and political aspects; it is the culmination of the antisemitism which grew out of the special conditions of the nation-state. Yet its violent form foreshadowed future developments, so that the main actors of the Affair sometimes seem to be staging a huge dress rehearsal for a performance that had to be put off for more than three decades. It drew together all the open or subterranean, political or social sources which had brought the Jewish question into a predominant position in the nineteenth century; its premature outburst, on the other hand, kept it within the framework of a typical nineteenth-century ideology which, although it survived all French governments and political crises, never quite fitted into twentieth-century political conditions. When, after the 1940 defeat, French antisemitism got its supreme chance under the Vichy government, it had a definitely antiquated and, for major purposes, rather useless character, which German Nazi writers never forgot to point out.[49] It had no influence on the formation of Nazism and remains more significant in itself than as an active historical factor in the final catastrophe.

The principal reason for these wholesome limitations was that France's antisemitic parties, though violent on the domestic scene, had no supra-

<hr/>

[49] See especially Walfried Vernunft, "Die Hintergründe des französischen Antisemitismus," in *Nationalsozialistische Monatshefte*, Juni, 1939.

national aspirations. They belonged after all to the oldest and most fully developed nation-state in Europe. None of the antisemites ever tried seriously to organize a "party above parties" or to seize the state as a party and for no other purpose but party interests. The few attempted *coups d'état* which might be credited to the alliance between antisemites and higher army officers were ridiculously inadequate and obviously contrived.[50] In 1898 some nineteen members of Parliament were elected through antisemitic campaigns, but this was a peak which was never reached again and from which the decline was rapid.

It is true, on the other hand, that this was the earliest instance of the success of antisemitism as a catalytic agent for all other political issues. This can be attributed to the lack of authority of the Third Republic, which had been voted in with a very slight majority. In the eyes of the masses, the state had lost its prestige along with the monarchy, and attacks on the state were no longer a sacrilege. The early outburst of violence in France bears a striking resemblance to similar agitation in the Austrian and German Republics after the first World War. The Nazi dictatorship has been so frequently connected with so-called "state-worship" that even historians have become somewhat blind to the truism that the Nazis took advantage of the complete breakdown of state worship, originally prompted by the worship of a prince who sits on the throne by the grace of God, and which hardly ever occurs in a Republic. In France, fifty years before Central European countries were affected by this universal loss of reverence, state worship had suffered many defeats. It was much easier to attack the Jews and the government together there than in Central Europe where the Jews were attacked in order to attack the government.

French antisemitism, moreover, is as much older than its European counterparts as is French emancipation of the Jews, which dates back to the end of the eighteenth century. The representatives of the Age of Enlightenment who prepared the French Revolution despised the Jews as a matter of course; they saw in them the backward remnants of the Dark Ages, and they hated them as the financial agents of the aristocracy. The only articulate friends of the Jews in France were conservative writers who denounced anti-Jewish attitudes as "one of the favorite theses of the eighteenth century." [51] For the more liberal or radical writer it had become almost a tradition to warn against the Jews as barbarians who still lived in the patriarchal form of government and recognized no other state.[52] During and after the French Revolution, the French clergy and French aristocrats added their voices to the general anti-Jewish sentiment, though for other and more material reasons. They accused the revolutionary government of having ordered the sale of clerical property to pay "the Jews and merchants to whom the government

[50] See Chapter iv.
[51] See J. de Maistre, *Les Soirées de St. Petersburg,* 1821, II, 55.
[52] Charles Fourier, *Nouveau Monde Industriel,* 1829, Vol. V of his *Oeuvres Complètes,* 1841, p. 421. For Fourier's anti-Jewish doctrines, see also Edmund Silberner, "Charles Fourier on the Jewish Question" in *Jewish Social Studies,* October, 1946.

is indebted." [53] These old arguments, somehow kept alive through the never-ending struggle between Church and State in France, supported the general violence and embitterment which had been touched off by other and more modern forces at the end of the century.

Mainly because of the strong clerical support of antisemitism, the French socialist movement finally decided to take a stand against antisemitic propaganda in the Dreyfus Affair. Until then, however, nineteenth-century French leftist movements had been outspoken in their antipathy to the Jews. They simply followed the tradition of eighteenth-century enlightenment which was the source of French liberalism and radicalism, and they considered anti-Jewish attitudes an integral part of anticlericalism. These sentiments on the left were strengthened first by the fact that the Alsatian Jews continued to live from lending money to peasants, a practice which had already prompted Napoleon's decree of 1808. After conditions had changed in Alsace, leftist antisemitism found a new source of strength in the financial policies of the house of Rothschild, which played a large part in the financing of the Bourbons, maintained close connections with Louis Philippe, and flourished under Napoleon III.

Behind these obvious and rather superficial incentives to anti-Jewish attitudes there was a deeper cause, which was crucial to the whole structure of the specifically French brand of radicalism, and which almost succeeded in turning the whole French leftist movement against the Jews. Bankers were much stronger in the French economy than in other capitalist countries, and France's industrial development, after a brief rise during the reign of Napoleon III, lagged so far behind other nations that pre-capitalist socialist tendencies continued to exert considerable influence. The lower middle classes which in Germany and Austria became antisemitic only during the seventies and eighties, when they were already so desperate that they could be used for reactionary politics as well as for the new mob policies, had been antisemitic in France some fifty years earlier, when, with the help of the working class, they carried the revolution of 1848 to a brief victory. In the forties, when Toussenel published his *Les Juifs, Rois de l'Epoque,* the most important book in a veritable flood of pamphlets against the Rothschilds, it was enthusiastically received by the entire left-wing press, which at the time was the organ of the revolutionary lower middle classes. Their sentiments, as expressed by Toussenel, though less articulate and less sophisticated, were not very different from those of the young Marx, and Toussenel's attack on the Rothschilds was only a less gifted and more elaborate variation of the letters from Paris which Boerne had written fifteen years before.[54] These Jews, too, mistook the Jewish banker for a

[53] See the newspaper *Le Patriote Français,* No. 457, November 8, 1790. Quoted from Clemens August Hoberg, "Die geistigen Grundlagen des Antisemitismus im modernen Frankreich," in *Forschungen zur Judenfrage,* 1940, Vol. IV.

[54] Marx's essay on the Jewish question is sufficiently well known not to warrant quotation. Since Boerne's utterances, because of their merely polemical and un-theoretical character, are being forgotten today, we quote from the 72nd letter from

central figure in the capitalist system, an error which has exerted a certain influence on the municipal and lower government bureaucracy in France up to our own time.[55]

However this outburst of popular anti-Jewish feeling, nourished by an economic conflict between Jewish bankers and their desperate clientele, lasted no longer as an important factor in politics than similar outbursts with purely economic or social causes. The twenty years of Napoleon III's rule over a French Empire were an age of prosperity and security for French Jewry much like the two decades before the outbreak of the first World War in Germany and Austria.

The only brand of French antisemitism which actually remained strong, and outlasted social antisemitism as well as the contemptuous attitudes of anticlerical intellectuals, was tied up with a general xenophobia. Especially after the first World War, foreign Jews became the stereotypes for all foreigners. A differentiation between native Jews and those who "invaded" the country from the East has been made in all Western and Central European countries. Polish and Russian Jews were treated exactly the same way in Germany and Austria as Rumanian and German Jews were treated in France, just as Jews from Posen in Germany or from Galicia in Austria were regarded with the same snobbish contempt as Jews from Alsace were in France. But only in France did this differentiation assume such importance on the domestic scene. And this is probably due to the fact that the Rothschilds, who more than anywhere else were the butt of anti-Jewish attacks, had immigrated into France from Germany, so that up to the outbreak of the second World War it became natural to suspect the Jews of sympathies with the national enemy.

Nationalistic antisemitism, harmless when compared with modern movements, was never a monopoly of reactionaries and chauvinists in France. On this point, the writer Jean Giraudoux, the propaganda minister in Daladier's war cabinet, was in complete agreement [56] with Pétain and the

---

Paris (January, 1832): "Rothschild kissed the Pope's hand. . . . At last the order has come which God had planned when he created the world. A poor Christian kisses the Pope's feet, and a rich Jew kisses his hand. If Rothschild had gotten his Roman loan at 60 per cent, instead of 65, and could have sent the cardinal-chamberlain more than ten thousand ducats, they would have allowed him to embrace the Holy Father. . . . Would it not be the greatest luck for the world if all kings were deposed and the Rothschild family placed on the throne?" *Briefe aus Paris. 1830-1833*.

[55] This attitude is well described in the preface by the municipal councilor Paul Brousse to Cesare Lombroso's famous work on antisemitism (1899). The characteristic part of the argument is contained in the following: "The small shopkeeper needs credit, and we know how badly organized and how expensive credit is these days. Here too the small merchant places the responsibility on the Jewish banker. All the way down to the worker—*i.e.* only those workers who have no clear notion of scientific socialism—everybody thinks the revolution is being advanced if the general expropriation of capitalists is preceded by the expropriation of Jewish capitalists, who are the most typical and whose names are the most familiar to the masses."

[56] For the surprising continuity in French antisemitic arguments, compare, for instance, Charles Fourier's picture of the Jew "Iscariote" who arrives in France with 100,000 pounds, establishes himself in a town with six competitors in his field,

Vichy government, which also, no matter how hard it tried to please the Germans, could not break through the limitations of this outmoded antipathy for Jews. The failure was all the more conspicuous since the French had produced an outstanding antisemite who realized the full range and possibilities of the new weapon. That this man should be a prominent novelist is characteristic of conditions in France, where antisemitism in general had never fallen into the same social and intellectual disrepute as in other European countries.

Louis Ferdinand Céline had a simple thesis, ingenious and containing exactly the ideological imagination that the more rational French antisemitism had lacked. He claimed that the Jews had prevented the evolution of Europe into a political entity, had caused all European wars since 843, and had plotted the ruin of both France and Germany by inciting their mutual hostility. Céline proposed this fantastic explanation of history in his *Ecole des Cadavres,* written at the time of the Munich pact and published during the first months of the war. An earlier pamphlet on the subject, *Bagatelle pour un Massacre* (1938), although it did not include the new key to European history, was already remarkably modern in its approach; it avoided all restricting differentiations between native and foreign Jews, between good and bad ones, and did not bother with elaborate legislative proposals (a particular characteristic of French antisemitism), but went straight to the core of the matter and demanded the massacre of all Jews.

Céline's first book was very favorably received by France's leading intellectuals, who were half pleased by the attack on the Jews and half convinced that it was nothing more than an interesting new literary fancy.[57] For exactly the same reasons French home-grown Fascists did not take Céline seriously, despite the fact that the Nazis always knew he was the only true antisemite in France. The inherent good sense of French politicians and their deep-rooted respectability prevented their accepting a charlatan and crackpot. The result was that even the Germans, who knew better, had to continue to use such inadequate supporters as Doriot, a follower of Mussolini, and Pétain, an old French chauvinist with no comprehension whatever of modern problems, in their vain efforts to persuade the French people that extermination of the Jews would be a cure for everything under the sun. The way this situation developed during the years of French official,

---

crushes all the competing houses, amasses a great fortune, and returns to Germany (in *Théorie des quatre mouvements,* 1808, *Oeuvres Complètes,* 88 ff.) with Giraudoux's picture of 1939: "By an infiltration whose secret I have tried in vain to detect, hundreds of thousands of Ashkenasim, who escaped from the Polish and Rumanian Ghettos, have entered our country . . . eliminating our fellow citizens and, at the same time, ruining their professional customs and traditions . . . and defying all investigations of census, taxes and labor." In *Pleins Pouvoirs,* 1939.

[57] See especially the critical discussion in the *Nouvelle Revue Française* by Marcel Arland (February, 1938) who claims that Céline's position is essentially *"solide."* André Gide (April, 1938) thinks that Céline in depicting only the Jewish *"spécialité,"* has succeeded in painting not the reality but the very hallucination which reality provokes.

and even unofficial, readiness to co-operate with Nazi Germany, clearly indicates how ineffective nineteenth-century antisemitism was to the new political purposes of the twentieth, even in a country where it had reached its fullest development and had survived all other changes in public opinion. It did not matter that able nineteenth-century journalists like Edouard Drumont, and even great contemporary writers like Georges Bernanos, contributed to a cause that was much more adequately served by crackpots and charlatans.

That France, for various reasons, never developed a full-fledged imperialist party turned out to be the decisive element. As many French colonial politicians have pointed out,[58] only a French-German alliance would have enabled France to compete with England in the division of the world and to join successfully in the scramble for Africa. Yet France somehow never let herself be tempted into this competition, despite all her noisy resentment and hostility against Great Britain. France was and remained—though declining in importance—the *nation par excellence* on the Continent, and even her feeble imperialist attempts usually ended with the birth of new national independence movements. Since, moreover, her antisemitism had been nourished principally by the purely national French-German conflict, the Jewish issue was almost automatically kept from playing much of a role in imperialist policies, despite the conditions in Algeria, whose mixed population of native Jews and Arabs would have offered an excellent opportunity.[59] The simple and brutal destruction of the French nation-state by German aggression, the mockery of a German-French alliance on the basis of German occupation and French defeat, may have proved how little strength of her own the *nation par excellence* had carried into our times from a glorious past; it did not change her essential political structure.

v: *The Golden Age of Security*

ONLY TWO DECADES separated the temporary decline of the antisemitic movements from the outbreak of the first World War. This period has been adequately described as a "Golden Age of Security" [60] because only a few who lived in it felt the inherent weakness of an obviously outmoded political structure which, despite all prophecies of imminent doom, continued to function in spurious splendor and with inexplicable, monotonous stubbornness. Side by side, and apparently with equal stability, an anachronistic despotism in Russia, a corrupt bureaucracy in Austria, a stupid militarism

[58] See for instance René Pinon, *France et Allemagne*, 1912.

[59] Some aspects of the Jewish question in Algeria are treated in the author's article, "Why the Crémieux Decree was Abrogated," in *Contemporary Jewish Record*, April, 1943.

[60] The term is Stefan Zweig's, who thus named the period up to the first World War in *The World of Yesterday: An Autobiography*, 1943.

in Germany and a half-hearted Republic in continual crisis in France—all of them still under the shadow of the world-wide power of the British Empire—managed to carry on. None of these governments was especially popular, and all faced growing domestic opposition; but nowhere did there seem to exist an earnest political will for radical change in political conditions. Europe was much too busy expanding economically for any nation or social stratum to take political questions seriously. Everything could go on because nobody cared. Or, in the penetrating words of Chesterton, "everything is prolonging its existence by denying that it exists." [61]

The enormous growth of industrial and economic capacity produced a steady weakening of purely political factors, while at the same time economic forces became dominant in the international play of power. Power was thought to be synonymous with economic capacity before people discovered that economic and industrial capacity are only its modern prerequisites. In a sense, economic power could bring governments to heel because they had the same faith in economics as the plain businessmen who had somehow convinced them that the state's means of violence had to be used exclusively for protection of business interests and national property. For a very brief time, there was some truth in Walter Rathenau's remark that 300 men, who all know each other, held the destinies of the world in their hands. This odd state of affairs lasted exactly until 1914 when, through the very fact of war, the confidence of the masses in the providential character of economic expansion fell apart.

The Jews were more deluded by the appearances of the golden age of security than any other section of the European peoples. Antisemitism seemed to be a thing of the past; the more the governments lost in power and prestige, the less attention was paid to the Jews. While the state played an ever narrower and emptier representative role, political representation tended to become a kind of theatrical performance of varying quality until in Austria the theater itself became the focus of national life, an institution whose public significance was certainly greater than that of Parliament. The theatrical quality of the political world had become so patent that the theater could appear as the realm of reality.

The growing influence of big business on the state and the state's declining need for Jewish services threatened the Jewish banker with extinction and forced certain shifts in Jewish occupations. The first sign of the decline of the Jewish banking houses was their loss of prestige and power within the Jewish communities. They were no longer strong enough to centralize and, to a certain extent, monopolize the general Jewish wealth. More and more Jews left state finance for independent business. Out of food and clothing deliveries to armies and governments grew the Jewish food and grain commerce, and the garment industries in which they soon acquired a prominent position in all countries; pawnshops and general stores in small

[61] For a wonderful description of the British state of affairs, see G. K. Chesterton, *The Return of Don Quixote*, which did not appear until 1927 but was "planned and partly written before the War."

country towns were the predecessors of department stores in the cities. This does not mean that the relationship between Jews and governments ceased to exist, but fewer individuals were involved, so that at the end of this period we have almost the same picture as at the beginning: a few Jewish individuals in important financial positions with little or no connection with the broader strata of the Jewish middle class.

More important than the expansion of the independent Jewish business class was another shift in the occupational structure. Central and Western European Jewries had reached a saturation point in wealth and economic fortune. This might have been the moment for them to show that they actually wanted money for money's or for power's sake. In the former case, they might have expanded their businesses and handed them down to their descendants; in the latter they might have entrenched themselves more firmly in state business and fought the influence of big business and industry on governments. But they did neither. On the contrary, the sons of the well-to-do businessmen and, to a lesser extent, bankers, deserted their fathers' careers for the liberal professions or purely intellectual pursuits they had not been able to afford a few generations before. What the nation-state had once feared so much, the birth of a Jewish intelligentsia, now proceeded at a fantastic pace. The crowding of Jewish sons of well-to-do parents into the cultural occupations was especially marked in Germany and Austria, where a great proportion of cultural institutions, like newspapers, publishing, music, and theater, became Jewish enterprises.

What had been made possible through the traditional Jewish preference and respect for intellectual occupations resulted in a real break with tradition and the intellectual assimilation and nationalization of important strata of Western and Central European Jewry. Politically, it indicated emancipation of Jews from state protection, growing consciousness of a common destiny with their fellow-citizens, and a considerable loosening of the ties that had made Jews an inter-European element. Socially, the Jewish intellectuals were the first who, as a group, needed and wanted admittance to non-Jewish society. Social discrimination, a small matter to their fathers who had not cared for social intercourse with Gentiles, became a paramount problem for them.

Searching for a road into society, this group was forced to accept social behavior patterns set by individual Jews who had been admitted into society during the nineteenth century as exceptions to the rule of discrimination. They quickly discovered the force that would open all doors, the "radiant Power of Fame" (Stefan Zweig), which a hundred years' idolatry of genius had made irresistible. What distinguished the Jewish pursuit of fame from the general fame idolatry of the time was that Jews were not primarily interested in it for themselves. To live in the aura of fame was more important than to become famous; thus they became outstanding reviewers, critics, collectors, and organizers of what was famous. The "radiant power" was a very real social force by which the socially homeless were able to establish a home. The Jewish intellectuals, in other words, tried, and to a certain extent succeeded, in becoming the living tie binding famous individuals into a society of the renowned, an international society by definition, for spiritual achievement transcends national boundaries. The general weakening of political factors, for two decades having brought about a situation in which reality and appearance, political reality and theatrical performance could easily parody each other, now enabled them to become the representatives of a nebulous international society in which national prejudices no longer seemed valid. And paradoxically enough, this international society seemed to be the only one that recognized the nationalization and assimilation of its Jewish members; it was far easier for an Austrian Jew to be accepted as an Austrian in France than in Austria. The spurious world citizenship of this generation, this fictitious nationality which they claimed as soon as their Jewish origin was mentioned, in part already resembled those passports which later granted their owner the right to sojourn in every country except the one that issued it.

By their very nature, these circumstances could not but bring Jews into prominence just when their activities, their satisfaction and happiness in the world of appearance, proved that, as a group, they wanted in fact neither money nor power. While serious statesmen and publicists now bothered with the Jewish question less than at any time since the emancipation, and while antisemitism almost entirely disappeared from the open political scene, Jews became the symbols of Society as such and the objects of hatred for all those whom society did not accept. Antisemitism, having lost its ground in the special conditions that had influenced its development during the nineteenth century, could be freely elaborated by charlatans and crackpots into that weird mixture of half-truths and wild superstitions which emerged in Europe after 1914, the ideology of all frustrated and resentful elements.

Since the Jewish question in its social aspect turned into a catalyst of social unrest, until finally a disintegrated society recrystallized ideologically around a possible massacre of Jews, it is necessary to outline some of the main traits of the social history of emancipated Jewry in the bourgeois society of the last century.

CHAPTER THREE

The Jews and Society

T HE JEWS' political ignorance, which fitted them so well for their special role and for taking roots in the state's sphere of business, and their prejudices against the people and in favor of authority, which blinded them to the political dangers of antisemitism, caused them to be oversensitive toward all forms of social discrimination. It was difficult to see the decisive difference between political argument and mere antipathy when the two developed side by side. The point, however, is that they grew out of exactly opposite aspects of emancipation: political antisemitism developed because the Jews were a separate body, while social discrimination arose because of the growing equality of Jews with all other groups.

Equality of condition, though it is certainly a basic requirement for justice, is nevertheless among the greatest and most uncertain ventures of modern mankind. The more equal conditions are, the less explanation there is for the differences that actually exist between people; and thus all the more unequal do individuals and groups become. This perplexing consequence came fully to light as soon as equality was no longer seen in terms of an omnipotent being like God or an unavoidable common destiny like death. Whenever equality becomes a mundane fact in itself, without any gauge by which it may be measured or explained, then there is one chance in a hundred that it will be recognized simply as a working principle of a political organization in which otherwise unequal people have equal rights; there are ninety-nine chances that it will be mistaken for an innate quality of every individual, who is "normal" if he is like everybody else and "abnormal" if he happens to be different. This perversion of equality from a political into a social concept is all the more dangerous when a society leaves but little space for special groups and individuals, for then their differences become all the more conspicuous.

The great challenge to the modern period, and its peculiar danger, has been that in it man for the first time confronted man without the protection of differing circumstances and conditions. And it has been precisely this new concept of equality that has made modern race relations so difficult, for there we deal with natural differences which by no possible and conceivable change of conditions can become less conspicuous. It is because equality demands that I recognize each and every individual as my equal, that the conflicts between different groups, which for reasons of their own are reluctant to grant each other this basic equality, take on such terribly cruel forms.

Hence the more equal the Jewish condition, the more surprising were Jewish differences. This new awareness led to social resentment against the Jews and at the same time to a peculiar attraction toward them; the combined reactions determined the social history of Western Jewry. Discrimination, however, as well as attraction, were politically sterile. They neither produced a political movement against the Jews nor served in any way to protect them against their enemies. They did succeed, though, in poisoning the social atmosphere, in perverting all social intercourse between Jews and Gentiles, and had a definite effect on Jewish behavior. The formation of a Jewish type was due to both—to special discrimination and to special favor.

Social antipathy for Jews, with its varying forms of discrimination, did no great political harm in European countries, for genuine social and economic equality was never achieved. To all appearances new classes developed as groups to which one belonged by birth. There is no doubt that it was only in such a framework that society could suffer the Jews to establish themselves as a special clique.

The situation would have been entirely different if, as in the United States, equality of condition had been taken for granted; if every member of society—from whatever stratum—had been firmly convinced that by ability and luck he might become the hero of a success story. In such a society, discrimination becomes the only means of distinction, a kind of universal law according to which groups may find themselves outside the sphere of civic, political, and economic equality. Where discrimination is not tied up with the Jewish issue only, it can become a crystallization point for a political movement that wants to solve all the natural difficulties and conflicts of a multinational country by violence, mob rule, and the sheer vulgarity of race concepts. It is one of the most promising and dangerous paradoxes of the American Republic that it dared to realize equality on the basis of the most unequal population in the world, physically and historically. In the United States, social antisemitism may one day become the very dangerous nucleus for a political movement.[1] In Europe, however, it had little influence on the rise of political antisemitism.

[1] Although Jews stood out more than other groups in the homogeneous populations of European countries, it does not follow that they are more threatened by discrimination than other groups in America. In fact, up to now, not the Jews but the Negroes—by nature and history the most unequal among the peoples of America—have borne the burden of social and economic discrimination.

This could change, however, if a political movement ever grew out of this merely social discrimination. Then Jews might very suddenly become the principal objects of hatred for the simple reason that they, alone among all other groups, have themselves, within their history and their religion, expressed a well-known principle of separation. This is not true of the Negroes or Chinese, who are therefore less endangered politically, even though they may differ more from the majority than the Jews.

I: *Between Pariah and Parvenu*

THE PRECARIOUS balance between society and state, upon which the nation-state rested socially and politically, brought about a peculiar law governing Jewish admission to society. During the 150 years when Jews truly lived amidst, and not just in the neighborhood of, Western European peoples, they always had to pay with political misery for social glory and with social insult for political success. Assimilation, in the sense of acceptance by non-Jewish society, was granted them only as long as they were clearly distinguished exceptions from the Jewish masses even though they still shared the same restricted and humiliating political conditions, or later only when, after an accomplished emancipation and resulting social isolation, their political status was already challenged by antisemitic movements. Society, confronted with political, economic, and legal equality for Jews, made it quite clear that none of its classes was prepared to grant them social equality, and that only exceptions from the Jewish people would be received. Jews who heard the strange compliment that they were exceptions, exceptional Jews, knew quite well that it was this very ambiguity—that they were Jews and yet presumably not *like* Jews—which opened the doors of society to them. If they desired this kind of intercourse, they tried, therefore, "to be and yet not to be Jews." [2]

The seeming paradox had a solid basis in fact. What non-Jewish society demanded was that the newcomer be as "educated" as itself, and that, although he not behave like an "ordinary Jew," he be and produce something out of the ordinary, since, after all, he was a Jew. All advocates of emancipation called for assimilation, that is, adjustment to and reception by, society, which they considered either a preliminary condition to Jewish emancipation or its automatic consequence. In other words, whenever those who actually tried to improve Jewish conditions attempted to think of the Jewish question from the point of view of the Jews themselves, they immediately approached it merely in its social aspect. It has been one of the most unfortunate facts in the history of the Jewish people that only its enemies, and almost never its friends, understood that the Jewish question was a political one.

The defenders of emancipation tended to present the problem as one of "education," a concept which originally applied to Jews as well as non-Jews.[3] It was taken for granted that the vanguard in both camps would con-

---

[2] This surprisingly apt observation was made by the liberal Protestant theologian H. E. G. Paulus in a valuable little pamphlet, *Die jüdische Nationalabsonderung nach Ursprung, Folgen und Besserungsmitteln*, 1831. Paulus, much attacked by Jewish writers of the time, advocated a gradual individual emancipation on the basis of assimilation.

[3] This attitude is expressed in Wilhelm v. Humboldt's "Expert Opinion" of 1809: "The state should not exactly teach respect for the Jews, but should abolish an in-

sist of specially "educated," tolerant, cultured persons. It followed, of course, that the particularly tolerant, educated and cultured non-Jews could be bothered socially only with exceptionally educated Jews. As a matter of course, the demand, among the educated, for the abolition of prejudice was very quickly to become a rather one-sided affair, until only the Jews, finally, were urged to educate themselves.

This, however, is only one side of the matter. Jews were exhorted to become educated enough not to behave like ordinary Jews, but they were, on the other hand, accepted only because they were Jews, because of their foreign, exotic appeal. In the eighteenth century, this had its source in the new humanism which expressly wanted "new specimens of humanity" (Herder), intercourse with whom would serve as an example of possible intimacy with all types of mankind. To the enlightened Berlin of Mendelssohn's time, the Jews served as living proof that all men are human. For this generation, friendship with Mendelssohn or Markus Herz was an ever-renewed demonstration of the dignity of man. And because Jews were a despised and oppressed people, they were for it an even purer and more exemplary model of mankind. It was Herder, an outspoken friend of the Jews, who first used the later misused and misquoted phrase, "strange people of Asia driven into our regions." [4] With these words, he and his fellow-humanists greeted the "new specimens of humanity" for whom the eighteenth century had "searched the earth," [5] only to find them in their age-old neighbors. Eager to stress the basic unity of mankind, they wanted to show the origins of the Jewish people as more alien, and hence more exotic, than they actually were, so that the demonstration of humanity as a universal principle might be more effective.

For a few decades at the turn of the eighteenth century, when French Jewry already enjoyed emancipation and German Jewry had almost no hope or desire for it, Prussia's enlightened intelligentsia made "Jews all over the world turn their eyes to the Jewish community in Berlin" [6] (and not in Paris!). Much of this was due to the success of Lessing's *Nathan the Wise,* or to its misinterpretation, which held that the "new specimens of humanity," because they had become examples of mankind, must also be more intensely human individuals.[7] Mirabeau was strongly influenced by this idea and used to cite Mendelssohn as his example.[8] Herder hoped that educated Jews would

---

human and prejudiced way of thinking etc. . . ." In Ismar Freund, *Die Emancipation der Juden in Preussen,* Berlin, 1912, II, 270.

[4] J. G. Herder, "Über die politische Bekehrung der Juden" in *Adrastea und das 18. Jahrhundert,* 1801-03.

[5] Herder, *Briefe zur Beförderung der Humanität* (1793-97), 40. Brief.

[6] Felix Priebatsch, "Die Judenpolitik des fürstlichen Absolutismus im 17. und 18. Jahrhundert," in *Forschungen und Versuche zur Geschichte des Mittelalters und der Neuzeit,* 1915, p. 646.

[7] Lessing himself had no such illusions. His last letter to Moses Mendelssohn expressed most clearly what he wanted: "the shortest and safest way to that European country without either Christians or Jews." For Lessing's attitude toward Jews, see Franz Mehring, *Die Lessinglegende,* 1906.

[8] See Honoré Q. R. de Mirabeau, *Sur Moses Mendelssohn,* London, 1788.

show a greater freedom from prejudice because "the Jew is free of certain political judgments which it is very hard or impossible for us to abandon." Protesting against the habit of the time of granting "concessions of new mercantile advantages," he proposed education as the true road to emancipation of Jews from Judaism, from "the old and proud national prejudices, . . . customs that do not belong to our age and constitutions," so that Jews could become "purely humanized," and of service to "the development of the sciences and the entire culture of mankind." [9] At about the same time, Goethe wrote in a review of a book of poems that their author, a Polish Jew, did "not achieve more than a Christian *étudiant en belles lettres,*" and complained that where he had expected something genuinely new, some force beyond shallow convention, he had found ordinary mediocrity.[10]

One can hardly overestimate the disastrous effect of this exaggerated good will on the newly Westernized, educated Jews and the impact it had on their social and psychological position. Not only were they faced with the demoralizing demand that they be exceptions to their own people, recognize "the sharp difference between them and the others," and ask that such "separation . . . be also legalized" by the governments; [11] they were expected even to become exceptional specimens of humanity. And since this, and not Heine's conversion, constituted the true "ticket of admission" into cultured European society, what else could these and future generations of Jews do but try desperately not to disappoint anybody? [12]

In the early decades of this entry into society, when assimilation had not yet become a tradition to follow, but something achieved by few and exceptionally gifted individuals, it worked very well indeed. While France was the land of political glory for the Jews, the first to recognize them as citizens, Prussia seemed on the way to becoming the country of social splendor. Enlightened Berlin, where Mendelssohn had established close connections with many famous men of his time, was only a beginning. His connections with non-Jewish society still had much in common with the scholarly ties that had bound Jewish and Christian learned men together in nearly all periods of European history. The new and surprising element was that

[9] J. G. Herder, "Ueber die politische Bekehrung der Juden," *op. cit.*

[10] Johann Wolfgang v. Goethe's review of Isachar Falkensohn Behr, *Gedichte eines polnischen Juden,* Mietau and Leipzig, 1772, in *Frankfurter Gelehrte Anzeigen.*

[11] Friedrich Schleiermacher, *Briefe bei Gelegenheit der politisch theologischen Aufgabe und des Sendschreibens jüdischer Hausväter,* 1799, in *Werke,* 1846, Abt. I, Band V, 34.

[12] This does not, however, apply to Moses Mendelssohn, who hardly knew the thoughts of Herder, Goethe, Schleiermacher, and other members of the younger generation. Mendelssohn was revered for his uniqueness. His firm adherence to his Jewish religion made it impossible for him to break ultimately with the Jewish people, which his successors did as a matter of course. He felt he was "a member of an oppressed people who must beg for the good will and protection of the governing nation" (see his "Letter to Lavater," 1770, in *Gesammelte Schriften,* Vol. VII, Berlin, 1930); that is, he always knew that the extraordinary esteem for his person paralleled an extraordinary contempt for his people. Since he, unlike Jews of following generations, did not share this contempt, he did not consider himself an exception.

Mendelssohn's friends used these relationships for nonpersonal, ideological, or even political purposes. He himself explicitly disavowed all such ulterior motives and expressed time and again his complete satisfaction with the conditions under which he had to live, as though he had foreseen that his exceptional social status and freedom had something to do with the fact that he still belonged to "the lowliest inhabitants of the (Prussian king's) domain." [13]

This indifference to political and civil rights survived Mendelssohn's innocent relationships with the learned and enlightened men of his time; it was carried later into the salons of those Jewish women who gathered together the most brilliant society Berlin was ever to see. Not until after the Prussian defeat of 1806, when the introduction of Napoleonic legislation into large regions of Germany put the question of Jewish emancipation on the agenda of public discussion, did this indifference change into outright fear. Emancipation would liberate the educated Jews, together with the "backward" Jewish people, and their equality would wipe out that precious distinction, upon which, as they were very well aware, their social status was based. When the emancipation finally came to pass, most assimilated Jews escaped into conversion to Christianity, characteristically finding it bearable and not dangerous to be Jews before emancipation, but not after.

Most representative of these salons, and the genuinely mixed society they brought together in Germany, was that of Rahel Varnhagen. Her original, unspoiled, and unconventional intelligence, combined with an absorbing interest in people and a truly passionate nature, made her the most brilliant and the most interesting of these Jewish women. The modest but famous soirées in Rahel's "garret" brought together "enlightened" aristocrats, middle-class intellectuals, and actors—that is, all those who, like the Jews, did not belong to respectable society. Thus Rahel's salon, by definition and intentionally, was established on the fringe of society, and did not share any of its conventions or prejudices.

It is amusing to note how closely the assimilation of Jews into society followed the precepts Goethe had proposed for the education of his *Wilhelm Meister,* a novel which was to become the great model of middle-class education. In this book the young burgher is educated by noblemen and

[13] The Prussia which Lessing had described as "Europe's most enslaved country" was to Mendelssohn "a state in which one of the wisest princes who ever ruled men has made the arts and sciences flourish, has made national freedom of thought so general that its beneficent effects reach even the lowliest inhabitants of his domain." Such humble contentment is touching and surprising if one realizes that the "wisest prince" had made it very hard for the Jewish philosopher to get permission to sojourn in Berlin and, at a time when his *Münzjuden* enjoyed all privileges, did not even grant him the regular status of a "protected Jew." Mendelssohn was even aware that he, the friend of all educated Germany, would be subject to the same tax levied upon an ox led to the market if ever he decided to visit his friend Lavater in Leipzig, but no political conclusion regarding the improvement of such conditions ever occurred to him. (See the "Letter to Lavater," *op. cit.,* and his preface to his translation of Menasseh Ben Israel in *Gesammelte Schriften,* Vol. III, Leipzig, 1843-45.)

actors, so that he may learn how to present and represent his individuality, and thereby advance from the modest status of a burgher's son into a nobleman. For the middle classes and for the Jews, that is, for those who were actually outside of high aristocratic society, everything depended upon "personality" and the ability to express it. To know how to play the role of what one actually was, seemed the most important thing. The peculiar fact that in Germany the Jewish question was held to be a question of education was closely connected with this early start and had its consequence in the educational philistinism of both the Jewish and non-Jewish middle classes, and also in the crowding of Jews into the liberal professions.

The charm of the early Berlin salons was that nothing really mattered but personality and the uniqueness of character, talent, and expression. Such uniqueness, which alone made possible an almost unbounded communication and unrestricted intimacy, could be replaced neither by rank, money, success, nor literary fame. The brief encounter of true personalities, which joined a Hohenzollern prince, Louis Ferdinand, to the banker Abraham Mendelssohn; or a political publicist and diplomat, Friedrich Gentz, to Friedrich Schlegel, a writer of the then ultramodern romantic school—these were a few of the more famous visitors at Rahel's "garret"—came to an end in 1806 when, according to their hostess, this unique meeting place "foundered like a ship containing the highest enjoyment of life." Along with the aristocrats, the romantic intellectuals became antisemitic, and although this by no means meant that either group gave up all its Jewish friends, the innocence and splendor were gone.

The real turning point in the social history of German Jews came not in the year of the Prussian defeat, but two years later, when, in 1808, the government passed the municipal law giving full civic, though not political, rights to the Jews. In the peace treaty of 1807, Prussia had lost with her eastern provinces the majority of her Jewish population; the Jews left within her territory were "protected Jews" in any event, that is, they already enjoyed civic rights in the form of individual privileges. The municipal emancipation only legalized these privileges, and outlived the general emancipation decree of 1812; Prussia, having regained Posen and its Jewish masses after the defeat of Napoleon, practically rescinded the decree of 1812, which now would have meant political rights even for poor Jews, but left the municipal law intact.

Though of little political importance so far as the actual improvement of the Jews' status is concerned, these final emancipation decrees together with the loss of the provinces in which the majority of Prussian Jews lived, had tremendous social consequences. Before 1807, the protected Jews of Prussia had numbered only about 20 per cent of the total Jewish population. By the time the emancipation decree was issued, protected Jews formed the majority in Prussia, with only 10 per cent of "foreign Jews" left for contrast. Now the dark poverty and backwardness against which "exception Jews" of wealth and education had stood out so advantageously was no longer there. And this background, so essential as a basis of comparison for social success and psychological self-respect, never again became what it had been before Napoleon. When the Polish provinces were regained in 1816, the formerly "protected Jews" (now registered as Prussian citizens of Jewish faith) still numbered above 60 per cent.[14]

Socially speaking, this meant that the remaining Jews in Prussia had lost the native background against which they had been measured as exceptions. Now they themselves composed such a background, but a contracted one, against which the individual had to strain doubly in order to stand out at all. "Exception Jews" were once again simply Jews, not exceptions from but representatives of a despised people. Equally bad was the social influence of governmental interference. Not only the classes antagonistic to the government and therefore openly hostile to the Jews, but all strata of society, became more or less aware that Jews of their acquaintance were not so much individual exceptions as members of a group in whose favor the state was ready to take exceptional measures. And this was precisely what the "exception Jews" had always feared.

Berlin society left the Jewish salons with unmatched rapidity, and by 1808 these meeting-places had already been supplanted by the houses of the titled bureaucracy and the upper middle class. One can see, from any of the numerous correspondences of the time, that the intellectuals as well as the aristocrats now began to direct their contempt for the Eastern European Jews, whom they hardly knew, against the educated Jews of Berlin, whom they knew very well. The latter would never again achieve the self-respect that springs from a collective consciousness of being exceptional; henceforth, each one of them had to prove that although he was a Jew, yet he was not a Jew. No longer would it suffice to distinguish oneself from a more or less unknown mass of "backward brethren"; one had to stand out—as an individual who could be congratulated on being an exception—from *the* Jew," and thus from the people as a whole.

Social discrimination, and not political antisemitism, discovered the phantom of *"the* Jew." The first author to make the distinction between the Jewish individual and "the Jew in general, the Jew everywhere and nowhere" was an obscure publicist who had, in 1802, written a biting satire on Jewish society and its hunger for education, the magic wand for general social acceptance. Jews were depicted as a "principle" of philistine and upstart society.[15] This rather vulgar piece of literature not only was read with delight by quite a few prominent members of Rahel's salon, but even indirectly inspired a great romantic poet, Clemens von Brentano, to write a

---

[14] See Heinrich Silbergleit, *Die Bevölkerungs- und Berufsverhältnisse der Juden im Deutschen Reich,* Vol. I, Berlin, 1930.

[15] C. W. F. Grattenauer's widely read pamphlet *Wider die Juden* of 1802 had been preceded as far back as 1791 by another, *Ueber die physische und moralische Verfassung der heutigen Juden* in which the growing influence of the Jews in Berlin was already pointed out. Although the early pamphlet was reviewed in the *Allgemeine Deutsche Bibliothek,* 1792, Vol. CXII, almost nobody ever read it.

very witty paper in which again the philistine was identified with the Jew.[16]

With the early idyll of a mixed society something disappeared which was never, in any other country and at any other time, to return. Never again did any social group accept Jews with a free mind and heart. It would be friendly with Jews either because it was excited by its own daring and "wickedness" or as a protest against making pariahs of fellow-citizens. But social pariahs the Jews did become wherever they had ceased to be political and civil outcasts.

It is important to bear in mind that assimilation as a group phenomenon really existed only among Jewish intellectuals. It is no accident that the first educated Jew, Moses Mendelssohn, was also the first who, despite his low civic status, was admitted to non-Jewish society. The court Jews and their successors, the Jewish bankers and businessmen in the West, were never socially acceptable, nor did they care to leave the very narrow limits of their invisible ghetto. In the beginning they were proud, like all unspoiled upstarts, of the dark background of misery and poverty from which they had risen; later, when they were attacked from all sides, they had a vested interest in the poverty and even backwardness of the masses because it became an argument, a token of their own security. Slowly, and with misgivings, they were forced away from the more rigorous demands of Jewish law—they never left religious traditions altogether—yet demanded all the more orthodoxy from the Jewish masses.[17] The dissolution of Jewish communal autonomy made them that much more eager not only to protect Jewish communities against the authorities, but also to rule over them with the help of the state, so that the phrase denoting the "double dependence" of poor Jews on "both the government and their wealthy brethren" only reflected reality.[18]

The Jewish notables (as they were called in the nineteenth century) ruled

[16] Clemens Brentano's *Der Philister vor, in und nach der Geschichte* was written for and read to the so-called *Christlich-Deutsche Tischgesellschaft*, a famous club of writers and patriots, founded in 1808 for the struggle against Napoleon.

[17] Thus the Rothschilds in the 1820's withdrew a large donation from their native community of Frankfurt, in order to counteract the influence of reformers who wanted Jewish children to receive a general education. See Isaak Markus Jost, *Neuere Geschichte der Israeliten*, 1846, X, 102.

[18] *Op. cit.,* IX, 38.—The court Jews and the rich Jewish bankers who followed in their footsteps never wanted to leave the Jewish community. They acted as its representatives and protectors against public authorities; they were frequently granted official power over communities which they ruled from afar so that the old autonomy of Jewish communities was undermined and destroyed from within long before it was abolished by the nation-state. The first court Jew with monarchical aspirations in his own "nation" was a Jew of Prague, a purveyor of supplies to the Elector Maurice of Saxony in the sixteenth century. He demanded that all rabbis and community heads be selected from members of his family. (See Bondy-Dworsky, *Geschichte der Juden in Boehmen, Maehren und Schlesien,* Prague, 1906, II, 727.) The practice of installing court Jews as dictators in their communities became general in the eighteenth century and was followed by the rule of "notables" in the nineteenth century.

the Jewish communities, but they did not belong to them socially or even geographically. They stood, in a sense, as far outside Jewish society as they did outside Gentile society. Having made brilliant individual careers and been granted considerable privileges by their masters, they formed a kind of community of exceptions with extremely limited social opportunities. Naturally despised by court society, lacking business connections with the non-Jewish middle class, their social contacts were as much outside the laws of society as their economic rise had been independent of contemporary economic conditions. This isolation and independence frequently gave them a feeling of power and pride, illustrated by the following anecdote told in the beginning eighteenth century: "A certain Jew . . . , when gently reproached by a noble and cultured physician with (the Jewish) pride although they had no princes among them and no part in government . . . replied with insolence: We are not princes, but we govern them." [19]

Such pride is almost the opposite of class arrogance, which developed but slowly among the privileged Jews. Ruling as absolute princes among their own people, they still felt themselves to be *primi inter pares*. They were prouder of being a "privileged Rabbi of all Jewry" or a "Prince of the Holy Land" than of any titles their masters might offer them.[20] Until the middle of the eighteenth century, they would all have agreed with the Dutch Jew who said: *"Neque in toto orbi alicui nationi inservimus,"* and neither then nor later would they have understood fully the answer of the "learned Christian" who replied: "But this means happiness only for a few. The people considered as a *corpo* (*sic*) is hunted everywhere, has no self-government, is subject to foreign rule, has no power and no dignity, and wanders all over the world, a stranger everywhere." [21]

Class arrogance came only when business connections were established among state bankers of different countries; intermarriage between leading families soon followed, and culminated in a real international caste system, unknown thus far in Jewish society. This was all the more glaring to non-Jewish observers, since it took place when the old feudal estates and castes were rapidly disappearing into new classes. One concluded, very wrongly, that the Jewish people were a remnant of the Middle Ages and did not see that this new caste was of quite recent birth. It was completed only in the nineteenth century and comprised numerically no more than perhaps a hundred families. But since these were in the limelight, the Jewish people as a whole came to be regarded as a caste.[22]

Great, therefore, as the role of the court Jews had been in political history and for the birth of antisemitism, social history might easily neglect

[19] Johann Jacob Schudt, *Jüdische Merkwürdigkeiten,* Frankfurt a.M., 1715-1717, IV, Annex, 48.
[20] Selma Stern, *Jud Suess,* Berlin, 1929, pp. 18 f.
[21] Schudt, *op. cit.,* I, 19.
[22] Christian Friedrich Ruehs defines the whole Jewish people as a "caste of merchants." "Ueber die Ansprüche der Juden an das deutsche Bürgerrecht," in *Zeitschrift für die neueste Geschichte,* 1815.

them were it not for the fact that they had certain psychological traits and behavior patterns in common with Jewish intellectuals who were, after all, usually the sons of businessmen. The Jewish notables wanted to dominate the Jewish people and therefore had no desire to leave it, while it was characteristic of Jewish intellectuals that they wanted to leave their people and be admitted to society; they both shared the feeling that they were exceptions, a feeling perfectly in harmony with the judgment of their environment. The "exception Jews" of wealth felt like exceptions from the common destiny of the Jewish people and were recognized by the governments as exceptionally useful; the "exception Jews" of education felt themselves exceptions from the Jewish people and also exceptional human beings, and were recognized as such by society.

Assimilation, whether carried to the extreme of conversion or not, never was a real menace to the survival of the Jews.[23] Whether they were welcomed or rejected, it was because they were Jews, and they were well aware of it. The first generations of educated Jews still wanted sincerely to lose their identity as Jews, and Boerne wrote with a great deal of bitterness, "Some reproach me with being a Jew, some praise me because of it, some pardon me for it, but all think of it." [24] Still brought up on eighteenth-century ideas, they longed for a country without either Christians or Jews; they had devoted themselves to science and the arts, and were greatly hurt when they found out that governments which would give every privilege and honor to a Jewish banker, condemned Jewish intellectuals to starvation.[25] The conversions which, in the early nineteenth century, had been prompted by fear of being lumped together with the Jewish masses, now became a necessity for daily bread. Such a premium on lack of character forced a whole generation of Jews into bitter opposition against state and society. The "new specimens of humanity," if they were worth their salt, all became rebels, and since the most reactionary governments of the period were supported and financed by Jewish bankers, their rebellion was especially violent against the official representatives of their own people. The anti-Jewish denunciations of Marx and Boerne cannot be properly understood except in the light of this conflict between rich Jews and Jewish intellectuals.

This conflict, however, existed in full vigor only in Germany and did not survive the antisemitic movement of the century. In Austria, there was no Jewish intelligentsia to speak of before the end of the nineteenth century,

---

[23] A remarkable, though little-known, fact is that assimilation as a program led much more frequently to conversion than to mixed marriage. Unfortunately statistics cover up rather than reveal this fact because they consider all unions between converted and nonconverted Jewish partners to be mixed marriages. We know, however, that there were quite a number of families in Germany who had been baptized for generations and yet remained purely Jewish. That the converted Jew only rarely left his family and even more rarely left his Jewish surroundings altogether, accounts for this. The Jewish family, at any rate, proved to be a more conserving force than Jewish religion.

[24] *Briefe aus Paris.* 74th Letter, February, 1832.

[25] *Ibid.,* 72nd Letter.

when it felt immediately the whole impact of antisemitic pressure. These Jews, like their wealthy brethren, preferred to trust themselves to the Hapsburg monarchy's protection, and became socialist only after the first World War, when the Social Democratic party came to power. The most significant, though not the only, exception to this rule was Karl Kraus, the last representative of the tradition of Heine, Boerne, and Marx. Kraus's denunciations of Jewish businessmen on one hand, and Jewish journalism as the organized cult of fame on the other, were perhaps even more bitter than those of his predecessors because he was so much more isolated in a country where no Jewish revolutionary tradition existed. In France, where the emancipation decree had survived all changes of governments and regimes, the small number of Jewish intellectuals were neither the forerunners of a new class nor especially important in intellectual life. Culture as such, education as a program, did not form Jewish behavior patterns as it did in Germany.

In no other country had there been anything like the short period of true assimilation so decisive for the history of German Jews, when the real vanguard of a people not only accepted Jews, but was even strangely eager to associate with them. Nor did this attitude ever completely disappear from German society. To the very end, traces of it could easily be discerned, which showed, of course, that relations with Jews never came to be taken for granted. At best it remained a program, at worst a strange and exciting experience. Bismarck's well-known remark about "German stallions to be paired off with Jewish mares," is but the most vulgar expression of a prevalent point of view.

It is only natural that this social situation, though it made rebels out of the first educated Jews, would in the long run produce a specific kind of conformism rather than an effective tradition of rebellion.[26] Conforming to a society which discriminated against "ordinary" Jews and in which, at the same time, it was generally easier for an educated Jew to be admitted to fashionable circles than for a non-Jew of similar condition, Jews had to differentiate themselves clearly from the "Jew in general," and just as clearly to indicate that they were Jews; under no circumstances were they allowed simply to disappear among their neighbors. In order to rationalize an ambiguity which they themselves did not fully understand, they might pretend to "be a man in the street and a Jew at home."[27] This actually amounted to a feeling of being different from other men in the street because they were Jews, and different from other Jews at home because they were not like "ordinary Jews."

[26] The "conscious pariah" (Bernard Lazare) was the only tradition of rebellion which established itself, although those who belonged to it were hardly aware of its existence. See the author's "The Jew as Pariah. A Hidden Tradition," in *Jewish Social Studies*, Vol. VI, No. 2 (1944).

[27] It is not without irony that this excellent formula, which may serve as a motto for Western European assimilation, was propounded by a Russian Jew and first published in Hebrew. It comes from Judah Leib Gordon's Hebrew poem, *Hakitzah ami*, 1863. See S. M. Dubnow, *History of the Jews in Russia and Poland*, 1918, II, 228 f.

66   ANTISEMITISM

The behavior patterns of assimilated Jews, determined by this continuous concentrated effort to distinguish themselves, created a Jewish type that is recognizable everywhere. Instead of being defined by nationality or religion, Jews were being transformed into a social group whose members shared certain psychological attributes and reactions, the sum total of which was supposed to constitute "Jewishness." In other words, Judaism became a psychological quality and the Jewish question became an involved personal problem for every individual Jew.

In his tragic endeavor to conform through differentiation and distinction, the new Jewish type had as little in common with the feared "Jew in general" as with that abstraction, the "heir of the prophets and eternal promoter of justice on earth," which Jewish apologetics conjured up whenever a Jewish journalist was being attacked. The Jew of the apologists was endowed with attributes that are indeed the privileges of pariahs, and which certain Jewish rebels living on the fringe of society did possess—humanity, kindness, freedom from prejudice, sensitiveness to injustice. The trouble was that these qualities had nothing to do with the prophets and that, worse still, these Jews usually belonged neither to Jewish society nor to fashionable circles of non-Jewish society. In the history of assimilated Jewry, they played but an insignificant role. The "Jew in general," on the other hand, as described by professional Jew-haters, showed those qualities which the parvenu must acquire if he wants to arrive—inhumanity, greed, insolence, cringing servility, and determination to push ahead. The trouble in this case was that these qualities have also nothing to do with national attributes and that, moreover, these Jewish business-class types showed little inclination for non-Jewish society and played almost as small a part in Jewish social history. As long as defamed peoples and classes exist, parvenu- and pariah-qualities will be produced anew by each generation with incomparable monotony, in Jewish society and everywhere else.

For the formation of a social history of the Jews within nineteenth-century European society, it was, however, decisive that to a certain extent every Jew in every generation had somehow at some time to decide whether he would remain a pariah and stay out of society altogether, or become a parvenu, or conform to society on the demoralizing condition that he not so much hide his origin as "betray with the secret of his origin the secret of his people as well." [28] The latter road was difficult, indeed, as such secrets did not exist and had to be made up. Since Rahel Varnhagen's unique attempt to establish a social life outside of official society had failed, the way of the pariah and the parvenu were equally ways of extreme solitude, and the way of conformism one of constant regret. The so-called complex psychology of the average Jew, which in a few favored cases developed into a very modern sensitiveness, was based on an ambiguous situation. Jews felt simultaneously the pariah's regret at not having become a parvenu and the parvenu's bad conscience at having betrayed his people and exchanged equal rights for

[28] This formulation was made by Karl Kraus around 1912. See *Untergang der Welt durch schwarze Magie,* 1925.

personal privileges. One thing was certain: if one wanted to avoid all ambiguities of social existence, one had to resign oneself to the fact that to be a Jew meant to belong either to an overprivileged upper class or to an underprivileged mass which, in Western and Central Europe, one could belong to only through an intellectual and somewhat artificial solidarity.

The social destinies of average Jews were determined by their eternal lack of decision. And society certainly did not compel them to make up their minds, for it was precisely this ambiguity of situation and character that made the relationship with Jews attractive. The majority of assimilated Jews thus lived in a twilight of favor and misfortune and knew with certainty only that both success and failure were inextricably connected with the fact that they were Jews. For them the Jewish question had lost, once and for all, all political significance; but it haunted their private lives and influenced their personal decisions all the more tyrannically. The adage, "a man in the street and a Jew at home," was bitterly realized: political problems were distorted to the point of pure perversion when Jews tried to solve them by means of inner experience and private emotions; private life was poisoned to the point of inhumanity—for example in the question of mixed marriages—when the heavy burden of unsolved problems of public significance was crammed into that private existence which is much better ruled by the unpredictable laws of passion than by considered policies.

It was by no means easy not to resemble the "Jew in general" and yet remain a Jew; to pretend not to be like Jews and still show with sufficient clarity that one was Jewish. The average Jew, neither a parvenu nor a "conscious pariah" (Bernard Lazare), could only stress an empty sense of difference which continued to be interpreted, in all its possible psychological aspects and variations from innate strangeness to social alienation. As long as the world was somewhat peaceful, this attitude did not work out badly and for generations even became a *modus vivendi*. Concentration on an artificially complicated inner life helped Jews to respond to the unreasonable demands of society, to be strange and exciting, to develop a certain immediacy of self-expression and presentation which were originally the attributes of the actor and the virtuoso, people whom society has always half denied and half admired. Assimilated Jews, half proud and half ashamed of their Jewishness, clearly were in this category.

The process by which bourgeois society developed out of the ruins of its revolutionary traditions and memories added the black ghost of boredom to economic saturation and general indifference to political questions. Jews became people with whom one hoped to while away some time. The less one thought of them as equals, the more attractive and entertaining they became. Bourgeois society, in its search for entertainment and its passionate interest in the individual, insofar as he differed from the norm that is man, discovered the attraction of everything that could be supposed to be mysteriously wicked or secretly vicious. And precisely this feverish preference opened the doors of society to Jews; for within the framework of this society, Jewishness, after having been distorted into a psychological quality, could easily be perverted into a vice. The Enlightenment's genuine tolerance and curiosity for everything human was being replaced by a morbid lust for the exotic, abnormal, and different as such. Several types in society, one after the other, represented the exotic, the anomalous, the different, but none of them was in the least connected with political questions. Thus only the role of Jews in this decaying society could assume a stature that transcended the narrow limits of a society affair.

Before we follow the strange ways which led the "exception Jews," famous and notorious strangers, into the salons of the Faubourg St. Germain in *fin-de-siècle* France, we must recall the only great man whom the elaborate self-deception of the "exception Jews" ever produced. It seems that every commonplace idea gets one chance in at least one individual to attain what used to be called historical greatness. The great man of the "exception Jews" was Benjamin Disraeli.

II: *The Potent Wizard* [29]

BENJAMIN DISRAELI, whose chief interest in life was the career of Lord Beaconsfield, was distinguished by two things: first, the gift of the gods which we moderns banally call luck, and which other periods revered as a goddess named Fortune, and second, more intimately and more wondrously connected with Fortune than one may be able to explain, the great carefree innocence of mind and imagination which makes it impossible to classify the man as a careerist, though he never thought seriously of anything except his career. His innocence made him recognize how foolish it would be to feel *déclassé* and how much more exciting it would be for himself and for others, how much more useful for his career, to accentuate the fact that he was a Jew "by dressing differently, combing his hair oddly, and by queer manners of expression and verbiage." [30] He cared for admission to high and highest society more passionately and shamelessly than any other Jewish intellectual did; but he was the only one of them who discovered the secret of how to preserve luck, that natural miracle of pariahdom, and who knew from the beginning that one never should bow down in order to "move up from high to higher."

He played the game of politics like an actor in a theatrical performance, except that he played his part so well that he was convinced by his own make-believe. His life and his career read like a fairy-tale, in which he appeared as the prince—offering the blue flower of the romantics, now the primrose of imperialist England, to his princess, the Queen of England.

[29] The title phrase is taken from a sketch of Disraeli by Sir John Skleton in 1867. See W. F. Monypenny and G. E. Buckle, *The Life of Benjamin Disraeli, Earl of Beaconsfield*, New York, 1929, II, 292-93.
[30] Morris S. Lazaron, *Seed of Abraham*, New York, 1930, "Benjamin Disraeli," pp. 260 ff.

The British colonial enterprise was the fairyland upon which the sun never sets and its capital the mysterious Asiatic Delhi whence the prince wanted to escape with his princess from foggy prosaic London. This may have been foolish and childish; but when a wife writes to her husband as Lady Beaconsfield wrote to hers: "You know you married me for money, and I know that if you had to do it again you would do it for love," [31] one is silenced before a happiness that seemed to be against all the rules. Here was one who started out to sell his soul to the devil, but the devil did not want the soul and the gods gave him all the happiness of this earth.

Disraeli came from an entirely assimilated family; his father, an enlightened gentleman, baptized the son because he wanted him to have the opportunities of ordinary mortals. He had few connections with Jewish society and knew nothing of Jewish religion or customs. Jewishness, from the beginning, was a fact of origin which he was at liberty to embellish, unhindered by actual knowledge. The result was that somehow he looked at this fact much in the same way as a Gentile would have looked at it. He realized much more clearly than other Jews that being a Jew could be as much an opportunity as a handicap. And since, unlike his simple and modest father, he wanted nothing less than to become an ordinary mortal and nothing more than "to distinguish himself above all his contemporaries," [32] he began to shape his "olive complexion and coal-black eyes" until he with "the mighty dome of his forehead—no Christian temple, to be sure—(was) unlike any living creature one has met." [33] He knew instinctively that everything depended upon the "division between him and mere mortals," upon an accentuation of his lucky "strangeness."

All this demonstrates a unique understanding of society and its rules. Significantly, it was Disraeli who said, "What is a crime among the multitude is only a vice among the few" [34]—perhaps the most profound insight into the very principle by which the slow and insidious decline of nineteenth-century society into the depth of mob and underworld morality took place. Since he knew this rule, he knew also that Jews would have no better chances anywhere than in circles which pretended to be exclusive and to discriminate against them; for inasmuch as these circles of the few, together with the multitude, thought of Jewishness as a crime, this "crime" could be transformed at any moment into an attractive "vice." Disraeli's display of exoticism, strangeness, mysteriousness, magic, and power drawn from secret sources, was aimed correctly at this disposition in society. And it was his virtuosity at the social game which made him choose the Conservative Party, won him a seat in Parliament, the post of Prime Minister, and, last

---

[31] Horace B. Samuel, "The Psychology of Disraeli," in *Modernities,* London, 1914.

[32] J. A. Froude thus closes his biography of *Lord Beaconsfield,* 1890: "The aim with which he started in life was to distinguish himself above all his contemporaries, and wild as such an ambition must have appeared, he at last won the stake for which he played so bravely."

[33] Sir John Skleton, *op. cit.*

[34] In his novel *Tancred,* 1847.

but not least, the lasting admiration of society and the friendship of a Queen.

One of the reasons for his success was the sincerity of his play. The impression he made on his more unbiased contemporaries was a curious mixture of acting and "absolute sincerity and unreserve." [35] This could only be achieved by a genuine innocence that was partly due to an upbringing from which all specific Jewish influence had been excluded.[36] But Disraeli's good conscience was also due to his having been born an Englishman. England did not know Jewish masses and Jewish poverty, as she had admitted them centuries after their expulsion in the Middle Ages; the Portuguese Jews who settled in England in the eighteenth century were wealthy and educated. Not until the end of the nineteenth century, when the pogroms in Russia initiated the modern Jewish emigrations, did Jewish poverty enter London, and along with it the difference between the Jewish masses and their well-to-do brethren. In Disraeli's time the Jewish question, in its Continental form, was quite unknown, because only Jews welcome to the state lived in England. In other words, the English "exception Jews" were not so aware of being exceptions as their Continental brothers were. When Disraeli scorned the "pernicious doctrine of modern times, the natural equality of men," [37] he consciously followed in the footsteps of Burke who had "preferred the rights of an Englishman to the Rights of Man," but ignored the actual situation in which privileges for the few had been substituted for rights for all. He was so ignorant of the real conditions among the Jewish people, and so convinced of "the influence of the Jewish race upon modern communities," that he frankly demanded that the Jews "receive all that honour and favour from the northern and western races, which, in civilized and refined nations, should be the lot of those who charm the public taste and elevate the public feeling." [38] Since political influence of Jews in England centered around the English branch of the Rothschilds, he felt very proud about the Rothschilds' help in defeating Napoleon and did not see any reason why he should not be outspoken in his political opinions as a Jew.[39] As a baptized Jew, he was of course never an official spokesman for any Jewish community, but it remains true that he was the only Jew of his kind and his century who tried as well as he knew to represent the Jewish people politically.

Disraeli, who never denied that "the fundamental fact about (him) was that he was a Jew," [40] had an admiration for all things Jewish that was matched only by his ignorance of them. The mixture of pride and ignorance

---

[35] Sir John Skleton, *op. cit.*

[36] Disraeli himself reported: "I was not bred among my race and was nourished in great prejudice against them." For his family background, see especially Joseph Caro, "Benjamin Disraeli, Juden und Judentum," in *Monatsschrift für Geschichte und Wissenschaft des Judentums*, 1932, Jahrgang 76.

[37] *Lord George Bentinck. A Political Biography*, London, 1852, 496.

[38] *Ibid.*, p. 491.

[39] *Ibid.*, pp. 497 ff.

[40] Monypenny and Buckle, *op. cit.*, p. 1507.

in these matters, however, was characteristic of all the newly assimilated Jews. The great difference is that Disraeli knew even a little less of Jewish past and present and therefore dared to speak out openly what others betrayed in the half-conscious twilight of behavior patterns dictated by fear and arrogance.

The political result of Disraeli's ability to gauge Jewish possibilities by the political aspirations of a normal people was more serious; he almost automatically produced the entire set of theories about Jewish influence and organization that we usually find in the more vicious forms of antisemitism. First of all, he actually thought of himself as the "chosen man of the chosen race." [41] What better proof was there than his own career: a Jew without name and riches, helped only by a few Jewish bankers, was carried to the position of the first man in England; one of the less liked men of Parliament became Prime Minister and earned genuine popularity among those who for a long time had "regarded him as a charlatan and treated him as a pariah." [42] Political success never satisfied him. It was more difficult and more important to be admitted to London's society than to conquer the House of Commons, and it was certainly a greater triumph to be elected a member of Grillion's dining club—"a select coterie of which it has been customary to make rising politicians of both parties, but from which the socially objectionable are rigorously excluded" [43]—than to be Her Majesty's Minister. The delightfully unexpected climax of all these sweet triumphs was the sincere friendship of the Queen, for if the monarchy in England had lost most of its political prerogatives in a strictly controlled, constitutional nation-state, it had won and retained undisputed primacy in English society. In measuring the greatness of Disraeli's triumph, one should remember that Lord Robert Cecil, one of his eminent colleagues in the Conservative Party, could still, around 1850, justify a particularly bitter attack by stating that he was only "plainly speaking out what every one is saying of Disraeli in private and no one will say in public." [44] Disraeli's greatest victory was that finally nobody said in private what would not have flattered and pleased him if it had been said in public. It was precisely this unique rise to genuine popularity which Disraeli had achieved through a policy of seeing only the advantages, and preaching only the privileges, of being born a Jew.

Part of Disraeli's good fortune is the fact that he always fitted his time, and that consequently his numerous biographers understood him more completely than is the case with most great men. He was a living embodiment of ambition, that powerful passion which had developed in a century seemingly not allowing for any distinctions and differences. Carlyle, at any rate, who interpreted the whole world's history according to a nineteenth-century ideal of the hero, was clearly in the wrong when he refused a title from

[41] Horace S. Samuel, *op. cit.*
[42] Monypenny and Buckle, *op. cit.*, p. 147.
[43] *Ibid.*
[44] Robert Cecil's article appeared in the most authoritative organ of the Tories, the *Quarterly Review*. See Monypenny and Buckle, *op. cit.*, pp. 19-22.

Disraeli's hands.[45] No other man among his contemporaries corresponded to Carlyle's heroes as well as Disraeli, with his concept of greatness as such, emptied of all specific achievements; no other man fulfilled so exactly the demands of the late nineteenth century for genius in the flesh as this charlatan who took his role seriously and acted the great part of the Great Man with genuine naïveté and an overwhelming display of fantastic tricks and entertaining artistry. Politicians fell in love with the charlatan who transformed boring business transactions into dreams with an oriental flavor; and when society sensed an aroma of black magic in Disraeli's shrewd dealings, the "potent wizard" had actually won the heart of his time.

Disraeli's ambition to distinguish himself from other mortals and his longing for aristocratic society were typical of the middle classes of his time and country. Neither political reasons nor economic motives, but the impetus of his social ambition, made him join the Conservative Party and follow a policy that would always "select the Whigs for hostility and the Radicals for alliance." [46] In no European country did the middle classes ever achieve enough self-respect to reconcile their intelligentsia with their social status, so that aristocracy could continue to determine the social scale when it had already lost all political significance. The unhappy German philistine discovered his "innate personality" in his desperate struggle against caste arrogance, which had grown out of the decline of nobility and the necessity to protect aristocratic titles against bourgeois money. Vague blood theories and strict control of marriages are rather recent phenomena in the history of European aristocracy. Disraeli knew much better than the German philistines what was required to meet the demands of aristocracy. All attempts of the bourgeoisie to attain social status failed to convince aristocratic arrogance because they reckoned with individuals and lacked the most important element of caste conceit, the pride in privilege without individual effort and merit, simply by virtue of birth. The "innate personality" could never deny that its development demanded education and special effort of the individual. When Disraeli "summoned up a pride of race to confront a pride of caste," [47] he knew that the social status of the Jews, whatever else might be said of it, at least depended solely on the fact of birth and not on achievement.

Disraeli went even a step further. He knew that the aristocracy, which year after year had to see quite a number of rich middle-class men buy titles, was haunted by very serious doubts of its own value. He therefore defeated them at their game by using his rather trite and popular imagination to describe fearlessly how the Englishmen "came from a parvenu and hybrid race, while he himself was sprung from the purest blood in Europe," how "the life of a British peer (was) mainly regulated by Arabian laws and

[45] This happened as late as 1874. Carlyle is reported to have called Disraeli "a cursed Jew," "the worst man who ever lived." See Caro, *op. cit.*
[46] Lord Salisbury in an article in the *Quarterly Review*, 1869.
[47] E. T. Raymond, *Disraeli, The Alien Patriot*, London, 1925, p. 1.

Syrian customs," how "a Jewess is the queen of heaven" or that "the flower of the Jewish race is even now sitting on the right hand of the Lord God of Sabaoth." [48] And when he finally wrote that "there is no longer in fact an aristocracy in England, for the superiority of the animal man is an essential quality of aristocracy," [49] he had in fact touched the weakest point of modern aristocratic race theories, which were later to be the point of departure for bourgeois and upstart race opinions.

Judaism, and belonging to the Jewish people, degenerated into a simple fact of birth only among assimilated Jewry. Originally it had meant a specific religion, a specific nationality, the sharing of specific memories and specific hopes, and, even among the privileged Jews, it meant at least still sharing specific economic advantages. Secularization and assimilation of the Jewish intelligentsia had changed self-consciousness and self-interpretation in such a way that nothing was left of the old memories and hopes but the awareness of belonging to a chosen people. Disraeli, though certainly not the only "exception Jew" to believe in his own chosenness without believing in Him who chooses and rejects, was the only one who produced a full-blown race doctrine out of this empty concept of a historic mission. He was ready to assert that the Semitic principle "represents all that is spiritual in our nature," that "the vicissitudes of history find their main solution—all is race," which is "the key to history" regardless of "language and religion," for "there is only one thing which makes a race and that is blood" and there is only one aristocracy, the "aristocracy of nature" which consists of "an unmixed race of a first-rate organization." [50]

The close relationship of this to more modern race ideologies need not be stressed, and Disraeli's discovery is one more proof of how well they serve to combat feelings of social inferiority. For if race doctrines finally served much more sinister and immediately political purposes, it is still true that much of their plausibility and persuasiveness lay in the fact that they helped anybody feel himself an aristocrat who had been selected by birth on the strength of "racial" qualification. That these new selected ones did not belong to an elite, to a selected few—which, after all, had been inherent in the pride of a nobleman—but had to share chosenness with an ever-growing mob, did no essential harm to the doctrine, for those who did not belong to the chosen race grew numerically in the same proportion.

Disraeli's race doctrines, however, were as much the result of his extraordinary insight into the rules of society as the outgrowth of the specific secularization of assimilated Jewry. Not only was the Jewish intelligentsia caught up in the general secularization process, which in the nineteenth century had already lost the revolutionary appeal of the Enlightenment along with the confidence in an independent, self-reliant humanity and therefore remained without any protection against transformation of formerly genuine religious beliefs into superstitions. The Jewish intelligentsia was exposed also

[48] H. B. Samuel, *op. cit.*, Disraeli, *Tancred*, and *Lord George Bentinck*, respectively.
[49] In his novel *Coningsby*, 1844.
[50] See *Lord George Bentinck* and the novels *Endymion*, 1881, and *Coningsby*.

to the influences of the Jewish reformers who wanted to change a national religion into a religious denomination. To do so, they had to transform the two basic elements of Jewish piety—the Messianic hope and the faith in Israel's chosenness, and they deleted from Jewish prayerbooks the visions of an ultimate restoration of Zion, along with the pious anticipation of the day at the end of days when the segregation of the Jewish people from the nations of the earth would come to an end. Without the Messianic hope, the idea of chosenness meant eternal segregation; without faith in chosenness, which charged one specific people with the redemption of the world, Messianic hope evaporated into the dim cloud of general philanthropy and universalism which became so characteristic of specifically Jewish political enthusiasm.

The most fateful element in Jewish secularization was that the concept of chosenness was being separated from the Messianic hope, whereas in Jewish religion these two elements were two aspects of God's redemptory plan for mankind. Out of Messianic hope grew that inclination toward final solutions of political problems which aimed at nothing less than establishing a paradise on earth. Out of the belief in chosenness by God grew that fantastic delusion, shared by unbelieving Jews and non-Jews alike, that Jews are by nature more intelligent, better, healthier, more fit for survival—the motor of history and the salt of the earth. The enthusiastic Jewish intellectual dreaming of the paradise on earth, so certain of freedom from all national ties and prejudices, was in fact farther removed from political reality than his fathers, who had prayed for the coming of Messiah and the return of the people to Palestine. The assimilationists, on the other hand, who without any enthusiastic hope had persuaded themselves that they were the salt of the earth, were more effectively separated from the nations by this unholy conceit than their fathers had been by the fence of the Law, which, as it was faithfully believed, separated Israel from the Gentiles but would be destroyed in the days of the Messiah. It was this conceit of the "exception Jews," who were too "enlightened" to believe in God and, on the grounds of their exceptional position everywhere, superstitious enough to believe in themselves, that actually tore down the strong bonds of pious hope which had tied Israel to the rest of mankind.

Secularization, therefore, finally produced that paradox, so decisive for the psychology of modern Jews, by which Jewish assimilation—in its liquidation of national consciousness, its transformation of a national religion into a confessional denomination, and its meeting of the half-hearted and ambiguous demands of state and society by equally ambiguous devices and psychological tricks—engendered a very real Jewish chauvinism, if by chauvinism we understand the perverted nationalism in which (in the words of Chesterton) "the individual is himself the thing to be worshipped; the individual is his own ideal and even his own idol." From now on, the old religious concept of chosenness was no longer the essence of Judaism; it became instead the essence of Jewishness.

This paradox has found its most powerful and charming embodiment in Disraeli. He was an English imperialist and a Jewish chauvinist; but it is not difficult to pardon a chauvinism which was rather a play of imagination because, after all, "England was the Israel of his imagination"; [51] and it is not difficult, either, to pardon his English imperialism, which had so little in common with the single-minded resoluteness of expansion for expansion's sake, since he was, after all, "never a thorough Englishman and was proud of the fact." [52] All those curious contradictions which indicate so clearly that the potent wizard never took himself quite seriously and always played a role to win society and to find popularity, add up to a unique charm, they introduce into all his utterances an element of charlatan enthusiasm and day-dreaming which makes him utterly different from his imperialist followers. He was lucky enough to do his dreaming and acting in a time when Manchester and the businessmen had not yet taken over the imperial dream and were even in sharp and furious opposition to "colonial adventures." His superstitious belief in blood and race—into which he mixed old romantic folk credulities about a powerful supranational connection between gold and blood—carried no suspicion of possible massacres, whether in Africa, Asia, or Europe proper. He began as a not too gifted writer and remained an intellectual whom chance made a member of Parliament, leader of his party, Prime Minister, and a friend of the Queen of England.

Disraeli's notion of the Jews' role in politics dates back to the time when he was still simply a writer and had not yet begun his political career. His ideas on the subject were therefore not the result of actual experience, but he clung to them with remarkable tenacity throughout his later life.

In his first novel, *Alroy* (1833), Disraeli evolved a plan for a Jewish Empire in which Jews would rule as a strictly separated class. The novel shows the influence of current illusions about Jewish power-possibilities as well as the young author's ignorance of the actual power conditions of his time. Eleven years later, political experience in Parliament and intimate intercourse with prominent men taught Disraeli that "the aims of the Jews, whatever they may have been before and since, were, in his day, largely divorced from the assertion of political nationality in any form." [53] In a new novel, *Coningsby,* he abandoned the dream of a Jewish Empire and unfolded a fantastic scheme according to which Jewish money dominates the rise and fall of courts and empires and rules supreme in diplomacy. Never in his life did he give up this second notion of a secret and mysterious influence of the chosen men of the chosen race, with which he replaced his earlier dream of an openly constituted, mysterious ruler caste. It became the pivot of his political philosophy. In contrast to his much-admired Jewish bankers who granted loans to governments and earned commissions, Disraeli looked at the whole affair with the outsider's incomprehension that such power-possibilities could be handled day after day by people who were not ambitious for power. What he could not understand was that a Jewish banker was even

[51] Sir John Skleton, *op. cit.*
[52] Horace B. Samuel, *op. cit.*
[53] Monypenny and Buckle, *op. cit.,* p. 882.

less interested in politics than his non-Jewish colleagues; to Disraeli, at any rate, it was a matter of course that Jewish wealth was only a means for Jewish politics. The more he learned about the Jewish bankers' well-functioning organization in business matters and their international exchange of news and information, the more convinced he became that he was dealing with something like a secret society which, without anybody knowing it, had the world's destinies in its hands.

It is well known that the belief in a Jewish conspiracy that was kept together by a secret society had the greatest propaganda value for antisemitic publicity, and by far outran all traditional European superstitions about ritual murder and well-poisoning. It is of great significance that Disraeli, for exactly opposite purposes and at a time when nobody thought seriously of secret societies, came to identical conclusions, for it shows clearly to what extent such fabrications were due to social motives and resentments and how much more plausibly they explained events or political and economic activities than the more trivial truth did. In Disraeli's eyes, as in the eyes of many less well-known and reputable charlatans after him, the whole game of politics was played between secret societies. Not only the Jews, but every other group whose influence was not politically organized or which was in opposition to the whole social and political system, became for him powers behind the scenes. In 1863, he thought he witnessed "a struggle between the secret societies and the European millionaires; Rothschild hitherto has won." [54] But also "the natural equality of men and the abrogation of property are proclaimed by secret societies"; [55] as late as 1870, he could still talk seriously of forces "beneath the surface" and believe sincerely that "secret societies and their international energies, the Church of Rome and her claims and methods, the eternal conflict between science and faith" were at work to determine the course of human history. [56]

Disraeli's unbelievable naïveté made him connect all these "secret" forces with the Jews. "The first Jesuits were Jews; that mysterious Russian diplomacy which so alarms Western Europe is organized and principally carried on by Jews; that mighty revolution which is at this moment preparing in Germany and which will be in fact a second and greater Reformation . . . is entirely developing under the auspices of Jews," "men of Jewish race are found at the head of every one of (communist and socialist groups). The people of God co-operates with atheists; the most skilful accumulators of property ally themselves with communists, the peculiar and chosen race touch the hands of the scum and low castes of Europe! And all this because they wish to destroy that ungrateful Christendom which owes them even its name and whose tyranny they can no longer endure." [57] In Disraeli's imagination, the world had become Jewish.

[54] *Ibid.*, p. 73. In a letter to Mrs. Brydges Williams of July 21, 1863.
[55] *Lord George Bentinck*, p. 497.
[56] In his novel *Lothair*, 1870.
[57] *Lord George Bentinck*.

In this singular delusion, even that most ingenious of Hitler's publicity stunts, the cry of a secret alliance between the Jewish capitalist and the Jewish socialist, was already anticipated. Nor can it be denied that the whole scheme, imaginary and fantastic as it was, had a logic of its own. If one started, as Disraeli did, from the assumption that Jewish millionaires were makers of Jewish politics, if one took into account the insults Jews had suffered for centuries (which were real enough, but still stupidly exaggerated by Jewish apologetic propaganda), if one had seen the not infrequent instances when the son of a Jewish millionaire became a leader of the workers' movement and knew from experience how closely knit Jewish family ties were as a rule, Disraeli's image of a calculated revenge upon the Christian peoples was not so far-fetched. The truth was, of course, that the sons of Jewish millionaires inclined toward leftist movements precisely because their banker fathers had never come into an open class conflict with workers. They therefore completely lacked that class consciousness that the son of any ordinary bourgeois family would have had as a matter of course, while, on the other side, and for exactly the same reasons, the workers did not harbor those open or hidden antisemitic sentiments which every other class showed the Jews as a matter of course. Obviously leftist movements in most countries offered the only true possibilities for assimilation.

Disraeli's persistent fondness for explaining politics in terms of secret societies was based on experiences which later convinced many lesser European intellectuals. His basic experience had been that a place in English society was much more difficult to win than a seat in Parliament. English society of his time gathered in fashionable clubs which were independent of party distinctions. The clubs, although they were extremely important in the formation of a political elite, escaped public control. To an outsider they must have looked very mysterious indeed. They were secret insofar as not everybody was admitted to them. They became mysterious only when members of other classes asked admittance and were either refused or admitted after a plethora of incalculable, unpredictable, apparently irrational difficulties. There is no doubt that no political honor could replace the triumphs that intimate association with the privileged could give. Disraeli's ambitions, significantly enough, did not suffer even at the end of his life when he experienced severe political defeats, for he remained "the most commanding figure of London society." [58]

In his naïve certainty of the paramount importance of secret societies, Disraeli was a forerunner of those new social strata who, born outside the

[58] Monypenny and Buckle, *op. cit,* p. 1470. This excellent biography gives a correct evaluation of Disraeli's triumph. After having quoted Tennyson's *In Memoriam,* canto 64, it continues as follows: "In one respect Disraeli's success was more striking and complete than that suggested in Tennyson's lines; he not only scaled the political ladder to the topmost rung and 'shaped the whisper of the throne'; he also conquered Society. He dominated the dinner-tables and what we would call the salons of Mayfair . . . and his social triumph, whatever may be thought by philosophers of its intrinsic value, was certainly not less difficult of achievement for a despised outsider than his political, and was perhaps sweeter to his palate" (p. 1506).

framework of society, could never understand its rules properly. They found themselves in a state of affairs where the distinctions between society and politics were constantly blurred and where, despite seemingly chaotic conditions, the same narrow class interest always won. The outsider could not but conclude that a consciously established institution with definite goals achieved such remarkable results. And it is true that this whole society game needed only a resolute political will to transform its half-conscious play of interests and essentially purposeless machinations into a definite policy. This is what occurred briefly in France during the Dreyfus Affair, and again in Germany during the decade preceding Hitler's rise to power.

Disraeli, however, was not only outside of English, he was outside of Jewish, society as well. He knew little of the mentality of the Jewish bankers whom he so deeply admired, and he would have been disappointed indeed had he realized that these "exception Jews," despite exclusion from bourgeois society (they never really tried to be admitted), shared its foremost political principle that political activity centers around protection of property and profits. Disraeli saw, and was impressed by, only a group with no outward political organization, whose members were still connected by a seeming infinity of family and business connections. His imagination went to work whenever he had to deal with them and found everything "proved"— when, for instance, the shares of the Suez Canal were offered the English government through the information of Henry Oppenheim (who had learned that the Khedive of Egypt was anxious to sell) and the sale was carried through with the help of a four million sterling loan from Lionel Rothschild.

Disraeli's racial convictions and theories about secret societies sprang, in the last analysis, from his desire to explain something apparently mysterious and in fact chimerical. He could not make a political reality out of the chimerical power of "exception Jews"; but he could, and did, help transform chimeras into public fears and to entertain a bored society with highly dangerous fairy-tales.

With the consistency of most race fanatics, Disraeli spoke only with contempt of the "modern newfangled sentimental principle of nationality." [59] He hated the political equality at the basis of the nation-state and he feared for the survival of the Jews under its conditions. He fancied that race might give a social as well as political refuge against equalization. Since he knew the nobility of his time far better than he ever came to know the Jewish people, it is not surprising that he modeled the race concept after aristocratic caste concepts.

No doubt these concepts of the socially underprivileged could have gone far, but they would have had little significance in European politics had they not met with real political necessities when, after the scramble for Africa, they could be adapted to political purposes. This willingness to believe on the part of bourgeois society gave Disraeli, the only Jew of the nineteenth century, his share of genuine popularity. In the end, it was not his fault that the

[59] *Ibid.*, Vol. I, Book 3.

same trend that accounted for his singular great good fortune finally led to the great catastrophe of his people.

III: *Between Vice and Crime*

PARIS HAS rightly been called *la capitale du dixneuvième siècle* (Walter Benjamin). Full of promise, the nineteenth century had started with the French Revolution, for more than one hundred years witnessed the vain struggle against the degeneration of the *citoyen* into the *bourgeois,* reached its nadir in the Dreyfus Affair, and was given another fourteen years of morbid respite. The first World War could still be won by the Jacobin appeal of Clemenceau, France's last son of the Revolution, but the glorious century of the *nation par excellence* was at an end [60] and Paris was left; without political significance and social splendor, to the intellectual avant-garde of all countries. France played a very small part in the twentieth century, which started, immediately after Disraeli's death, with the scramble for Africa and the competition for imperialist domination in Europe. Her decline, therefore, caused partly by the economic expansion of other nations, and partly by internal disintegration, could assume forms and follow laws which seemed inherent in the nation-state.

To a certain extent, what happened in France in the eighties and nineties happened thirty and forty years later in all European nation-states. Despite chronological distances, the Weimar and Austrian Republics had much in common historically with the Third Republic, and certain political and social patterns in the Germany and Austria of the twenties and thirties seemed almost consciously to follow the model of France's *fin-de-siècle.*

Nineteenth-century antisemitism, at any rate, reached its climax in France and was defeated because it remained a national domestic issue without contact with imperialist trends, which did not exist there. The main features of this kind of antisemitism reappeared in Germany and Austria after the first World War, and its social effect on the respective Jewries was almost the same, although less sharp, less extreme, and more disturbed by other influences.[61]

[60] Yves Simon, *La Grande Crise de la République Française,* Montreal, 1941, p. 20: "The spirit of the French Revolution survived the defeat of Napoleon for more than a century. . . . It triumphed but only to fade unnoticed on November 11, 1918. The French Revolution? Its dates must surely be set at 1789-1918."

[61] The fact that certain psychological phenomena did not come out as sharply in German and Austrian Jews, may partly be due to the strong hold of the Zionist movement on Jewish intellectuals in these countries. Zionism in the decade after the first World War, and even in the decade preceding it, owed its strength not so much to political insight (and did not produce political convictions), as it did to its critical analysis of psychological reactions and sociological facts. Its influence was mainly pedagogical and went far beyond the relatively small circle of actual members of the Zionist movement.

The chief reason, however, for the choice of the salons of the Faubourg Saint-Germain as an example of the role of Jews in non-Jewish society is that nowhere else is there an equally grand society or a more truthful record of it. When Marcel Proust, himself half Jewish and in emergencies ready to identify himself as a Jew, set out to search for "things past," he actually wrote what one of his admiring critics has called an *apologia pro vita sua.* The life of this greatest writer of twentieth-century France was spent exclusively in society; all events appeared to him as they are reflected in society and reconsidered by the individual, so that reflections and reconsiderations constitute the specific reality and texture of Proust's world.[62] Throughout the *Remembrance of Things Past,* the individual and his reconsiderations belong to society, even when he retires into the mute and uncommunicative solitude in which Proust himself finally disappeared when he had decided to write his work. There his inner life, which insisted on transforming all worldly happenings into inner experience, became like a mirror in whose reflection truth might appear. The contemplator of inner experience resembles the onlooker in society insofar as neither has an immediate approach to life but perceives reality only if it is reflected. Proust, born on the fringe of society, but still rightfully belonging to it though an outsider, enlarged this inner experience until it included the whole range of aspects as they appeared to and were reflected by all members of society.

There is no better witness, indeed, of this period when society had emancipated itself completely from public concerns, and when politics itself was becoming a part of social life. The victory of bourgeois values over the citizen's sense of responsibility meant the decomposition of political issues into their dazzling, fascinating reflections in society. It must be added that Proust himself was a true exponent of this society, for he was involved in both of its most fashionable "vices," which he, "the greatest witness of dejudaized Judaism" interconnected in the "darkest comparison which ever has been made on behalf of Western Judaism": [63] the "vice" of Jewishness and the "vice" of homosexuality, and which in their reflection and individual reconsideration became very much alike indeed.[64]

It was Disraeli who had discovered that vice is but the corresponding reflection of crime in society. Human wickedness, if accepted by society, is changed from an act of will into an inherent, psychological quality which man cannot choose or reject but which is imposed upon him from without, and which rules him as compulsively as the drug rules the addict. In as-

[62] Compare the interesting remarks on this subject by E. Levinas, "L'Autre dans Proust" in *Deucalion,* No. 2, 1947.

[63] J. E. van Praag, "Marcel Proust, Témoin du Judaisme déjudaizé" in *Revue Juive de Genève,* 1937, Nos. 48, 49, 50.

A curious coincidence (or is it more than a coincidence?) occurs in the moving-picture *Crossfire* which deals with the Jewish question. The story was taken from Richard Brooks's *The Brick Foxhole,* in which the murdered Jew of *Crossfire* was a homosexual.

[64] For the following see especially *Cities of the Plain,* Part I, pp. 20-45.

similating crime and transforming it into vice, society denies all responsibility and establishes a world of fatalities in which men find themselves entangled. The moralistic judgment as a crime of every departure from the norm, which fashionable circles used to consider narrow and philistine, if demonstrative of inferior psychological understanding, at least showed greater respect for human dignity. If crime is understood to be a kind of fatality, natural or economic, everybody will finally be suspected of some special predestination to it. "Punishment is the right of the criminal," of which he is deprived if (in the words of Proust) "judges assume and are more inclined to pardon murder in inverts and treason in Jews for reasons derived from . . . racial predestination." It is an attraction to murder and treason which hides behind such perverted tolerance, for in a moment it can switch to a decision to liquidate not only all actual criminals but all who are "racially" predestined to commit certain crimes. Such changes take place whenever the legal and political machine is not separated from society so that social standards can penetrate into it and become political and legal rules. The seeming broadmindedness that equates crime and vice, if allowed to establish its own code of law, will invariably prove more cruel and inhuman than laws, no matter how severe, which respect and recognize man's independent responsibility for his behavior.

The Faubourg Saint-Germain, however, as Proust depicts it, was in the early stages of this development. It admitted inverts because it felt attracted by what it judged to be a vice. Proust describes how Monsieur de Charlus, who had formerly been tolerated, "notwithstanding his vice," for his personal charm and old name, now rose to social heights. He no longer needed to lead a double life and hide his dubious acquaintances, but was encouraged to bring them into the fashionable houses. Topics of conversation which he formerly would have avoided—love, beauty, jealousy—lest somebody suspect his anomaly, were now welcomed avidly "in view of the experience, strange, secret, refined and monstrous upon which he founded" his views.[65]

Something very similar happened to the Jews. Individual exceptions, ennobled Jews, had been tolerated and even welcomed in the society of the Second Empire, but now Jews as such were becoming increasingly popular. In both cases, society was far from being prompted by a revision of prejudices. They did not doubt that homosexuals were "criminals" or that Jews were "traitors"; they only revised their attitude toward crime and treason. The trouble with their new broadmindedness, of course, was not that they were no longer horrified by inverts but that they were no longer horrified by crime. They did not in the least doubt the conventional judgment. The best-hidden disease of the nineteenth century, its terrible boredom and general weariness, had burst like an abscess. The outcasts and the pariahs upon whom society called in its predicament were, whatever else they might have been, at least not plagued by ennui and, if we are to trust Proust's judgment, were the only ones in *fin-de-siècle* society who were still capable

[65] *Cities of the Plain,* Part II, chapter iii.

of passion. Proust leads us through the labyrinth of social connections and ambitions only by the thread of man's capacity for love, which is presented in the perverted passion of Monsieur de Charlus for Morel, in the devastating loyalty of the Jew Swann to his courtesan and in the author's own desperate jealousy of Albertine, herself the personification of vice in the novel. Proust made it very clear that he regarded the outsiders and newcomers, the inhabitants of *"Sodome et Ghomorre,"* not only as more human but as more normal.

The difference between the Faubourg Saint-Germain, which had suddenly discovered the attractiveness of Jews and inverts, and the mob which cried "Death to the Jews" was that the salons had not yet associated themselves openly with crime. This meant that on the one hand they did not yet want to participate actively in the killing, and on the other, still professed openly an antipathy toward Jews and a horror of inverts. This in turn resulted in that typically equivocal situation in which the new members could not confess their identity openly, and yet could not hide it either. Such were the conditions from which arose the complicated game of exposure and concealment, of half-confessions and lying distortions, of exaggerated humility and exaggerated arrogance, all of which were consequences of the fact that only one's Jewishness (or homosexuality) had opened the doors of the exclusive salons, while at the same time they made one's position extremely insecure. In this equivocal situation, Jewishness was for the individual Jew at once a physical stain and a mysterious personal privilege, both inherent in a "racial predestination."

Proust describes at great length how society, constantly on the lookout for the strange, the exotic, the dangerous, finally identifies the refined with the monstrous and gets ready to admit monstrosities—real or fancied—such as the strange, unfamiliar "Russian or Japanese play performed by native actors"; [66] the "painted, paunchy, tightly buttoned personage [of the invert], reminding one of a box of exotic and dubious origin from which escapes the curious odor of fruits the mere thought of tasting which stirs the heart"; [67] the "man of genius" who is supposed to emanate a "sense of the supernatural" and around whom society will "gather as though around a turning-table, to learn the secret of the Infinite." [68] In the atmosphere of this "necromancy," a Jewish gentleman or a Turkish lady might appear "as if they really were creatures evoked by the effort of a medium." [69]

Obviously the role of the exotic, the strange, and the monstrous could not be played by those individual "exception Jews" who, for almost a century, had been admitted and tolerated as "foreign upstarts" and on "whose friendship nobody would ever have dreamed of priding himself." [70] Much better suited of course were those whom nobody had ever known, who, in the first stage of their assimilation, were not identified with, and were not representative of, the Jewish community, for such identification with well-

[66] *Ibid.*
[67] *Ibid.*
[68] *The Guermantes Way,* Part I, chapter i.

[69] *Ibid.*
[70] *Ibid.*

known bodies would have limited severely society's imagination and expectations. Those who, like Swann, had an unaccountable flair for society and taste in general were admitted; but more enthusiastically embraced were those who, like Bloch, belonged to "a family of little repute, [and] had to support, as on the floor of the ocean, the incalculable pressure of what was imposed on him not only by the Christians upon the surface but by all the intervening layers of Jewish castes superior to his own, each of them crushing with its contempt the one that was immediately beneath it." Society's willingness to receive the utterly alien and, as it thought, utterly vicious, cut short that climb of several generations by which newcomers had "to carve their way through to the open air by raising themselves from Jewish family to Jewish family." [71] It was no accident that this happened shortly after native French Jewry, during the Panama scandal, had given way before the initiative and unscrupulousness of some German Jewish adventurers; the individual exceptions, with or without title, who more than ever before sought the society of antisemitic and monarchist salons where they could dream of the good old days of the Second Empire, found themselves in the same category as Jews whom they would never have invited to their houses. If Jewishness as exceptionalness was the reason for admitting Jews, then those were preferred who were clearly "a solid troop, homogeneous within itself and utterly dissimilar to the people who watched them go past," those who had not yet "reached the same stage of assimilation" as their upstart brethren.[72]

Although Benjamin Disraeli was still one of those Jews who were admitted to society because they were exceptions, his secularized self-representation as a "chosen man of the chosen race" foreshadowed and outlined the lines along which Jewish self-interpretation was to take place. If this, fantastic and crude as it was, had not been so oddly similar to what society expected of Jews, Jews would never have been able to play their dubious role. Not, of course, that they consciously adopted Disraeli's convictions or purposely elaborated the first timid, perverted self-interpretation of their Prussian predecessors of the beginning of the century; most of them were blissfully ignorant of all Jewish history. But wherever Jews were educated, secularized, and assimilated under the ambiguous conditions of society and state in Western and Central Europe, they lost that measure of political responsibility which their origin implied and which the Jewish notables had still felt, albeit in the form of privilege and rulership. Jewish origin, without religious and political connotation, became everywhere a psychological quality, was changed into "Jewishness," and from then on could be considered only in the categories of virtue or vice. If it is true that "Jewishness" could not have been perverted into an interesting vice without a prejudice which considered it a crime, it is also true that such perversion was made possible by those Jews who considered it an innate virtue.

✦

[71] *Within a Budding Grove,* Part II, "Placenames: The Place."
[72] *Ibid.*

Assimilated Jewry has been reproached with alienation from Judaism, and the final catastrophe brought upon it is frequently thought to have been a suffering as senseless as it was horrible, since it had lost the old value of martyrdom. This argument overlooks the fact that as far as the old ways of faith and life are concerned, "alienation" was equally apparent in Eastern European countries. But the usual notion of the Jews of Western Europe as "dejudaized" is misleading for another reason. Proust's picture, in contrast to the all too obviously interested utterances of official Judaism, shows that never did the fact of Jewish birth play such a decisive role in private life and everyday existence as among the assimilated Jews. The Jewish reformer who changed a national religion into a religious denomination with the understanding that religion is a private affair, the Jewish revolutionary who pretended to be a world citizen in order to rid himself of Jewish nationality, the educated Jew, "a man in the street and a Jew at home"—each one of these succeeded in converting a national quality into a private affair. The result was that their private lives, their decisions and sentiments, became the very center of their "Jewishness." And the more the fact of Jewish birth lost its religious, national, and social-economic significance, the more obsessive Jewishness became; Jews were obsessed by it as one may be by a physical defect or advantage, and addicted to it as one may be to a vice.

Proust's "innate disposition" is nothing but this personal, private obsession, which was so greatly justified by a society where success and failure depended upon the fact of Jewish birth. Proust mistook it for "racial predestination," because he saw and depicted only its social aspect and individual reconsiderations. And it is true that to the recording onlooker the behavior of the Jewish clique showed the same obsession as the behavior patterns followed by inverts. Both felt either superior or inferior, but in any case proudly different from other normal beings; both believed their difference to be a natural fact acquired by birth; both were constantly justifying, not what they did, but what they were; and both, finally, always wavered between such apologetic attitudes and sudden, provocative claims that they were an elite. As though their social position were forever frozen by nature, neither could move from one clique into another. The need to belong existed in other members of society too—"the question is not as for Hamlet, to be or not to be, but to belong or not to belong" [73]—but not to the same extent. A society disintegrating into cliques and no longer tolerating outsiders, Jews or inverts, as individuals but because of the special circumstances of their admission, looked like the embodiment of this clannishness.

Each society demands of its members a certain amount of acting, the ability to present, represent, and act what one actually is. When society disintegrates into cliques such demands are no longer made of the individual but of members of cliques. Behavior then is controlled by silent demands and not by individual capacities, exactly as an actor's performance must fit

[73] *Cities of the Plain*, Part II, chapter iii.

into the ensemble of all other roles in the play. The salons of the Faubourg Saint-Germain consisted of such an ensemble of cliques, each of which presented an extreme behavior pattern. The role of the inverts was to show their abnormality, of the Jews to represent black magic ("necromancy"), of the artists to manifest another form of supranatural and superhuman contact, of the aristocrats to show that they were not like ordinary ("bourgeois") people. Despite their clannishness, it is true, as Proust observed, that "save on the days of general disaster when the majority rally round the victim as the Jews rallied round Dreyfus," all these newcomers shunned intercourse with their own kind. The reason was that all marks of distinction were determined only by the ensemble of the cliques, so that Jews or inverts felt that they would lose their distinctive character in a society of Jews or inverts, where Jewishness or homosexuality would be the most natural, the most uninteresting, and the most banal thing in the world. The same, however, held true of their hosts who also needed an ensemble of counterparts before whom they could be different, nonaristocrats who would admire aristocrats as these admired the Jews or the homosexuals.

Although these cliques had no consistency in themselves and dissolved as soon as no members of other cliques were around, their members used a mysterious sign-language as though they needed something strange by which to recognize each other. Proust reports at length the importance of such signs, especially for newcomers. While, however, the inverts, masters at sign-language, had at least a real secret, the Jews used this language only to create the expected atmosphere of mystery. Their signs mysteriously and ridiculously indicated something universally known: that in the corner of the salon of the Princess So-and-So sat another Jew who was not allowed openly to admit his identity but who without this meaningless quality would never have been able to climb into that corner.

It is noteworthy that the new mixed society at the end of the nineteenth century, like the first Jewish salons in Berlin, again centered around nobility. Aristocracy by now had all but lost its eagerness for culture and its curiosity about "new specimens of humanity," but it retained its old scorn of bourgeois society. An urge for social distinction was its answer to political equality and the loss of political position and privilege which had been affirmed with the establishment of the Third Republic. After a short and artificial rise during the Second Empire, French aristocracy maintained itself only by social clannishness and half-hearted attempts to reserve the higher positions in the army for its sons. Much stronger than political ambition was an aggressive contempt for middle-class standards, which undoubtedly was one of the strongest motives for the admission of individuals and whole groups of people who had belonged to socially unacceptable classes. The same motive that had enabled Prussian aristocrats to meet socially with actors and Jews finally led in France to the social prestige of inverts. The middle classes, on the other hand, had not acquired social self-respect, although they had in the meantime risen to wealth and power. The absence of a political hierarchy in the nation-state and the victory of equality rendered "society secretly more hierarchical as it became outwardly more democratic." [74] Since the principle of hierarchy was embodied in the exclusive social circles of the Faubourg Saint-Germain, each society in France "reproduced the characteristics more or less modified, more or less in caricature of the society of the Faubourg Saint-Germain which it sometimes pretended . . . to hold in contempt, no matter what status or what political ideas its members might hold." Aristocratic society was a thing of the past in appearance only; actually it pervaded the whole social body (and not only of the people of France) by imposing "the key and the grammar of fashionable social life." [75] When Proust felt the need for an *apologia pro vita sua* and reconsidered his own life spent in aristocratic circles, he gave an analysis of society as such.

The main point about the role of Jews in this *fin-de-siècle* society is that it was the antisemitism of the Dreyfus Affair which opened society's doors to Jews, and that it was the end of the Affair, or rather the discovery of Dreyfus' innocence, that put an end to their social glory.[76] In other words, no matter what the Jews thought of themselves or of Dreyfus, they could play the role society had assigned them only as long as this same society was convinced that they belonged to a race of traitors. When the traitor was discovered to be the rather stupid victim of an ordinary frame-up, and the innocence of the Jews was established, social interest in Jews subsided as quickly as did political antisemitism. Jews were again looked upon as ordinary mortals and fell into the insignificance from which the supposed crime of one of their own had raised them temporarily.

It was essentially the same kind of social glory that the Jews of Germany and Austria enjoyed under much more severe circumstances immediately after the first World War. Their supposed crime then was that they had been guilty of the war, a crime which, no longer identified with a single act of a single individual, could not be refuted, so that the mob's evaluation of Jewishness as a crime remained undisturbed and society could continue to be delighted and fascinated by its Jews up to the very end. If there is any psychological truth in the scapegoat theory, it is as the effect of this social attitude toward Jews; for when antisemitic legislation forced society to oust the Jews, these "philosemites" felt as though they had to purge themselves of secret viciousness, to cleanse themselves of a stigma which they had mysteriously and wickedly loved. This psychology, to be sure, hardly explains why these "admirers" of Jews finally became their murderers, and it may

[74] *The Guermantes Way*, Part II, chapter ii.

[75] Ramon Fernandez, "La vie sociale dans l'oeuvre de Marcel Proust," in *Les Cahiers Marcel Proust*, No. 2, 1927.

[76] "But this was the moment when from the effects of the Dreyfus case there had arisen an antisemitic movement parallel to a more abundant movement towards the penetration of society by Israelites. The politicians had not been wrong in thinking that the discovery of the judicial error would deal a fatal blow to antisemitism. But provisionally at least a social antisemitism was on the contrary enhanced and exacerbated by it." See *The Sweet Cheat Gone*, chapter ii.

even be doubted that they were prominent among those who ran the death factories, although the percentage of the so-called educated classes among the actual killers is amazing. But it does explain the incredible disloyalty of precisely those strata of society which had known Jews most intimately and had been most delighted and charmed by Jewish friends.

As far as the Jews were concerned, the transformation of the "crime" of Judaism into the fashionable "vice" of Jewishness was dangerous in the extreme. Jews had been able to escape from Judaism into conversion; from Jewishness there was no escape. A crime, moreover, is met with punishment; a vice can only be exterminated. The interpretation given by society to the fact of Jewish birth and the role played by Jews in the framework of social life are intimately connected with the catastrophic thoroughness with which antisemitic devices could be put to work. The Nazi brand of antisemitism had its roots in these social conditions as well as in political circumstances. And though the concept of race had other and more immediately political purposes and functions, its application to the Jewish question in its most sinister aspect owed much of its success to social phenomena and convictions which virtually constituted a consent by public opinion.

The deciding forces in the Jews' fateful journey to the storm center of events were without doubt political; but the reactions of society to antisemitism and the psychological reflections of the Jewish question in the individual had something to do with the specific cruelty, the organized and calculated assault upon every single individual of Jewish origin, that was already characteristic of the antisemitism of the Dreyfus Affair. This passion-driven hunt of the "Jew in general," the "Jew everywhere and nowhere," cannot be understood if one considers the history of antisemitism as an entity in itself, as a mere political movement. Social factors, unaccounted for in political or economic history, hidden under the surface of events, never perceived by the historian and recorded only by the more penetrating and passionate force of poets or novelists (men whom society had driven into the desperate solitude and loneliness of the *apologia pro vita sua*) changed the course that mere political antisemitism would have taken if left to itself, and which might have resulted in anti-Jewish legislation and even mass expulsion but hardly in wholesale extermination.

Ever since the Dreyfus Affair and its political threat to the rights of French Jewry had produced a social situation in which Jews enjoyed an ambiguous glory, antisemitism appeared in Europe as an insoluble mixture of political motives and social elements. Society always reacted first to a strong antisemitic movement with marked preference for Jews, so that Disraeli's remark that "there is no race at this present . . . that so much delights and fascinates and elevates and ennobles Europe as the Jewish," became particularly true in times of danger. Social "philosemitism" always ended by adding to political antisemitism that mysterious fanaticism without which antisemitism could hardly have become the best slogan for organizing the masses. All the *déclassés* of capitalist society were finally ready to unite and establish mob organizations of their own; their propaganda and their attraction rested on the assumption that a society which had shown its willingness to incorporate crime in the form of vice into its very structure would by now be ready to cleanse itself of viciousness by openly admitting criminals and by publicly committing crimes.

CHAPTER FOUR

The Dreyfus Affair

1: *The Facts of the Case*

IT HAPPENED in France at the end of the year 1894. Alfred Dreyfus, a Jewish officer of the French General Staff, was accused and convicted of espionage for Germany. The verdict, lifelong deportation to Devil's Island, was unanimously adopted. The trial took place behind closed doors. Out of an allegedly voluminous dossier of the prosecution, only the so-called *"bordereau"* was shown. This was a letter, supposedly in Dreyfus' handwriting, addressed to the German military attaché, Schwartzkoppen. In July, 1895, Colonel Picquart became head of the Information Division of the General Staff. In May, 1896, he told the chief of the General Staff, Boisdeffre, that he had convinced himself of Dreyfus' innocence and of the guilt of another officer, Major Walsin-Esterhazy. Six months later, Picquart was removed to a dangerous post in Tunisia. At the same time, Bernard Lazare, on behalf of Dreyfus' brothers, published the first pamphlet of the Affair: *Une erreur judiciaire; la vérité sur l'affaire Dreyfus.* In June, 1897, Picquart informed Scheurer-Kestner, Vice-President of the Senate, of the facts of the trials and of Dreyfus' innocence. In November, 1897, Clemenceau started his fight for re-examination of the case. Four weeks later Zola joined the ranks of the Dreyfusards. *J'Accuse* was published by Clemenceau's newspaper in January, 1898. At the same time, Picquart was arrested. Zola, tried for calumny of the army, was convicted by both the ordinary tribunal and the Court of Appeal. In August, 1898, Esterhazy was dishonorably discharged because of embezzlement. He at once hurried to a British journalist and told him that he—and not Dreyfus—was the author of the *"bordereau,"* which he had forged in Dreyfus' handwriting on orders from Colonel Sandherr, his superior and former chief of the counterespionage division. A few days later Colonel Henry, another member of the same department, confessed forgeries of several other pieces of the secret Dreyfus dossier and committed suicide. Thereupon the Court of Appeal ordered an investigation of the Dreyfus case.

In June, 1899, the Court of Appeal annulled the original sentence against Dreyfus of 1894. The revision trial took place in Rennes in August. The sentence was made ten years' imprisonment because of "alleviating circumstances." A week later Dreyfus was pardoned by the President of the Republic. The World Exposition opened in Paris in April, 1900. In May, when the success of the Exposition was guaranteed, the Chamber of Deputies, with overwhelming majority, voted against any further revision of the Dreyfus case. In December of the same year all trials and lawsuits connected with the affair were liquidated through a general amnesty.

In 1903 Dreyfus asked for a new revision. His petition was neglected until 1906, when Clemenceau had become Prime Minister. In July, 1906, the Court of Appeal annulled the sentence of Rennes and acquitted Dreyfus of all charges. The Court of Appeal, however, had no authority to acquit; it should have ordered a new trial. Another revision before a military tribunal would, in all probability and despite the overwhelming evidence in favor of Dreyfus, have led to a new conviction. Dreyfus, therefore, was never acquitted in accordance with the law,[1] and the Dreyfus case was never really settled. The reinstatement of the accused was never recognized by the French people, and the passions that were originally aroused never entirely subsided. As late as 1908, nine years after the pardon and two years after Dreyfus was cleared, when, at Clemenceau's instance, the body of Emile Zola was transferred to the Pantheon, Alfred Dreyfus was openly attacked in the street. A Paris court acquitted his assailant and indicated that it "dissented" from the decision which had cleared Dreyfus.

Even stranger is the fact that neither the first nor the second World War has been able to bury the affair in oblivion. At the behest of the Action Française, the *Précis de l'Affaire Dreyfus* [2] was republished in 1924 and has since been the standard reference manual of the Anti-Dreyfusards. At the premiere of *L'Affaire Dreyfus* (a play written by Rehfisch and Wilhelm Herzog under the pseudonym of René Kestner) in 1931, the atmosphere of the nineties still prevailed with quarrels in the auditorium, stink-bombs in the stalls, the shock troops of the Action Française standing around to strike terror into actors, audience and bystanders. Nor did the government— Laval's government—act in any way differently than its predecessors some thirty years before: it gladly admitted it was unable to guarantee a single undisturbed performance, thereby providing a new late triumph for the Anti-Dreyfusards. The play had to be suspended. When Dreyfus died in 1935, the general press was afraid to touch the issue [3] while the leftist papers still spoke in the old terms of Dreyfus' innocence and the right wing of Dreyfus' guilt. Even today, though to a lesser extent, the Dreyfus Affair is still a kind of shibboleth in French politics. When Pétain was condemned the influential provincial newspaper *Voix du Nord* (of Lille) linked the

---

[1] The most extensive and still indispensable work on the subject is that of Joseph Reinach, *L'Affaire Dreyfus*, Paris, 1903-11, 7 vols. The most detailed among recent studies, written from a socialist viewpoint, is by Wilhelm Herzog, *Der Kampf einer Republik*, Zürich, 1933. Its exhaustive chronological tables are very valuable. The best political and historical evaluation of the affair is to be found in D. W. Brogan, *The Development of Modern France*, 1940, Books VI and VII. Brief and reliable is G. Charensol, *L'Affaire Dreyfus et la Troisième République*, 1930.

[2] Written by two officers and published under the pseudonym Henri Dutrait-Crozon.

[3] The *Action Française* (July 19, 1935) praised the restraint of the French press while voicing the opinion that "the famous champions of justice and truth of forty years ago have left no disciples."

Pétain case to the Dreyfus case and maintained that "the country remains divided as it was after the Dreyfus case," because the verdict of the court could not settle a political conflict and "bring to all the French peace of mind or of heart." [4]

While the Dreyfus Affair in its broader political aspects belongs to the twentieth century, the Dreyfus case, the various trials of the Jewish Captain Alfred Dreyfus, are quite typical of the nineteenth century, when men followed legal proceedings so keenly because each instance afforded a test of the century's greatest achievement, the complete impartiality of the law. It is characteristic of the period that a miscarriage of justice could arouse such political passions and inspire such an endless succession of trials and retrials, not to speak of duels and fisticuffs. The doctrine of equality before the law was still so firmly implanted in the conscience of the civilized world that a single miscarriage of justice could provoke public indignation from Moscow to New York. Nor was anyone, except in France itself, so "modern" as to associate the matter with political issues. [5] The wrong done to a single Jewish officer in France was able to draw from the rest of the world a more vehement and united reaction than all the persecutions of German Jews a generation later. Even Czarist Russia could accuse France of barbarism while in Germany members of the Kaiser's entourage would openly express an indignation matched only by the radical press of the 1930's. [6]

The *dramatis personae* of the case might have stepped out of the pages of Balzac: on the one hand, the class-conscious generals frantically covering up for the members of their own clique and, on the other, their antagonist, Picquart, with his calm, clear-eyed and slightly ironical honesty. Beside them stand the nondescript crowd of the men in Parliament, each terrified of what his neighbor might know; the President of the Republic, notorious patron of the Paris brothels, and the examining magistrates, living solely for the sake of social contacts. Then there is Dreyfus himself, actually a parvenu, continually boasting to his colleagues of his family fortune which he spent on women; his brothers, pathetically offering their entire fortune, and then reducing the offer to 150,000 francs, for the release of their kinsman, never quite sure whether they wished to make a sacrifice or simply to suborn the General Staff; and the lawyer Démange, really convinced of his

---

[4] See G. H. Archambault in *New York Times,* August 18, 1945, p. 5.

[5] The sole exceptions, the Catholic journals most of which agitated in all countries against Dreyfus, will be discussed below. American public opinion was such that in addition to protests an organized boycott of the Paris World Exposition scheduled for 1900 was begun. On the effect of this threat see below. For a comprehensive study see the master's essay on file at Columbia University by Rose A. Halperin, "The American Reaction to the Dreyfus Case," 1941. The author wishes to thank Professor S. W. Baron for his kindness in placing this study at her disposal.

[6] Thus, for example, H. B. von Buelow, the German chargé d'affaires at Paris, wrote to Reichchancellor Hohenlohe that the verdict at Rennes was a "mixture of vulgarity and cowardice, the surest signs of barbarism," and that France "has therewith shut herself out of the family of civilized nations," cited by Herzog, *op. cit.,* under date of September 12, 1899. In the opinion of von Buelow the *Affaire* was the "shibboleth" of German liberalism; see his *Denkwürdigkeiten,* Berlin, 1930-31, I, 428.

client's innocence but basing the defense on an issue of doubt so as to save himself from attacks and injury to his personal interests. Lastly, there is the adventurer Esterhazy, he of the ancient escutcheon, so utterly bored by this bourgeois world as to seek relief equally in heroism and knavery. An erstwhile second lieutenant of the Foreign Legion, he impressed his colleagues greatly by his superior boldness and impudence. Always in trouble, he lived by serving as duelist's second to Jewish officers and by blackmailing their wealthy coreligionists. Indeed, he would avail himself of the good offices of the chief rabbi himself in order to obtain the requisite introductions. Even in his ultimate downfall he remained true to the Balzac tradition. Not treason nor wild dreams of a great orgy in which a hundred thousand besotted Prussian Uhlans would run berserk through Paris [7] but a paltry embezzlement of a relative's cash sent him to his doom. And what shall we say of Zola, with his impassioned moral fervor, his somewhat empty pathos, and his melodramatic declaration, on the eve of his flight to London, that he had heard the voice of Dreyfus begging him to bring this sacrifice? [8]

All this belongs typically to the nineteenth century and by itself would never have survived two World Wars. The old-time enthusiasm of the mob for Esterhazy, like its hatred of Zola, have long since died down to embers, but so too has that fiery passion against aristocracy and clergy which had once inflamed Jaurès and which had alone secured the final release of Dreyfus. As the Cagoulard affair was to show, officers of the General Staff no longer had to fear the wrath of the people when they hatched their plots for a coup d'état. Since the separation of Church and State, France, though certainly no longer clerical-minded, had lost a great deal of her anticlerical feeling, just as the Catholic Church had itself lost much of its political aspiration. Pétain's attempt to convert the republic into a Catholic state was blocked by the utter indifference of the people and by the lower clergy's hostility to clerico-fascism.

The Dreyfus Affair in its political implications could survive because two of its elements grew in importance during the twentieth century. The first is hatred of the Jews; the second, suspicion of the republic itself, of Parliament, and the state machine. The larger section of the public could still go on thinking the latter, rightly or wrongly, under the influence of the Jews and the power of the banks. Down to our times the term Anti-Dreyfusard can still serve as a recognized name for all that is antirepublican, antidemocratic, and antisemitic. A few years ago it still comprised everything, from the monarchism of the Action Française to the National Bolshevism of Doriot and the social Fascism of Déat. It was not, however, to these Fascist groups, numerically unimportant as they were, that the Third Republic owed its collapse. On the contrary, the plain, if paradoxical, truth is that their influence was never so slight as at the moment when the collapse actually took place.

---

[7] Théodore Reinach, Histoire sommaire de l'Affaire Dreyfus, Paris, 1924, p. 96.
[8] Reported by Joseph Reinach, as cited by Herzog, op. cit., under date of June 18, 1898.

What made France fall was the fact that she had no more true Dreyfusards, no one who believed that democracy and freedom, equality and justice could any longer be defended or realized under the republic.[9] At long last the republic fell like overripe fruit into the lap of that old Anti-Dreyfusard clique [10] which had always formed the kernel of her army, and this at a time when she had few enemies but almost no friends. How little the Pétain clique was a product of German Fascism was shown clearly by its slavish adherence to the old formulas of forty years before.

While Germany shrewdly truncated her and ruined her entire economy through the demarcation line, France's leaders in Vichy tinkered with the old Barrès formula of "autonomous provinces," thereby crippling her all the more. They introduced anti-Jewish legislation more promptly than any Quisling, boasting all the while that they had no need to import antisemitism from Germany and that their law governing the Jews differed in essential points from that of the Reich.[11] They sought to mobilize the Catholic clergy against the Jews, only to give proof that the priests have not only lost their political influence but are not actually antisemites. On the contrary, it was the very bishops and synods which the Vichy regime wanted to turn once more into political powers who voiced the most emphatic protest against the persecution of the Jews.

Not the Dreyfus case with its trials but the Dreyfus Affair in its entirety offers a foregleam of the twentieth century. As Bernanos pointed out in 1931,[12] "The Dreyfus affair already belongs to that tragic era which certainly was not ended by the last war. The affair reveals the same inhuman character, preserving amid the welter of unbridled passions and the flames of hate an inconceivably cold and callous heart." Certainly it was not in France that the true sequel to the affair was to be found, but the reason why France fell an easy prey to Nazi aggression is not far to seek. Hitler's propa-

<hr>

[9] That even Clemenceau no longer believed in it toward the end of his life is shown clearly by the remark quoted in René Benjamin, *Clémenceau dans la retraite,* Paris, 1930, p. 249: "Hope? Impossible! How can I go on hoping when I no longer believe in that which roused me, namely, democracy?"

[10] Weygand, a known adherent of the Action Française, was in his youth an Anti-Dreyfusard. He was one of the subscribers to the "Henry Memorial" established by the *Libre Parole* in honor of the unfortunate Colonel Henry, who paid with suicide for his forgeries while on the General Staff. The list of subscribers was later published by Quillard, one of the editors of *L'Aurore* (Clemenceau's paper), under the title of *Le Monument Henry,* Paris, 1899. As for Pétain, he was on the general staff of the military government of Paris from 1895 to 1899, at a time when nobody but a proven anti-Dreyfusard would have been tolerated. See Contamine de Latour, "Le Maréchal Pétain," in *Revue de Paris,* I, 57-69. D. W. Brogan, *op. cit.,* p. 382, pertinently observes that of the five World War I marshals, four (Foch, Pétain, Lyautey, and Fayolle) were bad republicans, while the fifth, Joffre, had well-known clerical leanings.

[11] The myth that Pétain's anti-Jewish legislation was forced upon him by the Reich, which took in almost the whole of French Jewry, has been exploded on the French side itself. See especially Yves Simon, *La Grande crise de la République Française: observations sur la vie politique des français de 1918 à 1938,* Montreal, 1941.

[12] Cf. Georges Bernanos, *La grande peur des bien-pensants, Edouard Drumont,* Paris, 1931, p. 262.

94 ANTISEMITISM

ganda spoke a language long familiar and never quite forgotten. That the "Caesarism" [13] of the *Action Française* and the nihilistic nationalism of Barrès and Maurras never succeeded in their original form is due to a variety of causes, all of them negative. They lacked social vision and were unable to translate into popular terms those mental phantasmagoria which their contempt for the intellect had engendered.

We are here concerned essentially with the political bearings of the Dreyfus Affair and not with the legal aspects of the case. Sharply outlined in it are a number of traits characteristic of the twentieth century. Faint and barely distinguishable during the early decades of the century, they have at last emerged into full daylight and stand revealed as belonging to the main trends of modern times. After thirty years of a mild, purely social form of anti-Jewish discrimination, it had become a little difficult to remember that the cry, "Death to the Jews," had echoed through the length and breadth of a modern state once before when its domestic policy was crystallized in the issue of antisemitism. For thirty years the old legends of world conspiracy had been no more than the conventional stand-by of the tabloid press and the dime novel and the world did not easily remember that not long ago, but at a time when the "Protocols of the Elders of Zion" were still unknown, a whole nation had been racking its brains trying to determine whether "secret Rome" or "secret Judah" held the reins of world politics.[14]

Similarly, the vehement and nihilistic philosophy of spiritual self-hatred [15] suffered something of an eclipse when a world at temporary peace with itself yielded no crop of outstanding criminals to justify the exaltation of brutality and unscrupulousness. The Jules Guérins had to wait nearly forty years before the atmosphere was ripe again for quasi-military storm troops. The *déclassés,* produced through nineteenth-century economy, had to grow numerically until they were strong minorities of the nations, before that *coup d'état,* which had remained but a grotesque plot [16] in France, could achieve reality in Germany almost without effort. The prelude to Nazism was played over the entire European stage. The Dreyfus case, therefore, is

[13] Waldemar Gurian, *Der integrale Nationalismus in Frankreich: Charles Maurras und die Action Française,* Frankfurt-am-Main, 1931, p. 92, makes a sharp distinction between the monarchist movement and other reactionary tendencies. The same author discusses the Dreyfus case in his *Die politischen und sozialen Ideen des französischen Katholizismus,* M. Gladbach, 1929.

[14] For the creation of such myths on both sides, Daniel Halévy, "Apologie pour notre passé," in *Cahiers de la quinzaine,* Series XL, No. 10, 1910.

[15] A distinctly modern note is struck in Zola's *Letter to France* of 1898: "We hear on all sides that the concept of liberty has gone bankrupt. When the Dreyfus business cropped up, this prevalent hatred of liberty found a golden opportunity. . . . Don't you see that the only reason why Scheurer-Kestner has been attacked with such fury is that he belongs to a generation which believed in liberty and worked for it? Today one shrugs one's shoulders at such things . . . 'Old greybeards,' one laughs, 'outmoded greathearts.' " Herzog, *op. cit.,* under date of January 6, 1898.

[16] The farcical nature of the various attempts made in the nineties to stage a *coup d'état* was clearly analyzed by Rosa Luxemburg in her article, "Die soziale Krise in Frankreich," in *Die Neue Zeit,* Vol. I, 1901.

more than a bizarre, imperfectly solved "crime," [17] an affair of staff officers disguised by false beards and dark glasses, peddling their stupid forgeries by night in the streets of Paris. Its hero is not Dreyfus but Clemenceau and it begins not with the arrest of a Jewish staff officer but with the Panama scandal.

II: *The Third Republic and French Jewry*

BETWEEN 1880 and 1888 the Panama Company, under the leadership of de Lesseps, who had constructed the Suez Canal, was able to make but little practical progress. Nevertheless, within France itself it succeeded during this period in raising no less than 1,335,538,454 francs in private loans.[18] This success is the more significant when one considers the carefulness of the French middle class in money matters. The secret of the company's success lies in the fact that its several public loans were invariably backed by Parliament. The building of the Canal was generally regarded as a public and national service rather than as a private enterprise. When the company went bankrupt, therefore, it was the foreign policy of the republic that really suffered the blow. Only after a few years did it become clear that even more important was the ruination of some half-million middle-class Frenchmen. Both the press and the Parliamentary Commission of Inquiry came to roughly the same conclusion: the company had already been bankrupt for several years. De Lesseps, they contended, had been living in hopes of a miracle, cherishing the dream that new funds would be somehow forthcoming to push on with the work. In order to win sanction for the new loans he had been obliged to bribe the press, half of Parliament, and all of the higher officials. This, however, had called for the employment of middlemen and these in turn had commanded exorbitant commissions. Thus, the very thing which had originally inspired public confidence in the enterprise, namely, Parliament's backing of the loans, proved in the end the factor which converted a not too sound private business into a colossal racket.

There were no Jews either among the bribed members of Parliament or on the board of the company. Jacques Reinach and Cornélius Herz, however, vied for the honor of distributing the baksheesh among the members of the Chamber, the former working on the right wing of the bourgeois parties and the latter on the radicals (the anticlerical parties of the petty bourgeoisie).[19] Reinach was the secret financial counsellor of the government during the

---

[17] Whether Colonel Henry forged the *bordereau* on orders from the chief of staff or upon his own initiative, is still unknown. Similarly, the attempted assassination of Labori, counsel for Dreyfus at the Rennes tribunal, has never been properly cleared up. Cf. Emile Zola, *Correspondance: lettres à Maître Labori*, Paris, 1929, p. 32, n. 1.
[18] Cf. Walter Frank, *Demokratie und Nationalismus in Frankreich*, Hamburg, 1933, p. 273.
[19] Cf. Georges Suarez, *La Vie orgueilleuse de Clémenceau*, Paris, 1930, p. 156.

eighties [20] and therefore handled its relations with the Panama Company, while Herz's role was a double one. On the one hand he served Reinach as liaison with the radical wings of Parliament, to which Reinach himself had no access; on the other this office gave him such a good insight into the extent of the corruption that he was able constantly to blackmail his boss and to involve him ever deeper in the mess.[21]

Naturally there were quite a number of smaller Jewish businessmen working for both Herz and Reinach. Their names, however, may well repose in the oblivion into which they have deservedly fallen. The more uncertain the situation of the company, the higher, naturally, was the rate of commission, until in the end the company itself received but little of the moneys advanced to it. Shortly before the crash Herz received for a single intra-parliamentary transaction an advance of no less than 600,000 francs. The advance, however, was premature. The loan was not taken up and the shareholders were simply 600,000 francs out of pocket.[22] The whole ugly racket ended disastrously for Reinach. Harassed by the blackmail of Herz he finally committed suicide.[23]

Shortly before his death, however, he had taken a step the consequences of which for French Jewry can scarcely be exaggerated. He had given the *Libre Parole,* Edouard Drumont's antisemitic daily, his list of suborned members of Parliament, the so-called "remittance men," imposing as the sole condition that the paper should cover up for him personally when it published its exposure. The *Libre Parole* was transformed overnight from a small and politically insignificant sheet into one of the most influential papers in the country, with 300,000 circulation. The golden opportunity proffered by Reinach was handled with consummate care and skill. The list of culprits was published in small installments so that hundreds of politicians had to live on tenterhooks morning after morning. Drumont's journal, and with it the entire antisemitic press and movement, emerged at last as a dangerous force in the Third Republic.

The Panama scandal, which, in Drumont's phrase, rendered the invisible visible, brought with it two revelations. First, it disclosed that the members of Parliament and civil servants had become businessmen. Secondly, it showed that the intermediaries between private enterprise (in this case, the company) and the machinery of the state were almost exclusively Jews.[24]

[20] Such, for instance, was the testimony of the former minister, Rouvier, before the Commission of Inquiry.

[21] Barrès (quoted by Bernanos, *op. cit.,* p. 271) puts the matter tersely: "Whenever Reinach had swallowed something, it was Cornélius Herz who knew how to make him disgorge it."

[22] Cf. Frank, *op. cit.,* in the chapter headed "Panama"; cf. Suarez, *op. cit.,* p. 155.

[23] The quarrel between Reinach and Herz lends to the Panama scandal an air of gangsterism unusual in the nineteenth century. In his resistance to Herz's blackmail Reinach went so far as to recruit the aid of former police inspectors in placing a price of ten thousand francs on the head of his rival; cf. Suarez, *op. cit.,* p. 157.

[24] Cf. Levaillant, "La Genèse de l'antisémitisme sous la troisième République," in *Revue des études juives,* Vol. LIII (1907), p. 97.

What was most surprising was that all these Jews who worked in such an intimate relationship with the state machinery were newcomers. Up to the establishment of the Third Republic, the handling of the finances of the state had been pretty well monopolized by the Rothschilds. An attempt by their rivals, Péreires Brothers, to wrest part of it from their hands by establishing the Crédit Mobilier had ended in a compromise. And in 1882, the Rothschild group was still powerful enough to drive into bankruptcy the Catholic Union Générale, the real purpose of which had been to ruin Jewish bankers.[25] Immediately after the conclusion of the peace treaty of 1871, whose financial provisions had been handled on the French side by Rothschild and on the German side by Bleichroeder, a former agent of the house, the Rothschilds embarked on an unprecedented policy: they came out openly for the monarchists and against the republic.[26] What was new in this was not the monarchist trend but the fact that for the first time an important Jewish financial power set itself in opposition to the current regime. Up to that time the Rothschilds had accommodated themselves to whatever political system was in power. It seemed, therefore, that the republic was the first form of government that really had no use for them.

Both the political influence and the social status of the Jews had for centuries been due to the fact that they were a closed group who worked directly for the state and were directly protected by it on account of their special services. Their close and immediate connection with the machinery of government was possible only so long as the state remained at a distance from the people, while the ruling classes continued to be indifferent to its management. In such circumstances the Jews were, from the state's point of view, the most dependable element in society just because they did not really belong to it. The parliamentary system allowed the liberal bourgeoisie to gain control of the state machine. To this bourgeoisie, however, the Jews had never belonged and they therefore regarded it with a not unwarranted suspicion. The regime no longer needed the Jews as much as before, since it was now possible to achieve through Parliament a financial expansion beyond the wildest dreams of the former more or less absolute or constitutional monarchs. Thus the leading Jewish houses gradually faded from the scene of finance politics and betook themselves more and more to the antisemitic salons of the aristocracy, there to dream of financing reactionary movements designed to restore the good old days.[27] Meanwhile, however, other Jewish circles, newcomers among Jewish plutocrats, were beginning to take an in-

[25] See Bernard Lazare, *Contre l'Antisémitisme: histoire d'une polémique,* Paris, 1896.

[26] On the complicity of the Haute Banque in the Orleanist movement see G. Charensol, *op. cit.* One of the spokesmen of this powerful group was Arthur Meyer, publisher of the *Gaulois.* A baptized Jew, Meyer belonged to the most virulent section of the Anti-Dreyfusards. See Clemenceau, "Le spectacle du jour," in *L'Iniquité,* 1899; see also the entries in Hohenlohe's diary, in Herzog, *op. cit.,* under date of June 11, 1898.

[27] On current leanings toward Bonapartism see Frank, *op. cit.,* p. 419, based upon unpublished documents taken from the archives of the German ministry of foreign affairs.

creasing part in the commercial life of the Third Republic. What the Rothschilds had almost forgotten and what had nearly cost them their power was the simple fact that once they withdrew, even for a moment, from active interest in a regime, they immediately lost their influence not only upon cabinet circles but upon the Jews. The Jewish immigrants were the first to see their chance.[28] They realized only too well that the republic, as it had developed, was not the logical sequel of a united people's uprising. Out of the slaughter of some 20,000 Communards, out of military defeat and economic collapse, what had in fact emerged was a regime whose capacity for government had been doubtful from its inception. So much, indeed, was this the case that within three years a society brought to the brink of ruin was clamoring for a dictator. And when it got one in President General MacMahon (whose only claim to distinction was his defeat at Sedan), that individual had promptly turned out to be a parliamentarian of the old school and after a few years (1879) resigned. Meanwhile, however, the various elements in society, from the opportunists to the radicals and from the coalitionists to the extreme right, had made up their minds what kind of policies they required from their representatives and what methods they ought to employ. The right policy was defense of vested interests and the right method was corruption.[29] After 1881, swindle (to quote Léon Say) became the only law.

It has been justly observed that at this period of French history every political party had its Jew, in the same way that every royal household once had its court Jew.[30] The difference, however, was profound. Investment of Jewish capital in the state had helped to give the Jews a productive role in the economy of Europe. Without their assistance the eighteenth-century development of the nation-state and its independent civil service would have been inconceivable. It was, after all, to these court Jews that Western Jewry owed its emancipation. The shady transactions of Reinach and his confederates did not even lead to permanent riches.[31] All they did was to shroud

[28] Jacques Reinach was born in Germany, received an Italian barony and was naturalized in France. Cornélius Herz was born in France, the son of Bavarian parents. Migrating to America in early youth, he acquired citizenship and amassed a fortune there. For further details, cf. Brogan, *op. cit.,* p. 268 ff.

Characteristic of the way in which native Jews disappeared from public office is the fact that as soon as the affairs of the Panama Company began to go badly, Lévy-Crémieux, its original financial adviser, was replaced by Reinach; see Brogan, *op. cit.,* Book VI, chapter 2.

[29] Georges Lachapelle, *Les Finances de la Troisième République,* Paris, 1937, pp. 54 ff., describes in detail how the bureaucracy gained control of public funds and how the Budget Commission was governed entirely by private interests.

With regard to the economic status of members of Parliament cf. Bernanos, *op. cit.,* p. 192: "Most of them, like Gambetta, lacked even a change of underclothes."

[30] As Frank remarks (*op. cit.,* pp. 321 ff.), the right had its Arthur Meyer, Boulangerism its Alfred Naquet, the opportunists their Reinachs, and the Radicals their Dr. Cornélius Herz.

[31] To these newcomers Drumont's charge applies (*Les Trétaux du succès,* Paris, 1901, p. 237): "Those great Jews who start from nothing and attain everything . . . they come from God knows where, live in a mystery, die in a guess. . . . They don't arrive, they jump up. . . . They don't die, they fade out."

in even deeper darkness the mysterious and scandalous relations between business and politics. These parasites upon a corrupt body served to provide a thoroughly decadent society with an exceedingly dangerous alibi. Since they were Jews it was possible to make scapegoats of them when public indignation had to be allayed. Afterwards things could go on the same old way. The antisemites could at once point to the Jewish parasites on a corrupt society in order to "prove" that all Jews everywhere were nothing but termites in the otherwise healthy body of the people. It did not matter to them that the corruption of the body politic had started without the help of Jews; that the policy of businessmen (in a bourgeois society to which Jews had not belonged) and their ideal of unlimited competition had led to the disintegration of the state in party politics; that the ruling classes had proved incapable any longer of protecting their own interests, let alone those of the country as a whole. The antisemites who called themselves patriots introduced that new species of national feeling which consists primarily in a complete whitewash of one's own people and a sweeping condemnation of all others.

The Jews could remain a separate group outside of society only so long as a more or less homogeneous and stable state machine had a use for them and was interested in protecting them. The decay of the state machine brought about the dissolution of the closed ranks of Jewry, which had so long been bound up with it. The first sign of this appeared in the affairs conducted by newly naturalized French Jews over whom their native-born brethren had lost control in much the same way as occurred in the Germany of the inflation period. The newcomers filled the gaps between the commercial world and the state.

Far more disastrous was another process which likewise began at this time and which was imposed from above. The dissolution of the state into factions, while it disrupted the closed society of the Jews, did not force them into a vacuum in which they could go on vegetating outside of state and society. For that the Jews were too rich and, at a time when money was one of the salient requisites of power, too powerful. Rather did they tend to become absorbed into the variety of social "sets," in accordance with their political leanings or, more frequently, their social connections. This, however, did not lead to their disappearance. On the contrary, they maintained certain relations with the state machine and continued, albeit in a crucially different form, to manipulate the business of the state. Thus, despite their known opposition to the Third Republic, it was none other than the Rothschilds who undertook the placement of the Russian loan while Arthur Meyer, though baptized and an avowed monarchist, was among those involved in the Panama scandal. This meant that the newcomers in French Jewry who formed the principal links between private commerce and the machinery of government were followed by the native-born. But if the Jews had previously constituted a strong, close-knit group, whose usefulness for the state was obvious, they were now split up into cliques, mutually antagonistic but all bent on the same purpose of helping society to batten on the state.

III: *Army and Clergy Against the Republic*

SEEMINGLY REMOVED from all such factors, seemingly immune from all corruption, stood the army, a heritage from the Second Empire. The republic had never dared to dominate it, even when monarchistic sympathies and intrigues came to open expression in the Boulanger crisis. The officer class consisted then as before of the sons of those old aristocratic families whose ancestors, as emigrés, had fought against their fatherland during the revolutionary wars. These officers were strongly under the influence of the clergy who ever since the Revolution had made a point of supporting reactionary and antirepublican movements. Their influence was perhaps equally strong over those officers who were of somewhat lower birth but who hoped, as a result of the Church's old practice of marking talent without regard to pedigree, to gain promotion with the help of the clergy.

In contrast to the shifting and fluid cliques of society and Parliament, where admission was easy and allegiance fickle, stood the rigorous exclusiveness of the army, so characteristic of the caste system. It was neither military life, professional honor, nor *esprit de corps* that held its officers together to form a reactionary bulwark against the republic and against all democratic influences; it was simply the tie of caste.[32] The refusal of the state to democratize the army and to subject it to the civil authorities entailed remarkable consequences. It made the army an entity outside of the nation and created an armed power whose loyalties could be turned in directions which none could foretell. That this caste-ridden power, if but left to itself, was neither for nor against anyone is shown clearly by the story of the almost burlesque *coups d'état* in which, despite statements to the contrary, it was really unwilling to take part. Even its notorious monarchism was, in the final analysis, nothing but an excuse for preserving itself as an independent interest-group, ready to defend its privileges "without regard to and in despite of, even against the republic." [33] Contemporary journalists and later historians have made valiant efforts to explain the conflict between military and civil powers during the Dreyfus Affair in terms of an antagonism between "businessmen and soldiers." [34] We know today, however, how unjustified is this indirectly antisemitic interpretation. The intelligence department of the General Staff were themselves reasonably expert at business. Were they not trafficking as

[32] See the excellent anonymous article, "The Dreyfus Case: A Study of French Opinion," in *The Contemporary Review,* Vol. LXXIV (October, 1898).

[33] See Luxemburg, *loc. cit.:* "The reason the army was reluctant to make a move was that it wanted to show its opposition to the civil power of the republic, without at the same time losing the force of that opposition by committing itself to a monarchy."

[34] It is under this caption that Maximilian Harden (a German Jew) described the Dreyfus case in *Die Zukunft* (1898). Walter Frank, the antisemitic historian, employs the same slogan in the heading of his chapter on Dreyfus while Bernanos (*op. cit.,* p. 413) remarks in the same vein that "rightly or wrongly, democracy sees in the military its most dangerous rival."

openly in forged *bordereaux* and selling them as nonchalantly to foreign military attachés as a leather merchant might traffic in skins and then become President of the Republic, or the son-in-law of the President traffic in honors and distinctions? [35] Indeed, the zeal of Schwartzkoppen, the German attaché, who was anxious to discover more military secrets than France had to hide, must have been a positive source of embarrassment to these gentlemen of the counterespionage service who, after all, could sell no more than they produced.

It was the great mistake of Catholic politicians to imagine that, in pursuit of their European policy, they could make use of the French army simply because it appeared to be antirepublican. The Church was, in fact, slated to pay for this error with the loss of its entire political influence in France.[36] When the department of intelligence finally emerged as a common fake factory, as Esterhazy, who was in a position to know, described the Deuxième Bureau,[37] no one in France, not even the army, was so seriously compromised as the Church. Toward the end of the last century the Catholic clergy had been seeking to recover its old political power in just those quarters where, for one or another reason, secular authority was on the wane among the people. Cases in point were those of Spain, where a decadent feudal aristocracy had brought about the economic and cultural ruin of the country, and Austria-Hungary, where a conflict of nationalities was threatening daily to disrupt the state. And such too was the case in France, where the nation appeared to be sinking fast into the slough of conflicting interests.[38] The army—left in a political vacuum by the Third Republic—gladly accepted the guidance of the Catholic clergy which at least provided for civilian leadership without which the military lose their *"raison d'être* (which) is to defend the principle embodied in civilian society"—as Clemenceau put it.

The Catholic Church then owed its popularity to the widespread popular skepticism which saw in the republic and in democracy the loss of all order, security, and political will. To many the hierarchic system of the Church seemed the only escape from chaos. Indeed, it was this, rather than any religious revivalism, which caused the clergy to be held in respect.[39] As a matter of fact, the staunchest supporters of the Church at that period were the exponents of that so-called "cerebral" Catholicism, the "Catholics without faith," who were henceforth to dominate the entire monarchist and ex-

[35] The Panama scandal was preceded by the so-called "Wilson affair." The President's son-in-law was found conducting an open traffic in honors and decorations.

[36] See Father Edouard Lecanuet, *Les Signes avant-coureurs de la séparation, 1894-1910,* Paris, 1930.

[37] See Bruno Weil, *L'Affaire Dreyfus,* Paris, 1930, p. 169.

[38] Cf. Clemenceau, "La Croisade," *op. cit.:* "Spain is writhing under the yoke of the Roman Church. Italy appears to have succumbed. The only countries left are Catholic Austria, already in her death-struggle, and the France of the Revolution, against which the papal hosts are even now deployed."

[39] Cf. Bernanos, *op. cit.,* p. 152: "The point cannot be sufficiently repeated: the real beneficiaries of that movement of reaction which followed the fall of the empire and the defeat were the clergy. Thanks to them national reaction assumed after 1873 the character of a religious revival."

treme nationalist movement. Without believing in their other-worldly basis, these "Catholics" clamored for more power to all authoritarian institutions. This, indeed, had been the line first laid down by Drumont and later endorsed by Maurras.[40]

The large majority of the Catholic clergy, deeply involved in political maneuvers, followed a policy of accommodation. In this, as the Dreyfus Affair makes clear, they were conspicuously successful. Thus, when Victor Basch took up the cause for a retrial his house at Rennes was stormed under the leadership of three priests,[41] while no less distinguished a figure than the Dominican Father Didon called on the students of the Collège D'Arcueil to "draw the sword, terrorize, cut off heads and run amok." [42] Similar too was the outlook of the three hundred lesser clerics who immortalized themselves in the "Henry Memorial," as the *Libre Parole's* list of subscribers to a fund for the benefit of Madame Henry (widow of the Colonel who had committed suicide while in prison [43]) was called, and which certainly is a monument for all time to the shocking corruption of the upper classes of the French people at that date. During the period of the Dreyfus crisis it was not her regular clergy, not her ordinary religious orders, and certainly not her *homines religiosi* who influenced the political line of the Catholic Church. As far as Europe was concerned, her reactionary policies in France, Austria, and Spain, as well as her support of antisemitic trends in Vienna, Paris, and Algiers were probably an immediate consequence of Jesuit influence. It was the Jesuits who had always best represented, both in the written and spoken word, the antisemitic school of the Catholic clergy.[44] This is largely the consequence of their statutes according to which each novice must prove that he has no Jewish blood back to the fourth generation.[45] And since the beginning of the nineteenth century the direction of the Church's international policy had passed into their hands.[46]

[40] On Drumont and the origin of "cerebral Catholicism," see Bernanos, *op. cit.,* pp. 127 ff.

[41] Cf. Herzog, *op. cit.,* under date of January 21, 1898.

[42] See Lecanuet, *op. cit.,* p. 182.

[43] See above, note 10.

[44] The Jesuits' magazine *Civiltà Cattolica* was for decades the most outspokenly antisemitic and one of the most influential Catholic magazines in the world. It carried anti-Jewish propaganda long before Italy went Fascist, and its policy was not affected by the anti-Christian attitude of the Nazis. See Joshua Starr, "Italy's Antisemites," in *Jewish Social Studies,* 1939.

According to L. Koch, S.J.: "Of all orders, the Society of Jesus through its constitution is best protected against any Jewish influences." In *Jesuiten-Lexikon,* Paderborn, 1934, article "Juden."

[45] Originally, according to the Convention of 1593, all Christians of Jewish descent were excluded. A decree of 1608 stipulated reinvestigations back to the fifth generation; the last provision of 1923 reduced this to four generations. These requirements can be waived by the chief of the order in individual cases.

[46] Cf. H. Boehmer, *Les Jésuites,* translated from the German, Paris, 1910, p. 284: "Since 1820 . . . no such thing as independent national churches able to resist the Jesuit-dictated orders of the Pope has existed. The higher clergy of our day have pitched their tents in front of the Holy See and the Church has become what Bellarmin, the

We have already observed how the dissolution of the state machinery facilitated the entry of the Rothschilds into the circles of the antisemitic aristocracy. The fashionable set of Faubourg Saint-Germain opened its doors not only to a few ennobled Jews, but their baptized sycophants, the antisemitic Jews, were also suffered to drift in as well as complete new-comers.[47] Curiously enough, the Jews of Alsace, who like the Dreyfus family had moved to Paris following the cession of that territory, took an especially prominent part in this social climb. Their exaggerated patriotism came out most markedly in the way they strove to dissociate themselves from Jewish immigrants. The Dreyfus family belonged to that section of French Jewry which sought to assimilate by adopting its own brand of antisemitism.[48] This adjustment to the French aristocracy had one inevitable result: the Jews tried to launch their sons upon the same higher military careers as were pursued by those of their new-found friends. It was here that the first cause of friction arose. The admission of the Jews into high society had been relatively peaceful. The upper classes, despite their dreams of a restored monarchy, were a politically spineless lot and did not bother unduly one way or the other. But when the Jews began seeking equality in the army, they came face to face with the determined opposition of the Jesuits who were not prepared to tolerate the existence of officers immune to the influence of the confessional.[49] Moreover, they came up against an inveterate caste spirit, which the easy atmosphere of the salons had led them to forget, a caste spirit which, already strengthened by tradition and calling, was still further fortified by uncompromising hostility to the Third Republic and to the civil administration.

A modern historian has described the struggle between Jews and Jesuits as a "struggle between two rivals," in which the "higher Jesuit clergy and the Jewish plutocracy stood facing one another in the middle of France like two invisible lines of battle." [50] The description is true insofar as the Jews

great Jesuit controversialist, always demanded it should become, an absolute monarchy whose policies can be directed by the Jesuits and whose development can be determined by pressing a button."

[47] Cf. Clemenceau, "Le spectacle du jour," in *op. cit.*: "Rothschild, friend of the entire antisemitic nobility . . . of a piece with Arthur Meyer, who is more papist than the Pope."

[48] On the Alsatian Jews, to whom Dreyfus belonged, see André Foucault, *Un nouvel aspect de l'Affaire Dreyfus,* in Les Oeuvres Libres, 1938, p. 310: "In the eyes of the Jewish bourgeoisie of Paris they were the incarnation of nationalist *raideur* . . . that attitude of distant disdain which the gentry affects towards its parvenu co-religionists. Their desire to assimilate completely to Gallic modes, to live on intimate terms with our old-established families, to occupy the most distinguished positions in the state, and the contempt which they showed for the commercial elements of Jewry, for the recently naturalized 'Polaks' of Galicia, gave them almost the appearance of traitors against their own race. . . . The Dreyfuses of 1894? Why, they were anti-semites!"

[49] Cf. "K.V.T." in *The Contemporary Review,* LXXIV, 598: "By the will of the democracy all Frenchmen are to be soldiers; by the will of the Church Catholics only are to hold the chief commands."

[50] Herzog, *op. cit.,* p. 35.

found in the Jesuits their first unappeasable foes, while the latter came promptly to realize how powerful a weapon antisemitism could be. This was the first attempt and the only one prior to Hitler to exploit the "major political concept" [51] of antisemitism on a Pan-European scale. On the other hand, however, if it is assumed that the struggle was one of two equally matched "rivals" the description is palpably false. The Jews sought no higher degree of power than was being wielded by any of the other cliques into which the republic had split. All they desired at the time was sufficient influence to pursue their social and business interests. They did not aspire to a political share in the management of the state. The only organized group who sought that were the Jesuits. The trial of Dreyfus was preceded by a number of incidents which show how resolutely and energetically the Jews tried to gain a place in the army and how common, even at that time, was the hostility toward them. Constantly subjected to gross insult, the few Jewish officers there were were obliged always to fight duels while Gentile comrades were unwilling to act as their seconds. It is, indeed, in this connection that the infamous Esterhazy first comes upon the scene as an exception to the rule.[52]

It has always remained somewhat obscure whether the arrest and condemnation of Dreyfus was simply a judicial error which just happened by chance to light up a political conflagration, or whether the General Staff deliberately planted the forged *bordereau* for the express purpose of at last branding a Jew as a traitor. In favor of the latter hypothesis is the fact that Dreyfus was the first Jew to find a post on the General Staff and under existing conditions this could only have aroused not merely annoyance but positive fury and consternation. In any case anti-Jewish hatred was unleashed even before the verdict was returned. Contrary to custom, which demanded the withholding of all information in a spy case still *sub iudice,* officers of the General Staff cheerfully supplied the *Libre Parole* with details of the case and the name of the accused. Apparently they feared lest Jewish influence with the government lead to a suppression of the trial and a stifling of the whole business. Some show of plausibility was afforded these fears by the fact that certain circles of French Jewry were known at the time to be seriously concerned about the precarious situation of Jewish officers.

[51] Cf. Bernanos, *op. cit.,* p. 151: "So, shorn of ridiculous hyperbole, antisemitism showed itself for what it really is: not a mere piece of crankiness, a mental quirk, but a major political concept."

[52] See Esterhazy's letter of July, 1894, to Edmond de Rothschild, quoted by J. Reinach, *op. cit.,* II, 53 ff.: "I did not hesitate when Captain Crémieux could find no Christian officer to act as his second." Cf. T. Reinach, *Histoire sommaire de l'Affaire Dreyfus,* pp. 60 ff. See also Herzog, *op. cit.,* under date of 1892 and June, 1894, where these duels are listed in detail and all of Esterhazy's intermediaries named. The last occasion was in September, 1896, when he received 10,000 francs. This misplaced generosity was later to have disquieting results. When, from the comfortable security of England, Esterhazy at length made his revelations and thereby compelled a revision of the case, the antisemitic press naturally suggested that he had been paid by the Jews for his self-condemnation. The idea is still advanced as a major argument in favor of Dreyfus' guilt.

It must also be remembered that the Panama scandal was then fresh in the public mind and that following the Rothschild loan to Russia distrust of the Jews had grown considerably.[53] War Minister Mercier was not only lauded by the bourgeois press at every fresh turn of the trial but even Jaurès' paper, the organ of the socialists, congratulated him on "having opposed the formidable pressure of corrupt politicians and high finance." [54] Characteristically this encomium drew from the *Libre Parole* the unstinted commendation, "Bravo, Jaurès!" Two years later, when Bernard Lazare published his first pamphlet on the miscarriage of justice, Jaurès' paper carefully refrained from discussing its contents but charged the socialist author with being an admirer of Rothschild and probably a paid agent.[55] Similarly, as late as 1897, when the fight for Dreyfus' reinstatement had already begun, Jaurès could see nothing in it but the conflict of two bourgeois groups, the opportunists and the clerics. Finally, even after the Rennes retrial Wilhelm Liebknecht, the German Social Democrat, still believed in the guilt of Dreyfus because he could not imagine that a member of the upper classes could ever be the victim of a false verdict.[56]

The skepticism of the radical and socialist press, strongly colored as it was by anti-Jewish feelings, was strengthened by the bizarre tactics of the Dreyfus family in its attempt to secure a retrial. In trying to save an innocent man they employed the very methods usually adopted in the case of a guilty one. They stood in mortal terror of publicity and relied exclusively on back-door maneuvers.[57] They were lavish with their cash and treated Lazare, one of their most valuable helpers and one of the greatest figures in the case, as if he were their paid agent.[58] Clemenceau, Zola, Picquart, and Labori—to

[53] Herzog, *op. cit.*, under date of 1892 shows at length how the Rothschilds began to adapt themselves to the republic. Curiously enough the papal policy of coalitionism, which represents an attempt at rapprochement by the Catholic Church, dates from precisely the same year. It is therefore not impossible that the Rothschild line was influenced by the clergy. As for the loan of 500 million francs to Russia, Count Münster pertinently observed: "Speculation is dead in France. . . . The capitalists can find no way of negotiating their securities . . . and this will contribute to the success of the loan. . . . The big Jews believe that if they make money they will best be able to help their small-time brethren. The result is that, though the French market is glutted with Russian securities, Frenchmen are still giving good francs for bad roubles"; Herzog, *ibid.*

[54] Cf. J. Reinach, *op. cit.,* I, 471.

[55] Cf. Herzog, *op. cit.,* p. 212.

[56] Cf. Max J. Kohler, "Some New Light on the Dreyfus Case," in *Studies in Jewish Bibliography and Related Subjects in Memory of A. S. Freidus,* New York, 1929.

[57] The Dreyfus family, for instance, summarily rejected the suggestion of Arthur Lévy, the writer, and Lévy-Bruhl, the scholar, that they should circulate a petition of protest among all leading figures of public life. Instead they embarked on a series of personal approaches to any politician with whom they happened to have contact; cf. Dutrait-Crozon, *op. cit.,* p. 51. See also Foucault, *op. cit.,* p. 309: "At this distance, one may wonder at the fact that the French Jews, instead of working on the papers secretly, did not give adequate and open expression to their indignation."

[58] Cf. Herzog, *op. cit.,* under date of December, 1894 and January, 1898. See also Charensol, *op. cit.,* p. 79, and Charles Péguy, "Le Portrait de Bernard Lazare," in *Cahiers de la quinzaine,* Series XI, No. 2 (1910).

name but the more active of the Dreyfusards—could in the end only save their good names by dissociating their efforts, with greater or less fuss and publicity, from the more concrete aspects of the issue.[59]

There was only one basis on which Dreyfus could or should have been saved. The intrigues of a corrupt Parliament, the dry rot of a collapsing society, and the clergy's lust for power should have been met squarely with the stern Jacobin concept of the nation based upon human rights—that republican view of communal life which asserts that (in the words of Clemenceau) by infringing on the rights of one you infringe on the rights of all. To rely on Parliament or on society was to lose the fight before beginning it. For one thing the resources of Jewry were in no way superior to those of the rich Catholic bourgeoisie; for another all of the higher strata of society, from the clerical and aristocratic families of the Faubourg Saint-Germain to the anticlerical and radical petty bourgeoisie, were only too willing to see the Jews formally removed from the body politic. In this way, they reckoned, they would be able to purge themselves of possible taint. The loss of Jewish social and commercial contacts seemed to them a price well worth paying. Similarly, as the utterances of Jaurès indicate, the Affair was regarded by Parliament as a golden opportunity for rehabilitating, or rather regaining, its time-honored reputation for incorruptibility. Last, but by no means least, in the countenancing of such slogans as "Death to the Jews" or "France for the French" an almost magic formula was discovered for reconciling the masses to the existent state of government and society.

IV: *The People and the Mob*

IF IT IS the common error of our time to imagine that propaganda can achieve all things and that a man can be talked into anything provided the talking is sufficiently loud and cunning, in that period it was commonly believed that the "voice of the people was the voice of God," and that the task of a leader was, as Clemenceau so scornfully expressed it,[60] to follow that voice shrewdly.

[59] Labori's withdrawal, after Dreyfus' family had hurriedly withdrawn the brief from him while the Rennes tribunal was still sitting, caused a major scandal. An exhaustive, if greatly exaggerated, account will be found in Frank, *op. cit.,* p. 432. Labori's own statement, which speaks eloquently for his nobility of character, appeared in *La Grande Revue* (February, 1900). After what had happened to his counsel and friend Zola at once broke relations with the Dreyfus family. As for Picquart, the *Echo de Paris* (November 30, 1901) reported that after Rennes he had nothing more to do with the Dreyfuses. Clemenceau in face of the fact that the whole of France, or even the whole world, grasped the real meaning of the trials better than the accused or his family, was more inclined to consider the incident humorous; cf. Weil, *op. cit.,* pp. 307-8.

[60] Cf. Clemenceau's article, February 2, 1898, in *op. cit.* On the futility of trying to win the workers with antisemitic slogans and especially on the attempts of Léon Daudet, see the Royalist writer Dimier, *Vingt ans d'Action Française,* Paris, 1926.

Both views go back to the same fundamental error of regarding the mob as identical with rather than as a caricature of the people. The mob is primarily a group in which the residue of all classes are represented. This makes it so easy to mistake the mob for the people, which also comprises all strata of society. While the people in all great revolutions fight for true representation, the mob always will shout for the "strong man," the "great leader." For the mob hates society from which it is excluded, as well as Parliament where it is not represented. Plebiscites, therefore, with which modern mob leaders have obtained such excellent results, are an old concept of politicians who rely upon the mob. One of the more intelligent leaders of the Anti-Dreyfusards, Déroulède, clamored for a "Republic through plebiscite."

High society and politicians of the Third Republic had produced the French mob in a series of scandals and public frauds. They now felt a tender sentiment of parental familiarity with their offspring, a feeling mixed with admiration and fear. The least society could do for its offspring was to protect it verbally. While the mob actually stormed Jewish shops and assailed Jews in the streets, the language of high society made real, passionate violence look like harmless child's play.[61] The most important of the contemporary documents in this respect is the "Henry Memorial" and the various solutions it proposed to the Jewish question: Jews were to be torn to pieces like Marsyas in the Greek myth; Reinach ought to be boiled alive; Jews should be stewed in oil or pierced to death with needles; they should be "circumcised up to the neck." One group of officers expressed great impatience to try out a new type of gun on the 100,000 Jews in the country. Among the subscribers were more than 1,000 officers, including four generals in active service, and the minister of war, Mercier. The relatively large number of intellectuals [62] and even of Jews in the list is surprising. The upper classes knew that the mob was flesh of their flesh and blood of their blood. Even a Jewish historian of the time, although he had seen with his own eyes that Jews are no longer safe when the mob rules the street, spoke with secret admiration of the "great collective movement." [63] This only shows how deeply most Jews were rooted in a society which was attempting to eliminate them.

If Bernanos, with reference to the Dreyfus Affair, describes antisemitism as a major political concept, he is undoubtedly right with respect to the mob.

[61] Very characteristic in this respect are the various depictions of contemporary society in J. Reinach, *op. cit.*, I, 233 ff.; III, 141: "Society hostesses fell in step with Guérin. Their language (which scarcely outran their thoughts) would have struck horror in the Amazon of Damohey . . ." Of special interest in this connection is an article by André Chevrillon, "Huit Jours à Rennes," in *La Grande Revue*, February, 1900. He relates, *inter alia*, the following revealing incident: "A physician speaking to some friends of mine about Dreyfus, chanced to remark, 'I'd like to torture him.' 'And I wish,' rejoined one of the ladies, 'that he were innocent. Then he'd suffer more.' "

[62] The intellectuals include, strangely enough, Paul Valéry, who contributed three francs *"non sans réflexion."*

[63] J. Reinach, *op. cit.*, I, 233.

It had been tried out previously in Berlin and Vienna, by Ahlwardt and Stoecker, by Schoenerer and Lueger, but nowhere was its efficacy more clearly proved than in France. There can be no doubt that in the eyes of the mob the Jews came to serve as an object lesson for all the things they detested. If they hated society they could point to the way in which the Jews were tolerated within it; and if they hated the government they could point to the way in which the Jews had been protected by or were identifiable with the state. While it is a mistake to assume that the mob preys only on Jews, the Jews must be accorded first place among its favorite victims.

Excluded as it is from society and political representation, the mob turns of necessity to extraparliamentary action. Moreover, it is inclined to seek the real forces of political life in those movements and influences which are hidden from view and work behind the scenes. There can be no doubt that during the nineteenth century Jewry fell into this category, as did Freemasonry (especially in Latin countries) and the Jesuits.[64] It is, of course, utterly untrue that any of these groups really constituted a secret society bent on dominating the world by means of a gigantic conspiracy. Nevertheless, it is true that their influence, however overt it may have been, was exerted beyond the formal realm of politics, operating on a large scale in lobbies, lodges, and the confessional. Ever since the French Revolution these three groups have shared the doubtful honor of being, in the eyes of the European mob, the pivotal point of world politics. During the Dreyfus crisis each was able to exploit this popular notion by hurling at the other charges of conspiring to world domination. The slogan, "secret Judah," is due, no doubt, to the inventiveness of certain Jesuits, who chose to see in the first Zionist Congress (1897) the core of a Jewish world conspiracy.[65] Similarly, the concept of "secret Rome" is due to the anticlerical Freemasons and perhaps to the indiscriminate slanders of some Jews as well.

The fickleness of the mob is proverbial, as the opponents of Dreyfus were to learn to their sorrow when, in 1899, the wind changed and the small group of true republicans, headed by Clemenceau, suddenly realized, with mixed feelings, that a section of the mob had rallied to their side.[66] In some eyes the two parties to the great controversy now seemed like "two rival gangs of charlatans squabbling for recognition by the rabble" [67] while actually the voice of the Jacobin Clemenceau had succeeded in bringing back one part of the French people to their greatest tradition. Thus the great scholar, Emile Duclaux, could write: "In this drama played before a whole people

[64] A study of European superstition would probably show that Jews became objects of this typically nineteenth-century brand of superstition fairly late. They were preceded by the Rosicrucians, Templars, Jesuits, and Freemasons. The treatment of nineteenth-century history suffers greatly from the lack of such a study.

[65] See "Il caso Dreyfus," in *Civiltà Cattolica* (February 5, 1898).—Among the exceptions to the foregoing statement the most notable is the Jesuit Pierre Charles Louvain, who has denounced the "Protocols."

[66] Cf. Martin du Gard, *Jean Barois,* pp. 272 ff., and Daniel Halévy, in *Cahiers de la quinzaine,* Series XI, cahier 10, Paris, 1910.

[67] Cf. Georges Sorel, *La Revolution dreyfusienne,* Paris, 1911, pp. 70-71.

and so worked up by the press that the whole nation ultimately took part in it, we see the chorus and anti-chorus of the ancient tragedy railing at each other. The scene is France and the theater is the world."

Led by the Jesuits and aided by the mob the army at last stepped into the fray confident of victory. Counterattack from the civil power had been effectively forestalled. The antisemitic press had stopped men's mouths by publishing Reinach's lists of the deputies involved in the Panama scandal.[68] Everything suggested an effortless triumph. The society and the politicians of the Third Republic, its scandals and affairs, had created a new class of *déclassés;* they could not be expected to fight against their own product; on the contrary, they were to adopt the language and outlook of the mob. Through the army the Jesuits would gain the upper hand over the corrupt civil power and the way would thus be paved for a bloodless *coup d'état.*

So long as there was only the Dreyfus family trying with bizarre methods to rescue their kinsman from Devil's Island, and so long as there were only Jews concerned about their standing in the antisemitic salons and the still more antisemitic army, everything certainly pointed that way. Obviously there was no reason to expect an attack on the army or on society from *that* quarter. Was not the sole desire of the Jews to continue to be accepted in society and suffered in the armed forces? No one in military or civilian circles needed to suffer a sleepless night on *their* account.[69] It was disconcerting, therefore, when it transpired that in the intelligence office of the General Staff there sat a high officer, who, though possessed of a good Catholic background, excellent military prospects, and the "proper" degree of antipathy toward the Jews, had yet not adopted the principle that the end justifies the means. Such a man, utterly divorced from social clannishness or professional ambition, was Picquart, and of this simple, quiet, politically disinterested spirit the General Staff was soon to have its fill. Picquart was no hero and certainly no martyr. He was simply that common type of citizen with an average interest in public affairs who in the hour of danger (though not a minute earlier) stands up to defend his country in the same unquestioning way as he discharges his daily duties.[70] Nevertheless, the cause only

[68] To what extent the hands of members of Parliament were tied is shown by the case of Scheurer-Kestner, one of their better elements and vice-president of the senate. No sooner had he entered his protest against the trial than *Libre Parole* proclaimed the fact that his son-in-law had been involved in the Panama scandal. See Herzog, *op. cit.,* under date of November, 1897.

[69] Cf. Brogan, *op. cit.,* Book VII, ch. 1: "The desire to let the matter rest was not uncommon among French Jews, especially among the richer French Jews."

[70] Immediately after he had made his discoveries Picquart was banished to a dangerous post in Tunis. Thereupon he made his will, exposed the whole business, and deposited a copy of the document with his lawyer. A few months later, when it was discovered that he was still alive, a deluge of mysterious letters came pouring in, compromising him and accusing him of complicity with the "traitor" Dreyfus. He was treated like a gangster who had threatened to "squeal." When all this proved of no avail, he was arrested, drummed out of the army, and divested of his decorations, all of which he endured with quiet equanimity.

grew serious when, after several delays and hesitations, Clemenceau at last became convinced that Dreyfus was innocent and the republic in danger. At the beginning of the struggle only a handful of well-known writers and scholars rallied to the cause, Zola, Anatole France, E. Duclaux, Gabriel Monod, the historian, and Lucien Herr, librarian of the Ecole Normale. To these must be added the small and then insignificant circle of young intellectuals who were later to make history in the *Cahiers de la quinzaine.*[71] That, however, was the full roster of Clemenceau's allies. There was no political group, not a single politician of repute, ready to stand at his side. The greatness of Clemenceau's approach lies in the fact that it was not directed against a particular miscarriage of justice, but was based upon such "abstract" ideas as justice, liberty, and civic virtue. It was based, in short, on those very concepts which had formed the staple of old-time Jacobin patriotism and against which much mud and abuse had already been hurled. As time wore on and Clemenceau continued, unmoved by threats and disappointments, to enunciate the same truths and to embody them in demands, the more "concrete" nationalists lost ground. Followers of men like Barrès, who had accused the supporters of Dreyfus of losing themselves in a "welter of metaphysics," came to realize that the abstractions of the "Tiger" were actually nearer to political realities than the limited intelligence of ruined businessmen or the barren traditionalism of fatalistic intellectuals.[72] Where the concrete approach of the realistic nationalists eventually led them is illustrated by the priceless story of how Charles Maurras had "the honor and pleasure," after the defeat of France, of falling in during his flight to the south with a female astrologer who interpreted to him the political meaning of recent events and advised him to collaborate with the Nazis.[73]

Although antisemitism had undoubtedly gained ground during the three years following the arrest of Dreyfus, before the opening of Clemenceau's campaign, and although the anti-Jewish press had attained a circulation comparable to that of the chief papers, the streets had remained quiet. It was only when Clemenceau began his articles in *L'Aurore,* when Zola published his *J'Accuse,* and when the Rennes tribunal set off the dismal succession of trials and retrials that the mob stirred into action. Every stroke of the Dreyfusards (who were known to be a small minority) was followed by a more or less violent disturbance on the streets.[74] The organization of the mob by the General Staff was remarkable. The trail leads straight from

71 To this group, led by Charles Péguy, belonged the youthful Romain Rolland, Suarez, Georges Sorel, Daniel Halévy, and Bernard Lazare.

72 Cf. M. Barrès, *Scènes et doctrines du nationalisme,* Paris, 1899.

73 See Yves Simon, *op. cit.,* pp. 54-55.

74 The faculty rooms of Rennes University were wrecked after five professors had declared themselves in favor of a retrial. After the appearance of Zola's first article Royalist students demonstrated outside the offices of *Figaro,* after which the paper desisted from further articles of the same type. The publisher of the pro-Dreyfus *La Bataille* was beaten up on the street. The judges of the Court of Cassation, which finally set aside the verdict of 1894, reported unanimously that they had been threatened with "unlawful assault." Examples could be multiplied.

the army to the *Libre Parole* which, directly or indirectly, through its articles or the personal intervention of its editors, mobilized students, monarchists, adventurers, and plain gangsters and pushed them into the streets. If Zola uttered a word, at once his windows were stoned. If Scheurer-Kestner wrote to the colonial minister, he was at once beaten up on the streets while the papers made scurrilous attacks on his private life. And all accounts agree that if Zola, when once charged, had been acquitted he would never have left the courtroom alive.

The cry, "Death to the Jews," swept the country. In Lyon, Rennes, Nantes, Tours, Bordeaux, Clermont-Ferrant, and Marseille—everywhere, in fact—antisemitic riots broke out and were invariably traceable to the same source. Popular indignation broke out everywhere on the same day and at precisely the same hour.[75] Under the leadership of Guérin the mob took on a military complexion. Antisemitic shock troops appeared on the streets and made certain that every pro-Dreyfus meeting should end in bloodshed. The complicity of the police was everywhere patent.[76]

The most modern figure on the side of the Anti-Dreyfusards was probably Jules Guérin. Ruined in business, he had begun his political career as a police stool pigeon, and acquired that flair for discipline and organization which invariably marks the underworld. This he was later able to divert into political channels, becoming the founder and head of the Ligue Antisémite. In him high society found its first criminal hero. In its adulation of Guérin bourgeois society showed clearly that in its code of morals and ethics it had broken for good with its own standards. Behind the Ligue stood two members of the aristocracy, the Duke of Orléans and the Marquis de Morès. The latter had lost his fortune in America and became famous for organizing the butchers of Paris into a manslaughtering brigade.

Most eloquent of these modern tendencies was the farcical siege of the so-called Fort Chabrol. It was here, in this first of "Brown Houses," that the cream of the Ligue Antisémite foregathered when the police decided at last to arrest their leader. The installations were the acme of technical perfection. "The windows were protected by iron shutters. There was a system of electric bells and telephones from cellar to roof. Five yards or so behind the massive entrance, itself always kept locked and bolted, there was a tall grill of cast iron. On the right, between the grill and the main entrance was a small door, likewise iron-plated, behind which sentries, handpicked from the butcher legions, mounted guard day and night." [77] Max Régis, instigator of the Algerian pogroms, is another who strikes a modern note. It was this youthful Régis who once called upon a cheering Paris rabble to "water the

[75] On January 18, 1898, antisemitic demonstrations took place at Bordeaux, Marseille, Clermont-Ferrant, Nantes, Rouen, and Lyon. On the following day student riots broke out in Rouen, Toulouse, and Nantes.

[76] The crudest instance was that of the police prefect of Rennes, who advised Professor Victor Basch, when the latter's house was stormed by a mob 2,000 strong, that he ought to hand in his resignation, as he could no longer guarantee his safety.

[77] Cf. Bernanos, *op. cit.,* p. 346.

tree of freedom with the blood of the Jews." Régis represented that section
of the movement which hoped to achieve power by legal and parliamentary
methods. In accordance with this program he had himself elected mayor of
Algiers and utilized his office to unleash the pogroms in which several Jews
were killed, Jewish women criminally assaulted and Jewish-owned stores
looted. It was to him also that the polished and cultured Edouard Drumont,
that most famous French antisemite, owed his seat in Parliament.

What was new in all this was not the activity of the mob; for that there
were abundant precedents. What was new and surprising at the time—though
all too familiar to us—was the organization of the mob and the hero-worship
enjoyed by its leaders. The mob became the direct agent of that "concrete"
nationalism espoused by Barrès, Maurras, and Daudet, who together formed
what was undoubtedly a kind of elite of the younger intellectuals. These men,
who despised the people and who had themselves but recently emerged from
a ruinous and decadent cult of estheticism, saw in the mob a living expression
of virile and primitive "strength." It was they and their theories which first
identified the mob with the people and converted its leaders into national
heroes.[78] It was their philosophy of pessimism and their delight in doom that
was the first sign of the imminent collapse of the European intelligentsia.

Even Clemenceau was not immune from the temptation to identify the
mob with the people. What made him especially prone to this error was
the consistently ambiguous attitude of the Labor party toward the question of "abstract" justice. No party, including the socialists, was ready to
make an issue of justice per se, "to stand, come what may, for justice, the
sole unbreakable bond of union between civilized men." [79] The socialists
stood for the interests of the workers, the opportunists for those of the liberal
bourgeoisie, the coalitionists for those of the Catholic higher classes, and
the radicals for those of the anticlerical petty bourgeoisie. The socialists had
the great advantage of speaking in the name of a homogeneous and united
class. Unlike the bourgeois parties they did not represent a society which
had split into innumerable cliques and cabals. Nevertheless, they were concerned primarily and essentially with the interests of their class. They were
not troubled by any higher obligation toward human solidarity and had no
conception of what communal life really meant. Typical of their attitude
was the observation of Jules Guesde, the counterpart of Jaurès in the French
party, that "law and honor are mere words."

The nihilism which characterized the nationalists was no monopoly of
the Anti-Dreyfusards. On the contrary, a large proportion of the socialists
and many of those who championed Dreyfus, like Guesde, spoke the same
language. If the Catholic *La Croix* remarked that "it is no longer a question
whether Dreyfus is innocent or guilty but only of who will win, the friends
of the army or its foes," the corresponding sentiment might well have been

---

[78] For these theories see especially Charles Maurras, *Au Signe de Flore; souvenirs
de la vie politique; l'Affaire Dreyfus et la fondation de l'Action Française,* Paris, 1931;
M. Barrès, *op. cit.;* Léon Daudet, *Panorama de la Troisième République,* Paris, 1936.
[79] Cf. Clemenceau, "A la dérive," in *op. cit.*

voiced, *mutatis mutandis,* by the partisans of Dreyfus.[80] Not only the mob but a considerable section of the French people declared itself, at best, quite uninterested in whether one group of the population was or was not to be excluded from the law.

As soon as the mob began its campaign of terror against the partisans of Dreyfus, it found the path open before it. As Clemenceau attests, the workers of Paris cared little for the whole affair. If the various elements of the bourgeoisie squabbled among themselves, that, they thought, scarcely affected their own interests. "With the open consent of the people," wrote Clemenceau, "they have proclaimed before the world the failure of their 'democracy.' Through them a sovereign people shows itself thrust from its throne of justice, shorn of its infallible majesty. For there is no denying that this evil has befallen us with the full complicity of the people itself. . . . The people is not God. Anyone could have foreseen that this new divinity would some day topple to his fall. A collective tyrant, spread over the length and breadth of the land, is no more acceptable than a single tyrant ensconced upon his throne." [81]

At last Clemenceau convinced Jaurès that an infringement of the rights of one man was an infringement of the rights of all. But in this he was successful only because the wrongdoers happened to be the inveterate enemies of the people ever since the Revolution, namely, the aristocracy and the clergy. It was *against* the rich and the clergy, not *for* the republic, not *for* justice and freedom that the workers finally took to the streets. True, both the speeches of Jaurès and the articles of Clemenceau are redolent of the old revolutionary passion for human rights. True, also, that this passion was strong enough to rally the people to the struggle, but first they had to be convinced that not only justice and the honor of the republic were at stake but also their own class "interests." As it was, a large number of socialists, both inside and outside the country, still regarded it as a mistake to meddle (as they put it) in the internecine quarrels of the bourgeoisie or to bother about saving the republic.

The first to wean the workers, at least partially, from this mood of indifference was that great lover of the people, Emile Zola. In his famous indictment of the republic he was also, however, the first to deflect from the presentation of precise political facts and to yield to the passions of the mob by raising the bogy of "secret Rome." This was a note which Clemenceau adopted only reluctantly, though Jaurès did with enthusiasm. The real achievement of Zola, which is hard to detect from his pamphlets, consists in the resolute and dauntless courage with which this man, whose life and works had exalted the people to a point "bordering on idolatry," stood up to challenge, combat, and finally conquer the masses, in whom, like Clemen-

---

[80] It was precisely this which so greatly disillusioned the champions of Dreyfus, especially the circle around Charles Péguy. This disturbing similarity between Dreyfusards and Anti-Dreyfusards is the subject matter of the instructive novel by Martin du Gard, *Jean Barois,* 1913.

[81] Preface to *Contre la Justice,* 1900.

ceau, he could all the time scarcely distinguish the mob from the people. "Men have been found to resist the most powerful monarchs and to refuse to bow down before them, but few indeed have been found to resist the crowd, to stand up alone before misguided masses, to face their implacable frenzy without weapons and with folded arms to dare a no when a yes is demanded. Such a man was Zola!" [82]

Scarcely had *J'Accuse* appeared when the Paris socialists held their first meeting and passed a resolution calling for a revision of the Dreyfus case. But only five days later some thirty-two socialist officials promptly came out with a declaration that the fate of Dreyfus, "the class enemy," was no concern of theirs. Behind this declaration stood large elements of the party in Paris. Although a split in its ranks continued throughout the Affair, the party numbered enough Dreyfusards to prevent the Ligue Antisémite from thenceforth controlling the streets. A socialist meeting even branded antisemitism "a new form of reaction." Yet a few months later when the parliamentary elections took place, Jaurès was not returned, and shortly afterwards, when Cavaignac, the minister of war, treated the Chamber to a speech attacking Dreyfus and commending the army as indispensable, the delegates resolved, with only two dissenting votes, to placard the walls of Paris with the text of that address. Similarly, when the great Paris strike broke out in October of the same year, Münster, the German ambassador, was able reliably and confidentially to inform Berlin that "as far as the broad masses are concerned, this is in no sense a political issue. The workers are simply out for higher wages and these they are bound to get in the end. As for the Dreyfus case, they have never bothered their heads about it." [83]

Who then, in broad terms, were the supporters of Dreyfus? Who were the 300,000 Frenchmen who so eagerly devoured Zola's *J'Accuse* and who followed religiously the editorials of Clemenceau? Who were the men who finally succeeded in splitting every class, even every family, in France into opposing factions over the Dreyfus issue? The answer is that they formed no party or homogeneous group. Admittedly they were recruited more from the lower than from the upper classes, as they comprised, characteristically enough, more physicians than lawyers or civil servants. By and large, however, they were a mixture of diverse elements: men as far apart as Zola and Péguy or Jaurès and Picquart, men who on the morrow would part company and go their several ways. "They come from political parties and religious communities who have nothing in common, who are even in conflict with each other. . . . Those men do not know each other. They have fought and on occasion will fight again. Do not deceive yourselves; those are the 'elite' of the French democracy." [84]

Had Clemenceau possessed enough self-confidence at that time to consider only those who heeded him the true people of France, he would not have

[82] Clemenceau, in a speech before the Senate several years later; cf. Weil, *op. cit.*, pp. 112-13.
[83] See Herzog, *op. cit.*, under date of October 10, 1898.
[84] "K.V.T.," *op. cit.*, p. 608.

fallen prey to that fatal pride which marked the rest of his career. Out of his experiences in the Dreyfus Affair grew his despair of the people, his contempt for men, finally his belief that he and he alone would be able to save the republic. He could never stoop to play the claque to the antics of the mob. Therefore, once he began to identify the mob with the people, he did indeed cut the ground from under his feet, and forced himself into that grim aloofness which thereafter distinguished him.

The disunity of the French people was apparent in each family. Characteristically enough, it found political expression only in the ranks of the Labor party. All others, as well as all parliamentary groups, were solidly against Dreyfus at the beginning of the campaign for a retrial. All this means, however, is that the bourgeois parties no longer represented the true feelings of the electorate, for the same disunity that was so patent among the socialists obtained among almost all sections of the populace. Everywhere a minority existed which took up Clemenceau's plea for justice, and this heterogeneous minority made up the Dreyfusards. Their fight against the army and the corrupt complicity of the republic which backed it was the dominating factor in French internal politics from the end of 1897 until the opening of the Exposition in 1900. It also exerted an appreciable influence on the nation's foreign policy. Nevertheless, this entire struggle, which was to result eventually in at least a partial triumph, took place exclusively outside of Parliament. In that so-called representative assembly, comprising as it did a full 600 delegates drawn from every shade and color both of labor and of the bourgeoisie, there were in 1898 but two supporters of Dreyfus and one of them, Jaurès, was not re-elected.

The disturbing thing about the Dreyfus Affair is that it was not only the mob which had to work along extraparliamentary lines. The entire minority, fighting as it was for Parliament, democracy, and the republic, was likewise constrained to wage its battle outside the Chamber. The only difference between the two elements was that while the one used the streets, the other resorted to the press and the courts. In other words, the whole of France's political life during the Dreyfus crisis was carried on outside Parliament. Nor do the several parliamentary votes in favor of the army and against a retrial in any way invalidate this conclusion. It is significant to remember that when parliamentary feeling began to turn, shortly before the opening of the Paris Exposition, Minister of War Gallifet was able to declare truthfully that this in no wise represented the mood of the country.[85] On the other hand the vote against a retrial must not be construed as an endorsement of the *coup d'état* policy which the Jesuits and certain radical antisemites were trying to introduce with the help of the army.[86] It was due, rather, to plain

[85] Gallifet, minister of war, wrote to Waldeck: "Let us not forget that the great majority of people in France are antisemitic. Our position would be, therefore, that on the one side we would have the entire army and the majority of Frenchmen, not to speak of the civil service and the senators; . . ." cf. J. Reinach, *op. cit.*, V, 579.

[86] The best known of such attempts is that of Déroulède who sought, while attending the funeral of President Paul Faure, in February, 1899, to incite General Roget to

resistance against any change in the status quo. As a matter of fact, an equally overwhelming majority of the Chamber would have rejected a military-clerical dictatorship.

Those members of Parliament who had learned to regard politics as the professional representation of vested interests were naturally anxious to preserve that state of affairs upon which their "calling" and their profits depended. The Dreyfus case revealed, moreover, that the people likewise wanted their representatives to look after their own special interests rather than to function as statesmen. It was distinctly unwise to mention the case in election propaganda. Had this been due solely to antisemitism the situation of the Dreyfusards would certainly have been hopeless. In point of fact, during the elections they already enjoyed considerable support among the working class. Nevertheless even those who sided with Dreyfus did not care to see this political question dragged into the elections. It was, indeed, because he insisted on making it the pivot of his campaign that Jaurès lost his seat.

If Clemenceau and the Dreyfusards succeeded in winning over large sections of all classes to the demand of a retrial, the Catholics reacted as a bloc; among them there was no divergence of opinion. What the Jesuits did in steering the aristocracy and the General Staff, was done for the middle and lower classes by the Assumptionists, whose organ, La Croix, enjoyed the largest circulation of all Catholic journals in France.[87] Both centered their agitation against the republic around the Jews. Both represented themselves as defenders of the army and the commonweal against the machinations of "international Jewry." More striking, however, than the attitude of the Catholics in France was the fact that the Catholic press throughout the world was solidly against Dreyfus. "All these journalists marched and are still marching at the word of command of their superiors." [88] As the case progressed, it became increasingly clear that the agitation against the Jews in France followed an international line. Thus the Civiltà Cattolica declared that Jews must be excluded from the nation everywhere, in France, Germany, Austria, and Italy. Catholic politicians were among the first to realize that latter-day power politics must be based on the interplay of colonial ambitions. They were therefore the first to link antisemitism to imperialism, declaring that the Jews were agents of England and thereby identifying antagonism toward them with Anglophobia.[89] The Dreyfus case, in which

---

mutiny. The German ambassadors and chargés d'affaires in Paris reported such attempts every few months. The situation is well summed up by Barrès, op. cit., p. 4: "In Rennes we have found our battlefield. All we need is soldiers or, more precisely, generals—or, still more precisely, a general." Only it was no accident that this general was non-existent.

[87] Brogan goes so far as to blame the Assumptionists for the entire clerical agitation.

[88] "K.V.T.," op. cit., p. 597.

[89] "The initial stimulus in the Affair very probably came from London, where the Congo-Nile mission of 1896-1898 was causing some degree of disquietude"; thus Maurras in Action Française (July 14, 1935). The Catholic press of London defended the Jesuits; see "The Jesuits and the Dreyfus Case," in The Month, Vol. XVIII (1899).

Jews were the central figures, thus afforded them a welcome opportunity to play their game. If England had taken Egypt from the French the Jews were to blame,[90] while the movement for an Anglo-American alliance was due, of course, to "Rothschild imperialism." [91] That the Catholic game was not confined to France became abundantly clear once the curtain was rung down on that particular scene. At the close of 1899, when Dreyfus had been pardoned and when French public opinion had turned round through fear of a projected boycott of the Exposition, only an interview with Pope Leo XIII was needed to stop the spread of antisemitism throughout the world.[92] Even in the United States, where championship of Dreyfus was particularly enthusiastic among the non-Catholics, it was possible to detect in the Catholic press after 1897 a marked resurgence of antisemitic feeling which, however, subsided overnight following the interview with Leo XIII.[93] The "grand strategy" of using antisemitism as an instrument of Catholicism had proved abortive.

v: *The Jews and the Dreyfusards*

THE CASE of the unfortunate Captain Dreyfus had shown the world that in every Jewish nobleman and multimillionaire there still remained something of the old-time pariah, who has no country, for whom human rights do not exist, and whom society would gladly exclude from its privileges. No one, however, found it more difficult to grasp this fact than the emancipated Jews themselves. "It isn't enough for them," wrote Bernard Lazare, "to reject any solidarity with their foreign-born brethren; they have also to go charging them with all the evils which their own cowardice engenders. They are not content with being more jingoist than the native Frenchmen; like all emancipated Jews everywhere, they have also of their own volition broken all ties of solidarity. Indeed, they go so far that for the three dozen or so men in France who are ready to defend one of their martyred brethren you can find some thousands ready to stand guard over Devil's Island, alongside the most rabid patriots of the country." [94] Precisely because they had played so small a part in the political development of the lands in which they lived, they had come, during the course of the century, to make a fetish of legal equality. To them it was the unquestionable basis of eternal security. When the Dreyfus Affair broke out to warn them that their security was menaced, they were deep in the process of a disintegrating assimilation, through which

---

[90] *Civiltà Cattolica*, February 5, 1898.
[91] See the particularly characteristic article of Rev. George McDermot, C.S.P., "Mr. Chamberlain's Foreign Policy and the Dreyfus Case," in the American monthly *Catholic World*, Vol. LXVII (September, 1898).
[92] Cf. Lecanuet, *op. cit.*, p. 188.
[93] Cf. Rose A. Halperin, *op. cit.*, pp. 59, 77 ff.
[94] Bernard Lazare, *Job's Dungheap*, New York, 1948, p. 97.

their lack of political wisdom was intensified rather than otherwise. They were rapidly assimilating themselves to those elements of society in which all political passions are smothered beneath the dead weight of social snobbery, big business, and hitherto unknown opportunities for profit. They hoped to get rid of the antipathy which this tendency had called forth by diverting it against their poor and as yet unassimilated immigrant brethren. Using the same tactics as Gentile society had employed against them they took pains to dissociate themselves from the so-called *Ostjuden*. Political antisemitism, as it had manifested itself in the pogroms of Russia and Rumania, they dismissed airily as a survival from the Middle Ages, scarcely a reality of modern politics. They could never understand that more was at stake in the Dreyfus Affair than mere social status, if only because more than mere social antisemitism had been brought to bear.

These then are the reasons why so few wholehearted supporters of Dreyfus were to be found in the ranks of French Jewry. The Jews, including the very family of the accused, shrank from starting a political fight. On just these grounds, Labori, counsel for Zola, was refused the defense before the Rennes tribunal, while Dreyfus' second lawyer, Démange, was constrained to base his plea on the issue of doubt. It was hoped thereby to smother under a deluge of compliments any possible attack from the army or its officers. The idea was that the royal road to an acquittal was to pretend that the whole thing boiled down to the possibility of a judicial error, the victim of which just happened by chance to be a Jew. The result was a second verdict and Dreyfus, refusing to face the true issue, was induced to renounce a retrial and instead to petition for clemency, that is, to plead guilty.[95] The Jews failed to see that what was involved was an organized fight against them on a political front. They therefore resisted the co-operation of men who were prepared to meet the challenge on this basis. How blind their attitude was is shown clearly by the case of Clemenceau. Clemenceau's struggle for justice as the foundation of the state certainly embraced the restoration of equal rights to the Jews. In an age, however, of class struggle on the one hand and rampant jingoism on the other, it would have remained a political abstraction had it not been conceived, at the same time, in actual terms of the oppressed fighting their oppressors. Clemenceau was one of the few true friends modern Jewry has known just because he recognized and proclaimed before the world that Jews were one of the oppressed peoples of Europe. The antisemite tends to see in the Jewish parvenu an upstart pariah; consequently in every huckster he fears a Rothschild and in every *shnorrer* a parvenu. But Clemenceau, in his consuming passion for justice, still saw the Rothschilds as members of a downtrodden people. His anguish over the

95 Cf. Fernand Labori, "Le mal politique et les partis," in *La Grande Revue* (October-December, 1901): "From the moment at Rennes when the accused pleaded guilty and the defendant renounced recourse to a retrial in the hope of gaining a pardon, the Dreyfus case as a great, universal human issue was definitely closed." In his article entitled "Le Spectacle du jour," Clemenceau speaks of the Jews of Algiers "in whose behalf Rothschild will not voice the least protest."

national misfortune of France opened his eyes and his heart even to those "unfortunates, who pose as leaders of their people and promptly leave them in the lurch," to those cowed and subdued elements who, in their ignorance, weakness and fear, have been so much bedazzled by admiration of the stronger as to exclude them from partnership in any active struggle and who are able to "rush to the aid of the winner" only when the battle has been won.[96]

VI: *The Pardon and Its Significance*

THAT THE Dreyfus drama was a comedy became apparent only in its final act. The *deus ex machina* who united the disrupted country, turned Parliament in favor of a retrial and eventually reconciled the disparate elements of the people from the extreme right to the socialists, was nothing other than the Paris Exposition of 1900. What Clemenceau's daily editorials, Zola's pathos, Jaurès' speeches, and the popular hatred of clergy and aristocracy had failed to achieve, namely, a change of parliamentary feeling in favor of Dreyfus, was at last accomplished by the fear of a boycott. The same Parliament that a year before had unanimously rejected a retrial, now by a two-thirds majority passed a vote of censure on an anti-Dreyfus government. In July, 1899, the Waldeck-Rousseau cabinet came to power. President Loubet pardoned Dreyfus and liquidated the entire affair. The Exposition was able to open under the brightest of commercial skies and general fraternization ensued: even socialists became eligible for government posts; Millerand, the first socialist minister in Europe, received the portfolio of commerce.

Parliament became the champion of Dreyfus! That was the upshot. For Clemenceau, of course, it was a defeat. To the bitter end he denounced the ambiguous pardon and the even more ambiguous amnesty. "All it has done," wrote Zola, "is to lump together in a single stinking pardon men of honor and hoodlums. All have been thrown into one pot." [97] Clemenceau remained, as at the beginning, utterly alone. The socialists, above all, Jaurès, welcomed both pardon and amnesty. Did it not insure them a place in the government and a more extensive representation of their special interests? A few months later, in May, 1900, when the success of the Exposition was assured, the real truth at last emerged. All these appeasement tactics were to be at the expense of the Dreyfusards. The motion for a further retrial was defeated 425 to 60, and not even Clemenceau's own government in 1906 could change the situation; it did not dare to entrust the retrial to a normal court of law. The (illegal) acquittal through the Court of Appeals was a compromise. But defeat for Clemenceau did not mean victory for the Church and the

[96] See Clemenceau's articles entitled "Le Spectacle du jour," "Et les Juifs!" "La Farce du syndicat," and "Encore les juifs!" in *L'Iniquité*.

[97] Cf. Zola's letter dated September 13, 1899, in *Correspondance: lettres à Maître Labori*.

army. The separation of Church and State and the ban on parochial education brought to an end the political influence of Catholicism in France. Similarly, the subjection of the intelligence service to the ministry of war, *i.e.*, to the civil authority, robbed the army of its blackmailing influence on cabinet and Chamber and deprived it of any justification for conducting police inquiries on its own account.

In 1909 Drumont stood for the Academy. Once his antisemitism had been lauded by the Catholics and acclaimed by the people. Now, however, the "greatest historian since Fustel" (Lemaître) was obliged to yield to Marcel Prévost, author of the somewhat pornographic *Demi-Vierges,* and the new "immortal" received the congratulations of the Jesuit Father Du Lac.[98] Even the Society of Jesus had composed its quarrel with the Third Republic. The close of the Dreyfus case marked the end of clerical antisemitism. The compromise adopted by the Third Republic cleared the defendant without granting him a regular trial, while it restricted the activities of Catholic organizations. Whereas Bernard Lazare had asked equal rights for both sides, the state had allowed one exception for the Jews and another which threatened the freedom of conscience of Catholics.[99] The parties which were really in conflict were both placed outside the law, with the result that the Jewish question on the one hand and political Catholicism on the other were banished thenceforth from the arena of practical politics.

Thus closes the only episode in which the subterranean forces of the nineteenth century enter the full light of recorded history. The only visible result was that it gave birth to the Zionist movement—the only political answer Jews have ever found to antisemitism and the only ideology in which they have ever taken seriously a hostility that would place them in the center of world events.

[98] Cf. Herzog, *op. cit.,* p. 97.

[99] Lazare's position in the Dreyfus Affair is best described by Charles Péguy, "Notre Jeunesse," in *Cahiers de la quinzaine,* Paris, 1910. Regarding him as the true representative of Jewish interests, Péguy formulates Lazare's demands as follows: "He was a partisan of the impartiality of the law. Impartiality of law in the Dreyfus case, impartial law in the case of the religious orders. This seems like a trifle; this can lead far. This led him to isolation in death." (Translation quoted from Introduction to Lazare's *Job's Dungheap.*) Lazare was one of the first Dreyfusards to protest against the law governing congregations.

Bibliography

Alhaiza, Adolphe, *Vérité sociologique gouvernementale et religieuse. Succinct résumé du Sociétarisme de Fourier comparé au socialisme de Marx*, Paris, 1919.

Alldag, Peter, *Der Hofjude*, Berlin, 1938.

Anchel, Robert, *Napoleon et les Juifs*, Paris, 1928; "Un Baron Juif au 18e siècle," *Souvenir et Science*, vol. 1.

Arendt, Hannah, "Why the Crémieux Decree Was Abrogated," *Contemporary Jewish Record*, April, 1943; "The Jew as Pariah. A Hidden Tradition," *Jewish Social Studies*, vol. 6, no. 2, 1944; "Organized Guilt," *Jewish Frontier*, January, 1945.

Arland, Marcel, "Review of F. Céline's *Bagatelle pour un Massacre*," *Nouvelle Revue Française*, February, 1938.

Aron, Robert, *The Vichy Regime 1940-1944*, New York, 1958.

Bainville, Jacques, *La troisième République*, 1935.

Baron, Salo W., *Die Judenfrage auf dem Wiener Kongress*, Vienna, 1920; *A Social and Religious History of the Jews*, New York, 1937; "The Jewish Question in the 19th Century," *Journal of Modern History*, vol. X, 1938; *Modern Nationalism and Religion*, 1947.

Barrès, Maurice, *Les Déracinés*, Paris, 1897; *Scènes et doctrines du nationalism*, Paris, 1899.

Basnage, J., *Histoire des Juifs*, La Haye, 1716.

Batault, Georges, *Le Problème juif. La renaissance de l'antisémitisme*, Paris, 1921.

Bauer, Bruno, *Die Judenfrage*, 1843.

Baumont, Maurice, *Aux Sources de l'Affaire: l'affaire Dreyfus d'après les archives diplomatiques*, Paris, 1959.

Beaurepaire, Guesnay de, *Le Panama et la République*, 1899.

Bécourt, Renault, *Conspiration universelle du Judaisme, entièrement dévoilée; dédiée à tous les souverains d'Europe, à leurs ministres, aux hommes d'Etat et généralement à toutes les classes de la société, menacée de ces perfides projets*, 1835.

Bédarrida, Jassuda, *Les Juifs en France, en Italie et en Espagne*, 1859.

Benjamin, René, *Clémenceau dans la retraite*, Paris, 1930.

Bernanos, Georges, *Las grande peur des bien-pensants*, Paris, 1931; *Les grands cimetières sous la lune*, Paris, 1938.

Berndorff, H. R., *Diplomatische Unterwelt*, 1930.

Bertholet, Alfred, *Die Stellung der Juden zu den Fremden*, 1896; *Kulturgeschichte Israels*, 1919.

Bismarck, Otto von, *Gedanken und Erinnerungen*, 1909-1921.

Bloom, R. I., *The Economic Activities of the Jews of Amsterdam in the 17th and 18th Centuries*, 1937.

Bloy, Léon, *Le Salut par les Juifs*, 1892.

Blum, Léon, *Souvenirs sur l'Affaire*, Paris, 1935.

Boehlich, W., *Der Berliner Antisemitismusstreit*, Frankfurt, 1965.

Boehlich, Walter, ed., *Der Berliner Antisemitismusstreit,* Frankfurt/M., 1965.

Boehmer, Heinrich, *Les Jésuites. Ouvrage traduit de l'allemand avec une introduction et des notes par G. Monod,* Paris, 1910.

Boerne, Ludwig, *Über die Judenverfolgung,* 1819; *Für die Juden,* 1819; *Briefe aus Paris, 1830-1833.*

Boh, Felix, *Der Konservatismus und die Judenfrage,* 1892.

Bondy-Dworsky, *Geschichte der Juden in Boehmen, Maehren und Schlesien,* Prague, 1906.

Boom, W. ten, *Entstehung des modernen Rassen-Antisemitismus,* Leipzig, 1928.

Bord, Gustave, *La Franc-Maçonnerie en France dès origines à 1815,* 1908.

Botzenhart, Erich, "Der politische Aufstieg des Judentums von der Emanzipation bis zur Revolution 1848," in *Forschungen zur Judenfrage,* vol. 3, 1938.

Bourgin, Georges, "Le Problème de la fonction économique des Juifs," *Souvenir et Science,* vol. 3, nos. 2-4, 1932.

Brentano, Clemens v., *Der Philister vor, in und nach der Geschichte,* 1811.

Brogan, D. W., *The Development of Modern France 1870-1939,* 1941. *The French Nation: From Napoleon to Pétain 1814-1940,* New York, 1958.

Bronner, Fritz, "Georg, Ritter v. Schoenerer," *Volk im Werden,* vol. 7, no. 3, 1939.

Brugerette, Joseph, *Le Comte de Montlosier,* 1931.

Buch, Willi, *Fünfzig Jahre antisemitische Bewegung,* Munich, 1937.

Buchholz, Friedrich, *Untersuchungen über den Geburtsadel,* Berlin, 1807.

Buelow, Bernhard von, *Denkwürdigkeiten,* Berlin, 1930-1931.

Buelow, Heinrich von, *Geschichte des Adels,* 1903.

Busch, Moritz, "Israel und die Gojim," *Die Grenzboten,* 1879-1881; *Bismarck: Some Secret Pages of his History,* London, 1898.

Byrnes, Robert, *Antisemitism in Modern France,* New Brunswick, 1950.

Capefigue, Jean, *Histoire des grandes opérations financières,* 1855-1858.

Capéran, Louis, *L'Anticléricalisme et l'Affaire Dreyfus,* Toulouse, 1948.

Caro, Georg, *Sozial- und Wirtschaftsgeschichte der Juden im Mittelalter und der Neuzeit,* 1908-1920.

Caro, Joseph, "Benjamin Disraeli, Juden und Judentum," *Monatsschrift für Geschichte und Wissenschaft des Judentums,* 1932.

"Il caso di Alfredo Dreyfus," *Civiltà Cattolica,* February 5, 1898.

Cassel, Selig, "Geschichte der Juden," in *Ersch und Gruber, Allgemeine Enzyklopädie der Wissenschaften und Künste,* section 2, vol. 27, 1850.

Céline, Ferdinand, *Bagatelle pour un massacre,* 1938; *L'Ecole des cadavres,* 1940.

Chabauty, E. A., *Les Juifs nos maîtres,* Paris, 1882.

Chamberlain, Houston Stewart, *The Foundations of the Nineteenth Century,* 1966, translation of the German edition of 1899.

Chapman, Guy, *The Dreyfus Case. A Reassessment,* London, 1955.

Charensol, Georges, *L'Affaire Dreyfus et la Troisième République,* Paris, 1930.

Chesterton, Gilbert K., *The Return of Don Quixote,* 1927.

Chevrillon, André, "Huit Jours à Rennes," *La Grande Revue,* February, 1900.

Clarke, Edwin, *Benjamin Disraeli,* London, 1926.

Clémenceau, Georges, *L'Iniquité,* 1899; *Vers la Réparation,* 1899; *Contre la Justice,* 1900; *Des Juges,* 1901.

Corti, Egon Cesar, Conte, The *Rise of the House of Rothschild,* New York, 1927.

Dairvaell, Mathieu, *Histoire édifiante et curieuse de Rothschild, Roi des Juifs, suivi du récit de la catastrophe du 18 Juillet par un témoin oculaire,* 1846; *Guerre aux fripons, chronique secrète de la Bourse et des chemins de fer par l'auteur de "Rothschild I, Roi des Juifs,"* 1846, 3rd ed.

Daudet, Léon, *Souvenirs des milieux littéraires, politiques et médicaux,* Paris, 1920; *Panorama de la Troisième Republique,* Paris, 1936.

Davidsohn, Ludwig, *Beiträge zur Sozial- und Wirtschaftsgeschichte der Berliner Juden vor der Emanzipation,* 1920.

Delitzsch, Franz, *Sind die Juden wirklich das auserwählte Volk?*, Leipzig, 1890.

Delitzsch, Friedrich, *Die grosse Täuschung*, 1920-1921.

Demachy, Edouard, *Les Rothschilds, une famille de financiers juifs au 19e siècle*, 1896.

Desachy, Paul, *Répertoire de l'Affaire Dreyfus*, 1894; *Bibliographie de l'Affaire Dreyfus*, 1905.

Diderot, Denis, "Juif," in *Encyclopédie*, vol. 9, 1765.

Diest Daber, Otto von, *Bismarck und Bleichroeder*, Munich, 1897.

Dilthey, Wilhelm, *Das Leben Schleiermachers*, 1870.

Dimier, Louis, *Vingt Ans d'Action Française*, Paris, 1926.

Disraeli, Benjamin, *Alroy*, 1833; *Coningsby*, 1844; *Tancred*, 1847; *Lord George Bentinck. A Political Biography*, 1852; *Lothair*, 1870; *Endymion*, 1881.

Dohm, Christian Wilhelm, *Über die bürgerliche Verbesserung der Juden*, 1781-1783; *Denkwürdigkeiten meiner Zeit*, Lemgo, 1814-1819.

Drumont, Edouard, *La France Juive*, 1885; *La dernière Bataille*, 1890; *La Fin d'un monde. De l'or, de la boue, du sang. Du Panama à l'anarchie*, 1896; *Le Testament d'un antisémite*, Paris, 1891; *Les Tréteaux du succès: les héros et les pitres*, Paris, 1901.

Dubnow, S. M., *Weltgeschichte des jüdischen Volkes*, 10 vols., 1929; *History of the Jews in Russia and Poland*. Translated from the Russian by I. Friedlaender, Philadelphia, 1918.

Duehring, Eugen Karl, *Die Judenfrage als Frage der Rassenschädlichkeit für Existenz, Sitte und Cultur der Völker mit einer weltgeschichtlichen Antwort*, 1880.

Dutrait-Crozon, Henri (pseudonym), *Précis de l'Affaire Dreyfus*, 1909, 2nd ed., 1924.

Ehrenberg, Richard, *Grosse Vermögen, ihre Entstehung und ihre Bedeutung*, Jena, 1902.

Eisemenger, J. A., *Entdecktes Judentum*, 1703. New edition by Schieferl, 1893.

Elbogen, Ismar, *Geschichte der Juden in Deutschland*, Berlin, 1935; "Die Messianische Idee in der alten jüdischen Geschichte," *Judaica* 1912, *Festschrift Hermann Cohen*.

Emden, Paul H., "The Story of the Vienna Creditanstalt," *Menorah Journal*, vol. 28, no. 1, 1940.

Ewald, Joh. Ludwig, *Ideen über die nötige Organisation der Israeliten in christlichen Staaten*, 1816.

Fernandez, Ramon, "La Vie sociale dans l'oeuvre de Marcel Proust," *Les Cahiers Marcel Proust*, no. 2, 1927.

Foucault, André, *Un nouvel Aspect de l'Affaire Dreyfus* (Les Oeuvres Libres), 1938.

Fourier, Charles, *Théorie des quatre mouvements*, 1808. *Nouveau Monde Industriel*, 1829.

Frank, Walter, *Demokratie und Nationalismus in Frankreich*, Hamburg, 1933; *Hofprediger Adolf Stoecker und die christlich-soziale Bewegung*, 1st ed., 1928, 2nd revised ed., 1935; "Neue Akten zur Affäre Dreyfus," *Preussische Jahrbücher*, 1933, vol. 233; "Apostata. Maximilian Harden und das wilhelminische Deutschland," in *Forschungen zur Judenfrage*, vol. 3, 1938; "Walter Rathenau und die blonde Rasse," *ibidem*, vol. 4, 1940; "Die Erforschung der Judenfrage. Rückblick und Ausblick," *ibidem*, vol. 5, 1941.

Frantz, Constantin, *Der Nationalliberalismus und die Judenherrschaft*, Munich, 1874.

Freemasonry, the Highway to Hell, London, 1761.—*Freimaurerei, Weg zur Hölle*, translated from the English, 1768.—*La Franche Maçonnerie n'est que le chemin de l'enfer*, translated from the German, Frankfurt, 1769.

Freund, Ismar, *Die Emanzipation der Juden in Preussen*, Berlin, 1912.

Fries, Jacob Friedrich, *Über die Gefährdung des Wohlstandes und Charakters der Deutschen durch die Juden*, Heidelberg, 1816.

Fritsch, Theodor E., *Antisemiten-Katechismus*, 1892; editor, *Die Zionistischen Protokolle*, mit einem Vor und Nachwort von Theodor Fritsch, 1924; *Handbuch der Judenfrage*, revised edition, 1935.

Froude, J. A., *Lord Beaconsfield*, London, 1890.

Gentz, Friedrich, *Briefwechsel mit Adam Müller,* Stuttgart, 1857.
Gide, André, "Review of F. Céline's *Bagatelle pour un massacre,*" *Nouvelle Revue Française,* April, 1938.
Giraudoux, Jean, *Pleins Pouvoirs,* 1939.
Glagau, Otto, *Der Börsen- und Gründungsschwindel,* Leipzig, 1876; *Der Bankrott des Nationalliberalismus und die Reaktion,* 8th ed., Berlin, 1878.
Goethe, Joh. Wolfgang von, "Isachar Falkensohn Behr, Gedichte eines polnischen Juden, 1772, Mietau und Leipzig," *Frankfurter Gelehrte Anzeigen; Wilhelm Meister.*
Goldberg, Isidor, "Finanz- und Bankwesen," in *Encyclopedia Judaica,* 1930.
Goldstein, Moritz, "Deutsch-Jüdischer Parnass," *Kunstwart,* March, 1912.
Graser, I. B., *Das Judentum und seine Reformen als Vorbedingung der vollständigen Aufnahme der Nation in den Staatsverband,* 1828.
Grattenauer, C. W. F., *Über die physische und moralische Verfassung der heutigen Juden. Stimme eines Kosmopoliten,* 1791. Reviewed in *Allgemeine deutsche Bibliothek,* vol. 112, 1792; *Wider die Juden,* 1802.
Grau, Wilhelm, *Die Judenfrage als Aufgabe der neuen deutschen Geschichte,* 1935; *Wilhelm v. Humboldt und das Problem der Juden,* Hamburg, 1935; "Geschichte der Judenfrage," *Historische Zeitschrift,* vol. 153, 1936.
Greenstone, Julius H., *The Messiah Idea in Jewish History,* Philadelphia, 1906.
Gressmann, Hugo, *Der Messias,* Göttingen, 1929.
Gruen, Karl, *Die Judenfrage,* 1844.
Grunwald, Max, *Samuel Oppenheimer und sein Kreis,* Vienna, 1913; "Contributions à l'histoire des impôts et des professions des Juifs de Bohème, Moravie et Silésie depuis le 16e siècle," *Revue des Etudes Juives,* vol. 82.
Gueneau, Louis, "La Première Voie Ferrée de Bourgogne," *Annales de Bourgogne,* 1930, 1931.
Gumplowicz, Ludwig, *Der Rassenkampt,* Innsbruck, 1883.
Gurian, Waldemar, *Die politischen und sozialen Ideen des französischen Katholizismus,* Munich-Gladbach, 1929; *Der integrale Nationalismus in Frankreich: Charles Maurras und die Action Française,* Frankfurt, 1931; "Antisemitism in Modern Germany," *Essays on Antisemitism,* ed. by K. S. Pinson, 1946.

Haeckel, Ernst, *Lebenswunder,* 1904.
Halévy, Daniel, "Apologie pour notre passé," *Cahiers de la Quinzaine,* sér. 11, no. 10, 1910.
Halperin, Rose A., *The American Reaction to the Dreyfus Case,* Master's Essay, Columbia University, 1941.
Harden, Maximilian, "Händler und Soldaten," *Die Zukunft,* 1898; "Zum Schutz der Republik," *ibid.,* July, 1922; "Tönt die Glocke Grabgesang?" *ibid.,* July-August, 1922; *Köpfe,* Berlin, 1910.
Hauser, Otto, *Die Rasse der Juden,* 1933.
Heckscher, Eli F., *Mercantilism,* London, 1935.
Herder, J. G., *Briefe zur Beförderung der Humanität,* 1793-1797; "Über die politische Bekehrung der Juden," in his *Adrastea und das 18. Jahrhundert,* 1801-1803.
Herzog, Wilhelm, *Der Kampf einer Republik,* Zürich, 1933; and Rehfisch, Hans José (pseudonym: René Kestner), *L'Affaire Dreyfus,* a play, 1931.
Hoberg, Clemens August, "Die geistigen Grundlagen des Antisemitismus im modernen Frankreich," in *Forschungen zur Judenfrage,* vol. 4, 1940.
Hohenlohe-Schillingsfürst, Chlodwig von, *Denkwürdigkeiten der Reichskanzlerzeit,* edited by Karl Alexander v. Müller (Deutsche Geschichtsquellen des 19. Jahrhunderts, vol. 28), Stuttgart, 1931.
Holst, Ludolf, *Das Judentum in allen dessen Teilen. Aus einem staatswissenschaftlichen Standpunkt betrachtet,* Mainz, 1821.
Humboldt, Wilhelm von, "Gutachten," 1809, in: J. Freund, *Die Emanzipation der Juden in Preussen,* Berlin, 1912; *Tagebücher,* ed. Leitzmann, Berlin, 1916-1918; *Wilhelm und Caroline von Humboldt in ihren Briefen,* Berlin, 1910.
Hyamson, A. M., *A History of the Jews in England,* 1928.

Jahn, F. L., *Deutsches Volkstum*, 1810.

Jöhlinger, Otto, *Bismarck und die Juden*, Berlin, 1921.

Johnson, Guy, *France and the Dreyfus Affair*, New York, 1967.

Jost, J. M., *Neuere Geschichte der Israeliten. 1815-1845*, Berlin, 1846.

Karbach, Oscar, "The Founder of Modern Political Antisemitism: Georg von Schoenerer," *Jewish Social Studies*, vol. 7, no. 1, January, 1945.

Katz, Jacob, *Die Entstehung der Judenassimilation in Deutschland und deren Ideologie*, Dissertation, Frankfurt/M., 1935; *Exclusiveness and Tolerance. Jewish and Gentile Relations in Medieval and Modern Times*, New York, 1962.

Kedward, Roderick, *The Dreyfus Affair*, New York, 1963.

Kleines Jahrbuch des Nützlichen und Angenehmen für Israeliten, 1847.

Koch, Ludwig, S. J., "Juden" in *Jesuitenlexikon*, Paderborn, 1934.

Koehler, Max, *Beiträge zur neueren jüdischen Wirtschaftsgeschichte. Die Juden in Halberstadt und Umgebung* (Studien zur Geschichte der Wirtschaft und Geisteskultur, vol. 3), 1927.

Kohler, Max J., "Some New Light on the Dreyfus Case," *Studies in Jewish Bibliography and Related Subjects in Memory of A. S. Freidus*, New York, 1929.

Krakauer, J., *Geschichte der Juden in Frankfurt/Main. 1150-1824*, 1925-1927.

Kraus, Karl, *Untergang de Welt durch schwarze Magie*, 1925.

Krueger, Hans K., *Berliner Romantik und Berliner Judentum*, Dissertation, 1939.

Krug, W. Traugott, "Über das Verhältnis verschiedener Religionsparteien zum Staate und über die Emanzipation der Juden," *Minerva*, vol. 148, 1828.

K.V.T., "The Dreyfus Case: A Study of French Opinion," *The Contemporary Review*, vol. 74, October, 1898.

Labori, Fernand, "Le Mal politique et les partis," *La Grande Revue*, October-December, 1901; "Notes de Plaidoiries pour le procès de Rennes," *ibid.*, February, 1900.

Lachapelle, Georges, *Les Finances de la Troisième République*, Paris, 1937.

La Serve, Fleury, "Les Juifs à Lyon," *Revue du Lyonnais*, vol. 7, 1838.

Lazare, Bernard, *L'Antisémitisme, son histoire et ses causes*, 1894; *Une Erreur judiciaire; la vérité sur l'affaire Dreyfus*, 1896; *Contre l'Antisémitisme; histoire d'une polémique*, Paris, 1896; *Job's Dungheap*, New York, 1948.

Lazaron, Morris S., *Seed of Abraham*, New York, 1930.

Lecanuet, Edouard, *Les Signes avant-coureurs de la séparation, 1894-1910*, Paris, 1930.

Lemoine, Albert, *Napoléon I et les Juifs*, Paris, 1900.

Lestschinsky, Jacob, "Die Umwandlung und Umschichtung des jüdischen Volkes im Laufe des letzten Jahrhunderts," *Weltwirtschaftliches Archiv*, vol. 30, Kiel, 1929.

Lesueur, E., *La Franc-Maçonnerie Artésienne au 18e siècle* (Bibliothèque Révolutionnaire), 1914.

Leuillot, Paul, "L'Usure judaïque en Alsace sous l'Empire et la Restauration," *Annales Historiques de la Révolution Française*, vol. 7, 1930.

Levaillant, I., "La Genèse de l'antisémitisme sous la Troisième République," *Revue des Etudes Juives*, vol. 53, 1907.

Levinas, E., "L'Autre dans Proust," *Deucalion*, no. 2, 1947.

Lewinsohn, Richard, *Jüdische Weltfinanz?*, 1925; *Wie sie gross und reich wurden*, Berlin, 1927.

Lombard de Langres, Vincent, *Sociétés secrètes en Allemagne . . . de l'assassinat Kotzebue*, Paris, 1819.

Lombroso, César, *L'Antisémitisme*, 2nd edition, 1899, Paris.

Lucien-Brun, Henry, *La Condition des Juifs en France depuis 1789*, Paris, 1900.

Luxemburg, Rosa, "Die sozialistische Krise in Frankreich," *Die Neue Zeit*, vol. I, 1901.

Maier, Hans, "Die Antisemiten," *Deutsches Parteiwesen*, no. 2, Munich, 1911.

Maistre, Comte J. M. de, *Les Soirées de St. Petersburg*, 1821.

Malet, Chevalier de, *Recherches politiques et historiques qui prouvent l'existence d'une secte révolutionnaire*, 1817.

Marburg, Fritz, *Der Antisemitismus in der deutschen Republik*, Vienna, 1931.

Marcus, Jacob R., *The Rise and Destiny of the German Jews*, 1934.

Marr, Wilhelm, *Sieg des Judentums über das Germanentum vom nicht konfessionellen Standpunkt aus betrachtet*, 2nd ed., Berlin, 1879.

Martin du Gard, Roger, *Jean Barois*, 1913.

Marwitz, Fr. August Ludwig von der, "Letzte Vorstellung der Stände des Lebusischen Kreises an den König," 1811, *Werke*, ed. Meusel, Berlin, 1908; "Über eine Reform des Adels," 1812, *ibid.;* "Von den Ursachen des Verfalls der preussischen Staaten" *ibid.*

Marx, Karl, "Zur Judenfrage," *Deutsch-französische Jahrbücher*, 1843.

Maurras, Charles, *Au Signe de Flore; Souvenirs de la vie politique; L'Affaire Dreyfus et la fondation de l'Action Française*, Paris, 1931; *Oeuvres Capitales*, Paris, 1954.

Mayer, Sigmund, *Die Wiener Juden; Kommerz, Kultur, Politik, 1700-1900*, 1917.

McDermot, George, C.S.P., "Mr. Chamberlain's Foreign Policy and the Dreyfus Case," *Catholic World*, vol. 67, September, 1898.

Mehring, Franz, *Die Lessinglegende*, 1906.

Mendelssohn, Moses, "Schreiben an Lavater," 1769, *Gesammelte Schriften*, Berlin, 1930, vol. 7; "Vorrede zur Uebersetzung von Menasseh ben Israel, *Rettung der Juden*," 1782, *Gesammelte Schriften*, Leipzig, 1843-1845, vol. 3.

Meyer, Rudolf, *Politische Gründer und die Korruption in Deutschland*, 1877.

Mirabeau, H. G. R. de, *Sur Moses Mendelssohn*, London, 1788.

Mommsen, Theodor, *Reden und Aufsätze*, Berlin, 1905.

Monypenny, W. F., and Buckle, G. E., *The Life of Benjamin Disraeli, Earl of Beaconsfield*, New York, 1929.

Morley, John, *Life of Gladstone*, 1903.

Much, Willi, *50 Jahre antisemitischer Bewegung*, Munich, 1937.

Mulert, Hermann, "Antisemitismus," *Die Religion in Geschichte und Gegenwart*, Tübingen, 1909.

Müller, Adam, *Ausgewählte Abhandlungen*, ed. J. Baxa, Jena, 1921.

Neuschäfer, Fritz Albrecht, *Georg, Ritter von Schoenerer*, Hamburg, 1935.

Nipperdey, Thomas, *Die Organisation der deutschen Parteien vor 1918*, Düsseldorf, 1961.

Paalzow, C. L., *Über das Bürgerrecht der Juden, übersetzt von einem Juden*, Berlin, 1803.

Paléologue, Maurice, "L'Antisémitisme, moyen du gouvernement sous Alexandre II et Alexandre III," *Annales Politiques et littéraires*, vol. 112, July, 1938; *Tagebuch der Affäre Dreyfus*, Stuttgart, 1957.

Parkes, James W., *The Emergence of the Jewish Problem, 1878-1939*, 1946.

Paulus, Heinrich, E. G., *Beiträge von jüdischen und christlichen Gelehrten zur Verbesserung der Bekenner des jüdischen Glaubens*, Frankfurt, 1817; *Die jüdische Nationalabsonderung nach Ursprung, Folgen und Besserungsmitteln*, 1831.

Péguy, Charles, "Notre Jeunesse," *Cahiers de la Quinzaine*, 1910; "A Portrait of Bernard Lazare," in Bernard Lazare, *Job's Dungheap*, New York, 1948.

Philipp, Alfred, *Die Juden und das Wirtschaftsleben. Eine antikritisch-bibliographische Studie zu W. Sombart, Die Juden und das Wirtschaftsleben*, Strasbourg, 1929.

Philippsohn, Ludwig, "Tagescontrolle," *Allgemeine Zeitung des Judentums*, 1839.

Picciotto, James, *Sketches of Anglo-Jewish History*, London, 1875.

Pichl, Eduard (pseudonym Herwig), *Georg Schoenerer*, 1938.

Pinner, Felix, *Deutsche Wirtschaftsführer*, 1924.

Praag, J. E. van, "Marcel Proust, Témoin du Judaisme déjudaisé," *Revue Juive de Genève*, nos. 48, 49, 50, 1937.

Précis historique sur l'Affaire du Panama, 1893.

Pribram, Alfred François, *Urkunden und Akten zur Geschichte der Juden in Wien*, Vienna, 1918.

Priebatsch, Felix, "Die Judenpolitik der fürstlichen Absolutismus im 17. und 18. Jahrhundert," *Forschungen und Versuche zur Geschichte des Mittelalters und der Neuzeit*, 1915.

Proust, Marcel, *Remembrance of Things Past*, 1932-1934.

Pulzer, Peter G., *The Rise of Political Anti-Semitism in Germany and Austria*, New York, 1964.

Quillard, P., *Le Monument Henry*, Paris, 1899.

Rachel, Hugo, *Das Berliner Wirtschaftsleben im Zeitalter des Frühkapitalismus*, Berlin, 1931; "Die Juden im Berliner Wirtschaftsleben zur Zeit des Merkantilismus," *Zeitschrift für die Geschichte der Juden in Deutschland*, vol. 2.

Rachfahl, Felix, "Das Judentum und die Genesis des modernen Kapitalismus," *Preussische Jahrbücher*, vol. 147, 1912.

Ramlow, Gerhard, *Ludwig von der Marwitz und die Anfänge konservativer Politik und Staatsauffassung in Preussen* (Historische Studien, no. 185).

Rathenau, Walter, *Staat und Judentum. Zur Kritik der Zeit*, Berlin, 1912; *Von kommenden Dingen*, 1917.

Raymond, E. T., *Disraeli. The Alien Patriot*, New York, 1925.

Reeves, John, *The Rothschilds. The Financial Rulers of Nations*, London, 1887.

Rehberg, August Wilhelm von, *Über den deutschen Adel*, Berlin, 1804.

Reinach, Joseph, *L'Affaire Dreyfus*, Paris, 1903-1911; "Le rôle d'Henri," *La Grande Revue*, 1900, vol. 1.

Reinach, Théodore, *Histoire sommaire de l'Affaire Dreyfus*, Paris, 1924.

Riesser, Gabriel, *Über die Stellung der Bekenner des mosaischen Glaubens, an die Deutschen aller Konfessionen*, 1831; *Betrachtungen über die Verhältnisse der jüdischen Untertanen in der Preussischen Monarchie*, 1834.

Robinson, John, *Proofs of a Conspiracy against the Religions and Governments of Europe*, London, 1797. American edition, 1798; German translation, 1800; French translation, 1798-1799.

Roth, Cecil, *The Magnificent Rothschild*, 1939.

Ruehs, Christian Friedrich, "Über die Ansprüche der Juden auf das deutsche Bürgerrecht," *Zeitschrift für die neueste Geschichte der Völker und Staatenkunde*, Berlin, 1815; *Die Rechte des Christentums und des deutschen Volkes verteidigt gegen die Ansprüche der Juden und ihrer Verfechter*, 1815.

Ruppin, Arthur, *Soziologie der Juden*, Berlin, 1930.

Samter, N., *Judentaufen im 19. Jahrhundert. Mit besonderer Berücksichtigung Preussens*, 1906.

Savigny, Friedrich Karl von, *Beitrag zur Rechtsgeschichte des Adels im neueren Europa*, 1836.

Sayou, André, "Les Juifs," *Revue Economique Internationale*, 1912.

Schaeffle, A. E. Fr., "Der 'grosse Börsenkrach' des Jahres 1873," *Zeitschrift für die gesamte Staatswissenschaft*, vol. 30, 1874.

Scharf-Scharffenstein, Hermann von, *Das geheime Treiben, der Einfluss und die Macht des Judentums in Frankreich seit 100 Jahren (1771-1871)*, Stuttgart, 1872.

Schay, Rudolf, *Juden in der deutschen Politik*, 1929.

Scheffer, Egon, *Der Siegeszug des Leihkapitals*, 1924.

Scheidler, K. H., "Judenemanzipation," in *Ersch und Gruber, Allgemeine Enzyklopaedie der Wissenschaften und Künste*, 1850, 2nd section, vol. 27.

Schlegel, Friedrich, *Philosophische Vorlesungen aus den Jahren 1804-1806*, Bonn, 1836.

Schleiermacher, Friedrich, *Briefe bei Gelegenheit der politischen theologischen Aufgabe und des Sendschreibens jüdischer Hausväter*, 1799, *Werke*, section I, vol. 5, 1846.

Schnee, H., *Die Hoffinanz und der moderne Staat*, 3 vols., Berlin, 1953-1955.

Schneider, K. H., "Judenemanzipation," in *Ersch und Gruber, Allgemeine Enzyklopaedie der Wissenschaften und Künste*, section 2, vol. 27, 1850.

Schudt, Johann Jacob, *Jüdische Merkwürdigkeiten*, Frankfurt, 1715-1717.
Schwertfeger, Bernhard, *Die Wahrheit über Dreyfus*, 1930.
S.F.S., "The Jesuits and the Dreyfus Case," *The Month*, vol. 93, February, 1899.
Shohet, D. M., *The Jewish Court in the Middle Ages*, New York, 1931.
Silbergleit, Heinrich, *Die Bevölkerungs- und Berufsverhältnisse der Juden im Deutschen Reich*, Berlin, 1930.
Silberner, Edmund, "Charles Fourier on the Jewish Question," *Jewish Social Studies*, October, 1946.
Simon, Yves, *La grande Crise de la République Française; observations sur la vie politique française de 1918-1938*, Montreal, 1941.
Sombart, Werner, *Die deutsche Volkswirtschaft im 19. Jahrhundert*, 1903; *Die Juden und das Wirtschaftsleben*, 1911; *Die Zukunft der Juden*, 1912; *Der Bourgeois*, 1913; *Studien zur Entwicklungsgeschichte des modernen Kapitalismus*, 1913.
Sonnenberg-Liebermann, Max von, *Beiträge zur Geschichte der antisemitischen Bewegung vom Jahre 1880-1885*, Berlin, 1885.
Sorel, Georges, *Réflexions sur la violence*, Paris, 1908; *La Révolution dreyfusienne*, Paris, 1911.
Stahl, F. J., *Der christliche Staat und sein Verhältnis zu Deismus und Judentum*, 1847.
Steinberg, A. S., "Die weltanschaulichen Voraussetzungen der jüdischen Geschichtsschreibung," *Dubnov-Festschrift*, 1930.
Stern, Selma, "Die Juden in der Handelspolitik Friedrich Wilhelms I. von Preussen," *Zeitschrift für die Geschichte der Juden in Deutschland*, vol. 5; *Der preussische Staat und die Juden*, 2 vols., Tübingen, 1962; *Jud Suess*, 1929; "Die Judenfrage in der Ideologie der Aufklärung und Romantik," *Der Morgen*, vol. 11, 1935; *The Court Jew*, Philadelphia, 1950.
Stoecker, Adolf, *Reden und Aufsätze*, Leipzig, 1913.
Strauss, Raphael, "The Jews in the Economic Evolution of Central Europe," *Jewish Social Studies*, vol. III, no. 1, 1941.
Suarez, Georges, *La Vie orgueilleuse de Clémenceau*, Paris, 1930.
Sundheimer, Paul, "Die jüdische Hochfinanz und der bayrische Staat im 18. Jahrhundert," *Finanzarchiv*, vol. 41, 1924.

Tama, D., *Transactions of the Parisian Sanhedrin*, London, 1807.
Thalheimer, Siegfried, *Macht und Gerechtigkeit—Ein Beitrag zur Geschichte des Falles Dreyfus*, München, 1958.
Théo-Daedalus (pseudonym), *L'Angleterre juive: Israël chez John Bull*, Bruxelles, 1913.
Thibaudet, Albert, *Les idées de Charles Maurras*, Paris, 1920.
Toussenel, Alphonse, *Les Juifs, rois de l'époque. L'histoire de la féodalité financière*, 3rd ed., 1846.
Treitschke, Heinrich von, "Unsere Aussichten," *Preussische Jahrbücher*, vol. 44, no. 5, 1879; "Herr Graetz und sein Judentum," *ibid.*, no. 6; "Erwidrung an Mommsen," *ibid.*, vol. 46, no. 6, 1881.

Ucko, Siegfried, "Geistesgeschichtliche Grundlagen der Wissenschaft des Judentums," *Zeitschrift für die Geschichte der Juden in Deutschland*, vol. 5, no. 1.

Vacher de Lapouge, George, *L'Aryen, son rôle social*, Paris, 1896; *Les Selections sociales*, Paris, 1896.
Vallée, Oscar de, *Manieurs d'argent, 1720-1857*, 1857.
Varigny, C. de, "Les grandes Fortunes en Angleterre," *Revue des deux Mondes*, June, 1888.
Varnhagen, August, *Tagebücher*, Leipzig, 1861.
Vernunft, Walfried, "Juden und Katholiken in Frankreich," *Nationalsozialistische Monatshefte*, October, 1938; "Die Hintergründe des französischen Antisemitismus," *ibid.*, June, 1939.

Voltaire, F. M. Arouet de, *Dictionnaire philosophique* (*Oeuvres complètes,* vol. 9, 1878); *Philosophie génerale: métaphysique, morale et Théologie* (*Oeuvres complètes,* vol. 40, 1785); *Essai sur les moeurs et l'esprit des nations* (*Oeuvres complètes,* vol. 12, 1878).

Waetjen, Hermann, "Das Judentum und die Anfänge der modernen Kolonisation," *Vierteljahrsschrift für Sozial- und Wirtschaftsgeschichte,* vol. 11.

Wagener, Hermann, "Das Judentum und der Staat," in *Wagener Staatslexikon,* 1815-1889; "Das Judentum in der Fremde," *ibid.*

Wawrzinek, Kurt, *Die Entstehung der deutschen Antisemitenparteien 1875-1890,* Berlin, 1927.

Weber, Eugen, *Action française—Royalism and Reaction in Twentieth-Century France,* Stanford, 1962.

Weber, Max, "Die Börse," in his *Gesammelte Aufsätze zur Soziologie und Sozialpolitik; Wirtschaftsgeschichte,* 1923; *Parlament und Regierung,* 1918.

Weil, Bruno, *L'Affaire Dreyfus,* Paris, 1930.

Weill, Alexandre, *Rothschild und die europäischen Staaten,* 1844.

Weill, George, "Les Juifs et le Saint-Simonisme," *Revue des Etudes Juives,* vol. 31.

Weinryb, S. B., *Neueste Wirtschaftsgeschichte der Juden in Russland und Polen* (*Historische Untersuchungen,* vol. 12), Berlin, 1934.

Zaccone, Pierre, *Histoire des sociétés secrètes politiques et religieuses depuis les temps les plus reculés jusqu'à nos jours,* 1847-1849.

Zielenziger, Kurt, *Die Juden in der deutschen Wirtschaft,* 1930.

Zola, Emile, "J'Accuse," *L'Aurore,* January 13, 1898; *Correspondance: lettres à Maître Labori,* Paris, 1929.

Zweig, Stefan, *The World of Yesterday: An Autobiography,* 1943.

Index

Authors are listed only in case of special discussion or reference. Subjects of footnotes are listed. Chapter headings and subheadings and bibliographical references are not included.

absolute monarchy, 14, 15 ff., 30
Action Française, 90, 92 ff., 116
Africa, 78, 79
Age of Enlightenment, *see* Enlightenment
Ahlwardt, Hermann, 108
Algeria, 50, 102, 111-12, 118
Alldeutscher Verband, *see* Pan-German League
Alliance Antijuive Universelle, 40
Alsace, 47, 103
anticlericalism, 47; in France, 95
Anti-Dreyfusards, 37, 90, 92-120 *passim*
antisemitic congresses, 39
antisemitic parties, xii; in Germany, 4, 38 ff.; supranational organizations, 39 f.; in Austria-Hungary, 44; in France, 45
antisemitism, explanations of, vii f.; 3-10, 86; history of, vii, xi; and nationalism, 3-4, 40, 48; Nazi brand of, 3 f., 87; in France, 4, 42, 45-50, 85, 102 f.; and nation-states, 4; in Austria-Hungary, 5, 42-45; and Jews, 7-8, 43, 46, 54, 87, 103, 120; Christian brand of, 7, 118; liberal, 20, 34; and aristocracy, 20, 31-33, 35, 46; laws of development, 25, 28, 39, 42, 54, 87; and working class, 25, 77; in Eastern Europe, 29; in Prussia, 29-35; and lower middle classes, 36 ff.; leftist, 34, 38, 42-50; in England, 70; and the pan-movements, 39; and socialists, 41; and French society, 79-88; and Third Republic, 89-120; clerical, 44, 46, 116 ff., 120; and Pan-Germanists, 44-45; in Germany, 46, 79; decline of, 50-53; and social discrimination, 54, 61, 79-88; in United States, 55; and secret societies, 76; post-World War I, 86; and Jesuits, 102, 104; and mob, 107 ff.; and imperialism, 116
Arabs, 50
aristocracy, 4, 16, 20 f.; in Germany and Prussia, 13, 18, 31 ff., 85; and Jews, 18,

20 f., 29, 31-33, 35, 72 f., 85, 103; and nation-state, 31; and middle classes, 31, 72; in Hungary, 42; and lower middle classes, 43; in Europe, 72; in England, 72 ff.; and race doctrines, 73; in Austria-Hungary, 79
"aristocracy of nature," 73-74
army, in France, 46, 100-106; and Parliament, 100; as a caste, 100; and nation-state, 100; Jews in, 103 f.
Assemblée Nationale, 18, 33
Assumptionists, 116
Austria, 44, 79
Austria-Hungary, 64-65, 101, 102; antisemitism in, 5, 42 ff.; Jewish bankers in, 16, 17, 37; and pan-movements, 45

Balzac, Honoré de, 91
Bank of England, 26
bankers, and capitalism, 47; Jewish, 15, 37, 62 ff., 75 f.; in Germany, 4; and nation-state, 11-28; and lower middle classes, 37, 47 ff.; and capitalism, 47; in France, 47 f.; and Jewish people, 51 f., 62; decline of, 51. *See also* financiers
Banque de France, 19
Barrès, Maurice, 93, 94, 96, 110, 112, 116
Basch, Victor, 102, 111
Bavaria, 16, 17
Beaconsfield, Lady, 69
Beaconsfield, Lord, *see* Disraeli, Benjamin
Benjamin, Walter, 79
Berlin society, 57-62, 85
Bernanos, Georges, 50, 93, 101, 104, 107
Bismarck, Otto von, 18, 20, 21, 22, 23, 32, 35, 43, 45, 65
Bleichroeder, Gerson, 18, 20, 21, 32, 35, 97
Boeckel, Otto, 38
Boerne, Ludwig, 47, 63, 64, 65
Boisdeffre, Charles le Mouton de, 89
Bolshevik movement or party or Bolshevism, 4, 6. *See also* totalitarianism

Books by Hannah Arendt
available in paperback editions
from Harcourt Brace Jovanovich, Inc.